THE CHARTISTS

The Chartists Studies Series from The Merlin Press
Series Editor: Owen R. Ashton

THE CHARTISTS
Perspectives & Legacies

MALCOLM CHASE

MERLIN PRESS

Published in 2015 by
The Merlin Press Ltd
99b Wallis Road
London
E9 5LN

www.merlinpress.co.uk

ISBN. 978-0-85036-625-9

Catalogue in publication data is available from the British Library

Printed in the UK by Imprint Digital, Exeter

CONTENTS

FOREWORD

Many debts have been incurred over the years these studies have evolved. First and foremost is to Shirley Chase who has helped nurture every one of these chapters, her interest never flagging at even repeated airings of their arguments and content. Second, I owe a great deal to a plethora of editors and anonymous referees, and third to participants in numerous seminars and conferences who commented on early iterations of the work presented here. The bracing scrutiny of generations of Chartism special subject students at the University of Leeds has also contributed a great deal. For their advice on specific issues or chapters I thank Joan Allen, Owen Ashton, Jeremy Burchardt, Margaret Escott, David Goodway, Allan Greer, John Harrison, Diana Poole, Stephen Roberts, Peter Searby, Martin Thornton and Eileen Yeo.

Chapter 1 is based on a lecture commemorating the 175th anniversary of the publication of the People's Charter, delivered at the Houses of Parliament in 2013 at the invitation of the All Party Parliamentary Group on Archives and History. I should like to thank the Group, especially Dr Hywel Francis, its Chair at the time, for this great honour. Chapter 3 develops a public lecture presented in Vancouver in 2010 at the invitation of the Department of History at Simon Fraser University, in memory of Ian Dyck. He was a dear friend and colleague, missed by us all. Ian and I jointly edited the collection *Living and Learning: Essays in Honour of J. F. C. Harrison* (1996) in which an earlier version of Chapter 4 in this volume originally appeared. Grateful acknowledgment is also extended to the following for permission to reproduce previously published material: Oxford University Press (chapters 5 and 12, first published in *English Historical Review*, volumes 106 [1991] and 118 [2003], respectively); Llafur, The Welsh People's History Society (chapter 6, first published in *Llafur* 10:3 [2011]); Cleveland & Teesside Local History Society (chapter 7, first published in *Cleveland History* 95 [2008]); the Society for the Study of Labour History (chapter 8, first published in *Labour History Review* 75:1 [2009]); Lawrence & Wishart (chapter 9, first published in D. Howell, K. Morgan, D. Kirby and W. Thompson, eds, *John Saville: Commitment and History – Themes from the Life and Work of a Socialist Historian* [2010]); and Palgrave Macmillan for chapters 10 (first published in D. Birch and M. Llewellyn, eds, *Culture and Difference in Nineteenth-Century Literature* [2010]) and 11 (first published in M. Cragoe and P. Readman, eds, *The Land Question in Britain* [2010]). Amendments to these pieces have been confined to standardizing citations, minimizing repetition and adding cross-references where appropriate. The overall arrangement is, I hope, a satisfactory whole ranging from the introductory overview of chapter 1 to the final chapter on an aspect of the mid-Victorian consensus with which Chartism was intimately connected.

ABBREVIATIONS

BPU	Birmingham Political Union
BSSLH	*Bulletin of the Society for the Study of Labour History*
DLB	*Dictionary of Labour Biography* volumes 1-10, J. Bellamy and J. Saville, eds, (London, Macmillan, 1972-2000); volume 11, K. Gildart, D. Howell and N. Kirk, eds, (London, Palgrave, 2003); volume 12, K. Gildart and D. Howell, eds, (London, Palgrave, 2005)
FLS	Freehold Land Society
LWMA	London Working Men's Association
LD	*London Dispatch*
NAUT	National Association of United Trades
NCA	National Charter Association
NCREC	National Central Registration and Election Committee
NDC	*Newcastle Daily Chronicle*
NL	*Northern Liberator*
NS	*Northern Star*
PP	Parliamentary Papers
RC	Royal Commission
SC	Select Committee
TNA	The National Archives, Kew (formerly the Public Record Office)

I

THE CHARTIST LEGACY
FOR PARLIAMENTARY DEMOCRACY

'I hold in my hand a charter, the people's charter'.[1]

These were the words of a delegate from the London Working Men's Association as he pulled from his pocket a copy of a document that was to become famous – one of the landmark texts in British political history. The occasion was a mass rally for parliamentary reform on Glasgow Green on 21 May 1838, organized by the city's trade unions. There were delegates present from across Scotland, but also from England, notably from the Birmingham Political Union which was spearheading a mass national petition for universal male suffrage. No one had heard of Chartism (it would be another eighteen months before the term was coined). Though media coverage of the rally was lavish, few newspapers commented on what the Londoner said. He had been the last to speak and it had started to rain. Thousands were already leaving the Green. And the Association, having chosen the occasion to launch their flagship publication, had failed to get it printed in time, so that the Charter in his hands was an uncorrected proof.

How was it that from this unpromising beginning on a wet Glasgow afternoon, there emerged a mass movement of unprecedented size and potency which at its peak in 1842 commanded the support of 3.3 million people? And why did *The People's Charter* so soon lend its name to the first, and arguably still the greatest, mass political movement in modern Britain?

The narrative of the movement that follows is different from the familiar account of mass petitions, the tragic Newport Rising of November 1839 and the disappointments of 1848. The approach here is made on the basis that Chartism, though it failed to secure any of the six points for parliamentary reform that were at the Charter's heart, made a profound and enduring difference. The Chartism that history textbooks largely ignore is not a movement that failed but a movement characterized by a multiplicity of small victories. Taking this approach in no way belittles the tragedy of Newport, or marginalizes the heroism of Chartists like William Cuffay (transported to Australia for life for his part in Chartism in 1848). Indeed, by thinking about why Chartism really matters for parliamentary democracy, we may understand better – and empathize with – those whom the movement projected as its martyrs.

There was nothing new about the *People's Charter* except, crucially, its title. It contained six points for parliamentary reform (universal male suffrage; no property qualification to become an MP; payment of MPs; equal sized constituencies; voting in secret; and annual parliaments) that had first been proposed as a package in 1777 in John Cartwright's *The Legislative Rights of the Commonalty Vindicated, or Take Your Choice!* Cartwright was strongly committed to annual parliaments. These he envisaged would offer a genuinely representative democracy in which MPs would be the mandated delegates of their constituents, rather than effectively unaccountable and subject only to re-election as infrequently as every seven years.

However, *The People's Charter* did more than merely reassert established demands. The punchy title was itself significant. The allusion to Magna Charta of 1215 was one which all politically aware contemporaries would have understood. Indeed, radical interest in 'the Great Charter of Liberties' had grown over the previous quarter of a century, fuelled by an explosion of reform publishing in the Regency years. At the French Revolution of 1830, France's new Declaration of Rights was widely referred to in English as 'the new Charter'. Taking a cue from this a leading London radical publisher issued *The New Charter* proposed '*as a Substitute for the Reform Bill*' in 1831. Magna Charta constituted the foundation stone of English liberties and the People's Charter was advanced as completing the edifice.

To understand why the Chartists were so abundantly confident that the People's Charter would remedy much more than just the yawning democratic deficit left after the 1832 Reform Act, we need to appreciate that annual parliaments were just as integral to their demands as universal male suffrage. Cartwright's insistence upon annual parliaments was not whimsical. It was a riposte to the celebrated declaration made by Edmund Burke to his Bristol electorate two years before, that a Member of Parliament's 'unbiased opinion, his mature judgment, his enlightened conscience, he ought not to sacrifice to you ... Your representative owes you, not his industry only, but his judgment; and he betrays, instead of serving you, if he sacrifices it to your opinion'.[2]

Burke's conception of an MP's relationship with his constituents worked within a parliamentary system that respected the independence of MPs, that lacked hard demarcations between parties and where the function of whips was to nurture rather than discipline supporters. However, during the nineteenth century radical reformers' adherence to the principle of annual parliaments swelled against the background of hardening party lines, ever more apparent after 1832; and for the Chartists in particular there was the additional conviction that a mass male electorate would increasingly be an educated one – not necessarily schooled in a formal sense (though we should not underestimate the extent to which Chartism was also an education movement) but able to refine its political judgment through access to a free press and the increasing prominence of the public platform in daily political life. Our image of nineteenth-century political debate is one dominated by a handful of extraordinary public speakers – 'Orator' Hunt, the Chartist leader Feargus O'Connor, Disraeli, Gladstone. We overlook too easily how routinized public debate was in the culture of even quite small communities, carefully regulated according to generally accepted rules of procedure, rules that were in turn imitated in the proceedings of a wide variety of political and educational endeavours, such as the ubiquitous mutual instruction societies which typically included the arts of public speaking in their curriculum.

Annual parliaments are scarcely less incompatible with the maximum span of parliaments set at five years, than they were with the Septennial Act repealed in 1911. At issue was not only a fundamentally contrasting concept of democratic procedure, but also the extent to which electors could trust the members that they sent to Westminster. The belief that Parliament was venial and incapable of passing any measure that was not in its members' direct interests was at the heart of early Chartism. Old Corruption, 'The Thing' as William Cobbett had called it, was still believed to prevail even after the 1832 Reform Act. That this act had changed nothing was a perception to which many political reformers beyond the Chartist movement adhered. The activities of the Anti-Corn Law League, for example, were predicated on the assumption that, following 1832, the aristocracy retained real control of Parliament and therefore needed to be persuaded – even forced if necessary – to relinquish that control. Following the repeal of the Corn Laws in 1846, many former Leaguers were for a time rudderless, thrashing around in an effort to develop a coherent campaign for land reform to revivify their deeper purposes.[3]

So for Chartism annual parliaments were about creating a democratically elected assembly that could be trusted to govern in accordance with the popular will. The internal governance of Chartism itself underlines the strength of this conviction. The norm was for localities to elect an executive and officers for only three months at a time, and for each general and executive meeting to elect its chairman from among those present. County or district bodies were elected for a similarly finite period, the culture of accountable delegacy requiring clear procedures by which members were mandated by, and required to report back to, their electorates.

It is important then that we do not shrink our understanding of what the Chartists meant by democracy to the six points.[4] Indeed these six were not consistently sacrosanct. It is commonplace during 1838-9 to come across references to the five points.[5] Many Chartists were equivocal about equal electoral districts, fearing that such a measure would lead to the disenfranchisement of some new constituencies created in 1832 (Whitby or Blackburn, for example) as well as Westminster being swamped by Irish members (at least until the tragedy of the Famine in the mid-1840s). This was a matter of practical politics rather than anti-Irish prejudice: Chartists consistently supported the restoration of a Dublin parliament, a policy that was formally embodied alongside the Charter in the text of the 1842 National Petition.

Even the secret ballot was occasionally seen as unmanly: it puts 'a mask on an honest face', O'Connor once said.[6] However few Chartists were prepared, even temporarily or pragmatically, to compromise on the four core points of the Charter, even to the extent that they refused overtures from middle-class reformers who, while sharing their opinion of Parliament, advocated triennial parliaments and enfranchising household heads alone. Among them was Joseph Hume MP. As architect of the repeal of the Combination Acts in 1824 he commanded widespread respect among working-class reformers. The Scotsman tried on several occasions to develop common ground between them and middle-class reformers with a four point 'Little Charter' (a vote for all household heads, triennial parliaments, the ballot and equal sized constituencies). But the implicit judgment here, that working men were unsuitable to be MPs, was anathema to Chartists; and although the Little Charter gained ground after the rejection of the third Chartist petition in 1848, it faired little better in the Commons than the six points had done.[7]

So we come to 'the elephant in the room' whenever Chartism as a blue print for democracy is discussed. Why did it seek the vote for men alone? Chartism was not inherently antagonistic to female suffrage, but the prevailing view was pragmatic, as the preface to The People's Charter candidly conceded that against the 'reasonable proposition' of female suffrage, 'we have no just argument to adduce but only to express our fears of entertaining it, lest the false estimate man entertains for this half of the human family may cause his ignorance and prejudice to be enlisted to retard the progress of his own freedom'.[8] Once universal male suffrage was won it was widely assumed female suffrage would eventually follow.

An important contextual point here is that the reality of political participation for nineteenth-century women was more complex than our lazy generalizations suppose. Women who were ratepayers in their own right did hold the right to vote in local elections. The extent to which they exercised it appears to have varied, according to customary interpretation and local economic circumstance. The rise of the seaside landlady, for example, boosted the female electorate in some coastal communities. Historians are only beginning to fathom the extent to which women participated in local elections.

We should not therefore be surprised by female participation in the Chartist movement. It is true that most Chartist women concentrated upon immediate practical issues concerning the quality of family life, doing so both through the NCA, which accepted men and women equally as members, and women-only Chartist groups: 'It is our duty, both as wives and mothers, to form a Female Association', the women of Elland, West Yorkshire, resolved in 1838, 'in order to give and receive instruction in political knowledge, and to co-operate with our husbands and sons in their great work of regeneration'.[9] The Ashton-under-Lyne Female Political Union was even more militant:

> We are determined that no man shall ever enjoy our hearts, or share our beds, that will not stand forward ... we do not despair of yet seeing intelligence, the necessary qualification for voting. And then Sisters, we shall be placed in our proper position in society, and enjoy the elective franchise as well as our kinsmen.[10]

Thus women signed Chartism's national petitions in large numbers. Where separately recorded for individual communities, women's signatures in 1839 ranged from around 13 to 20 per cent. In 1848, by contrast, the House of Commons Committee on Petitions (with no incentive to underestimate the figure since it saw women's signatures as discrediting Chartism) calculated the proportion to be only 8 per cent.

The contrast between the 1839 and 1848 National Petitions tells the story of a gradual transition from a movement genuinely rooted in the community, to one that increasingly espoused the male breadwinner ideal and the politics of respectability and which therefore closed off opportunities for women's participation. This leads me to suggest that Chartism was at its most politically potent in its early years, not because it was more readily disposed forcibly to agitate to achieve its objectives, but because of a moral authority rooted in the astonishing extent to which it mobilized whole communities.

There was much more to this movement than the six points. So great was its motivational force and so imaginative the popular response to it, that Chartism was the structure within which for a time the majority of industrial workers pursued their political and even cultural lives. Let me introduce you to a hypothetical family of committed Chartists. Their new-born child might be received into the movement at a special ceremony presided over by one of its leaders, and possibly given their name. Subsequently she or he might attend a Chartist Sunday School or have a subscription to the Chartist Land Plan taken out on their behalf. Meanwhile the parents would be immersed in the political and social life of the local branch of the NCA, the mother in a Chartist women's group and perhaps the father also in a trades union affiliated to Chartism. They might shop at a Chartist Co-op store. If a ratepayer, the father might be able to support Chartist candidates in local elections; if teetotal, they could join a Chartist Temperance Association. Prints of Chartist leaders would adorn their home; spare pennies subscribed to support Chartist prisoners and their dependents. Their main source of national news would be a Chartist weekly paper, usually *Northern Star*.

Every schoolchild knows that Chartist menfolk might join a clandestine group for arms drill. Much less appreciated is that in certain parliamentary boroughs they could also support Chartist candidates for Westminster. There were around fifty occasions on which Chartist candidates stood for parliament. Two were successful, Feargus O'Connor at Nottingham and Samuel Carter at Tavistock, though the latter was unseated on appeal because he could not meet the property qualification. Furthermore there were a couple of dozen instances of independent or progressive Liberal candidates receiving official Chartist endorsement – most of them were elected. And there were also countless occasions when Chartist candidates worked for one or the other of the two main political parties – Whig or Tory – typically with the objective of achieving a hung parliament, wherein those MPs who were favourably disposed to extending the suffrage might exercise particular influence.[11]

These details about Chartist participation in the parliamentary election process underline that this was a serious, constitutional movement. It was as much about contesting the parliamentary system on its own terms, as it was about demonstrating, sometimes riotously so, against that system. Chartists revered the institution of Parliament: that indeed is why they agitated so strenuously to reform it.

Few Britons at this time were not touched by this remarkable movement and it is almost inconceivable that there were any who had never heard of it, for Chartist localities could be found from west Cornwall right up to the Orkneys. The result was that the Chartists constituted a massive cross section of society: eighty distinct occupational groups are identified in the 1841 list of candidates for election to the movement's national executive, ranging from bakers and basket-makers to vets and wire-workers, as well as the textile workers and mechanics at the heart of Britain's industrial revolution.[12] Chartists were overwhelmingly working class but they also included a variety of the more comfortably off, such as the Reverend Arthur Wade, a Cambridge Doctor of Divinity. (He it was who presented the People's Charter to that rally in Glasgow in 1838.) Then there was the MP for Finsbury Thomas Slingsby Duncombe (an old Harrovian former Guards officer, and reputedly the best dressed man in the House of Commons). Almost all Britain's ethnic communities were represented in some way. William Cuffay was of Caribbean slave heritage; two other Londoners, arrested after a Chartist disturbance in Camberwell in 1848, David Duffy and Ben Prophett, were described as 'men of colour'. Arrested with them – and transported for his part in breaking into a pawnbrokers to cries of 'Hurrah for Liberty' – was Charles Lee, a Romany who had been born in a tent in the New Forest.[13] The Ayrshire Chartist John Taylor was Anglo-Indian (his mesmerizing good looks were ascribed to his Indian grandmother, Shanie Chanim from Sandila in Uttar Pradesh).

However, there appear to have been no Jewish Chartists – and we must frankly acknowledge that Chartism occasionally displayed that strand of economic anti-Semitism sadly so evident in much nineteenth century British politics. Nonetheless, *Northern Star* roundly condemned what it termed 'atrocious calumnies' committed against Jews in the Ottoman Empire; and in the 1850s Duncombe was a parliamentary campaigner for Jewish civil rights.[14]

In 1842 Duncombe presented the largest of the three Chartist petitions to Parliament, marshalling 3.3 million signatures (around a third of Britain's adult population and four times larger than the combined British and Irish electorate created by the Reform Act of 1832). This was the single largest petition ever laid before Parliament, occupying an estimated six miles of paper and weighing a third of a ton. On 2 May 1842, relays of burly London tradesmen carried it through the streets of London in a huge decorated box constructed for the purpose. Even *The Times* (no friend of Chartism) estimated the accompanying crowd at 50,000.

On entering Parliament, the petition jammed tight in the doorway into the Commons. After attempts to dismantle the door frame (authorized by the Speaker) failed, the petition had to be disassembled and taken in pieces into the House of Commons by members of the Chartists' National Convention. The mountain of paper, heaped onto the floor of the chamber, dwarfed the clerks' table upon which, technically, it was supposed to be placed. Procedure then required the Clerk to the House to read out all 3,000 words of a plea not only for parliamentary reform but also for other key Chartist demands. These included a clean-up of government corruption, disestablishment of the Church of England and home rule for Ireland. It was a deeply satisfying piece of political theatre.

Predictably less satisfying was the Commons' debate next day. Duncombe proposed that six members of the Chartist Convention should be allowed to speak to the petition at the bar of the House. The Tory Prime Minister Robert Peel and his Home Secretary both spoke opposing this; but their rhetoric failed to match that of the former Whig Cabinet member Thomas Macaulay. 'Universal suffrage would be fatal to all purposes for which government exists', he declared: 'it is utterly incompatible with the very existence of civilisation.' If Parliament was elected on the principles of the People's Charter, 'how is it possible to doubt that famine and pestilence would come before long to wind up the effects of such a state of things?'[15] Duncombe's motion was defeated by 287 to 49.

But the 1842 Petition was at least received with courtesy. In June 1839, the 1.3 million signatures accompanying the first mass petition had been greeted by laughter in the Commons. In April 1848 the inclusion of multiple names written by the same hands, along with pseudonyms, was used to discredit a two-million strong third petition. Neither of these features was exactly surprising in a society where literacy was low and many lived in fear of losing their jobs if their political views became known. But the background to the 1848 petition was one of revolution across Europe; of the Camberwell riots mentioned above in connection with Duffy, Prophett and Lee; of troops moved up from all over southern England into London, and of the royal family evacuated to the Isle of Wight. The political establishment was in no mood to receive Chartism with anything approaching courtesy in the spring of 1848. Draconian changes in the law of freedom of political assembly and speech (the Crown and Government Security Act, pushed through Parliament with a first reading on the very day the 1848 petition was presented) were one of the factors that led to the consequent decline of Chartism.[16]

It must be stressed that the decline of Chartism was not solely the consequence of official repression. To a considerable extent Chartism was predicated upon the unreformed Parliament being incapable of legislating in favour of anybody's economic interest except that of the social classes from which the Lords and Commons drew their members. The validity of such a premise was gradually eroded by the fiscal reforms passed by Peel's government in the 1840s, and by the Whig's Public Health Act of 1847. Chartists greatly admired Peel precisely because his conduct appeared to transcend the claims of both party and class. Three years before the repeal of the Corn Laws, Feargus O'Connor described Sir Robert Peel as 'now England's only great man. In their opposition they have nothing to stand against him.'[17] Significantly, Peel was among the subjects whose portraits were given away by the Chartist newspaper *Northern Star*, the only one who stood outside the orthodox pantheon of radical heroes.

The decline of Chartism and its complex causation have often been allowed to obscure the movement's true significance. I have argued elsewhere that the movement had a multitude of small endings and a multiplicity of small victories.[18] It is the dissemination of Chartist thinking in depth and breadth that concerns me here. Of course not all signatories to the petitions were immersed as deeply in Chartism as the hypothetical family described above: but support for the Charter was close to the norm among working men and women in the industrial regions of the English midlands and north, south Wales and west central Scotland. In the words of one Yorkshire workman, 'I had always been a Chartist since I knew what politics meant'.[19] And there were many other centres of intense Chartist activity outside those regions: for example Aberdeen, Dundee, Ipswich, Colchester, Brighton, Plymouth, Bristol, Cheltenham, Oxford and of course London.

Long after the 1848 petition, long even after the very last Chartist national convention in 1858, the People's Charter remained a tool to think with for those who sought to promote democracy in Britain. Its emotional charge was considerable: reforming personalities as widely contrasting as Charles Bradlaugh, the freethinker and atheist, and General Booth, founder of the Salvation Army, cited it among their inspirations.[20] For the leader of the Durham miners' trade union and an early Labour MP, John Wilson, writing in 1910, Chartism was 'ever-present to the progressive mind'. As late as 1935, Sylvia Pankhurst was criticizing the Labour Party for lacking 'the sturdy democratic fibre of the Chartists'.[21]

Why then should Chartism's legacy for democracy be judged important? Four areas particularly stand out. First, Chartism increased ordinary people's 'social capital'. It was an important provider of educational opportunities and also created space to develop organizational and public speaking skills. Second, it increased awareness among working people of what they had in common – despite the widely contrasting experiences of gender, geographical regions and different occupational groups. The message and the medium were alike central to this process. It was here that the tradition of a national press supportive of working-class issues was established. Chartist newspapers were lively: they offered not just news and commentary but fiction, poetry, extensive space for local reports and readers' letters, features for women and, even, children. *Northern Star* was the foremost Chartist paper (outselling *The Times* in 1839 and therefore the biggest selling newspaper in history at that point); but there were some 120 other Chartist and near-Chartist periodicals, a handful of which survived into the later decades of the nineteenth century. They were no longer Chartist papers, of course, but they still advocated reform politics. Notable among these titles was *Reynolds's News*, a Sunday paper closely associated with the cooperative movement, which did not close down until the 1960s.

Third, Chartism was one of the key forces in persuading Westminster to legislate against the prevailing interests of those who made up Parliament, and to bring forward instead social and economic measures to improve life for the people as a whole. One ventures to suggest that Robert Peel would not have achieved all that he did so fast under his own steam alone, if at all. A parliamentary majority for the reforms of the 1840s would have been less easily obtained. The movement also made authority, at both local and national levels, more cautious about applying any outright policy of repression. For example after Chartism, legal reversals suffered by trades unionism came from judicial interpretation of existing law, not from new legislation. Parliament was at worst disinclined to grant trade union rights and from 1859 it was increasingly well-disposed towards them. The landmark legislation was the Molestation of Workmen Act, which reformed the law of strikes and explicitly established a right to picket peacefully. It was passed by Parliament as a result of lobbying by the National Association of United Trades, founded in 1845. Two decades before the Trades Union Congress was formed, there was a nationwide co-ordinating body, established by trade unions affiliated to Chartism, supported by the Chartist press, and with Thomas Slingsby Duncombe (effectively a Chartist MP) as its president.[22]

Fourth, Chartism began the process by which local government was opened up to working men, both as voters and as elected representatives. The movement was a crucible for active citizenship. Chartist local councillors were elected in Leeds as early as 1841, a success that was widely imitated elsewhere. Three years earlier, Leeds Chartists had determined to 'make the Municipal Council of Leeds in miniature what we want the Commons House of Parliament to be'.[23] To return working-class candidates, it was necessary to organize closely and canvass thoroughly – so Chartism encouraged political awareness and habits of civic participation. The involvement of ex-Chartists in municipal and liberal politics was commonplace even into the 1880s. It was a natural consequence of Chartists continuing to be politically active in their local communities, once Chartism itself as a national movement dwindled to nothing. Commenting on the 1884 Reform Act, John Howe (a Colchester Liberal councillor and local leader of the carpenters' trades union) declared: 'I am an old Chartist; manhood suffrage was one of the points when I was a boy, and we have been fighting for it up to the present time. Every man should have the right to vote.' Seven years later, in 1891, John Howe became the first chairman of Colchester Trades Council. An even longer-serving political activist than Howe was another Colchester Chartist – Henry Clubb, the former secretary of the Colchester branch who, having emigrated to America, became a Michigan state senator and remarkably lived until 1921.[24]

Looking beyond local government to Parliament itself, no survey has ever been undertaken of the extent to which the post-1867 Reform Act intakes of MPs included men with earlier experience of Chartism. Logically there must have been several, maybe even many. There were two, coincidentally both called Carter. Samuel Carter, the Chartist elected for Tavistock in 1852 but then disqualifed, became Liberal MP for Coventry in 1868. And Robert Meek Carter, the Liberal MP elected for Leeds, had first entered politics as a Chartist municipal councillor in 1852. At work as a labourer on an East Riding farm from the age of six, Robert Carter received no education beyond that of an autodidact; much of it was acquired through Chartism after he moved to Leeds in the 1830s to work as a millhand.[25]

—o—

Inevitably a long-term perspective like that deployed here creates a teleology, a seemingly logical succession in a process of modernization. It is important therefore to consider 'the road not taken'. As Chartism 'modernized', grew less confrontational and left the streets and the hills behind in favour of indoor meetings, it moved away from being essentially the expression of community-based political concerns, which had mobilized women in numbers almost commensurate with men to defend the integrity of the working-class family in the face, particularly, of the New Poor Law. By the end of the 1840s it had evolved into a professionally staffed (that is *male* staffed) organization – a pressure group, even. The social and ideological context in which the Charter was situated had shifted decisively, away from communities and families towards a rather earnest subscriber-based organization that was characterized not by outdoors agitation but by indoor respectability. This process intermeshed with broader social changes that saw the accelerated evolution of the male breadwinner ideal, and almost a cult of domesticity. The late 1840s constituted the 'take-off' period of building societies, and saw a publishing explosion of cheap household manuals, as well as the Chartist Land Plan at the heart of which was a vision of the family in which women worked as carers and homemakers and men worked as providers.[26]

Of course the process summarized here was uneven and never neat or clear cut. However, as already indicated in considering the involvement of women in Chartism, wherever in the movement one looks, the involvement of women was thinner – both numerically and in intellectual substance – towards the end of the 1840s, than it had been at the decade's beginning. There's an important lesson here for those who care about democracy. Chartism was at its most potent as a political force when it was socially most inclusive. Even in the brief compass of the two decades in which there was formally a Chartist movement, we can see how the professionalization of politics tended to raise walls between 'grassroots' supporters and leaders, and between the electorate and the elected. Reflecting on present times in the light of Chartism, one ventures to suggest that there are processes at work within political organizations that are leading to the same end. In this connection it is important to reiterate that the sixth point of the Charter, annual parliaments, was central to the Chartist vision of what democracy should be. It was never realized and very few today would wish it otherwise. However, it is worth recalling the intentions behind it as we ponder declining election turnouts, the diminishing base of unpaid party activists, and the distance that remains between the parliamentary system and those to whom elected representatives are ultimately accountable.

Notes

1   *Scotch Reformers' Gazette*, 26 May 1838.
2   Speech to the Electors of Bristol, 3 Nov. 1774, in *The Works of the Right Hon. Edmund Burke* (London, 1834), vol. 1, p. 179.
3   See below, chapter 12.
4   E. Yeo, 'Some practices and problems of Chartist democracy', in J. Epstein and D. Thompson (eds), *The Chartist experience: studies in working-class radicalism and culture, 1830-60* (London, 1982), pp. 345-80.
5   For example in the work of James Watkins, discussed in chapter 7 below.

6   *NS* 17 March 1846.

7   In 1850 the House of Commons rejected Hume's motion promoting it by 242 votes to 96.

8   *The People's Charter* (London, 1838), p. 9.

9   *NS* 24 Mar. 1838.

10   *NS* 2 Feb. 1839.

11   See chapter 8 below.

12   D. J. V. Jones, *Chartism and the Chartists* (London, 1975), pp. 30-33.

13   D. Goodway, *London Chartism: 1838-48* (Cambridge, 1982), p. 116; H. Mayhew *London labour and the London poor*, vol.4 (London, 1862), pp. 376-7.

14   *NS* 2 May 1840; see also 22 Aug. 1846.

15   Hansard, House of Commons Debates, 3 May 1842 vol. 63 col. 45.

16   See chapter 9 below.

17   Quoted in M. Chase, *Chartism: A New History* (Manchester, 2007), pp. 273-4.

18   Chase, *Chartism*, chs 10 and 11; see also the conclusion to chapter 6 below.

19   J. Lawson, *Letters to the Young on Progress in Pudsey during the last sixty years* (Stannington, 1887), p. 132.

20   See below, chapter 10.

21   Wilson quoted in Chase, *Chartism*, p. 359; M. Davis, *Sylvia Pankhurst: A Life in Radical Politics* (London, 1999), p. 106.

22   Chase, *Chartism*, pp. 246-8, 253-5, 348-51. See also chapter 6 below.

23   Quoted in D. Fraser, *A History of Modern Leeds* (Manchester, 1982), p. 286.

24   A. F. J. Brown, *Chartism in Essex and Suffolk* (Chelmsford, 1982), p. 113; see also 78, 81, 116, 120-1. For Clubb see chapter 10 below.

25   See chapter 8 below.

26   See chapters 4, 5 and 12 below.

2

THE LEADING QUESTION
IN CHARTIST HISTORIOGRAPHY[1]

At the age of 76, well beyond the average lifespan for a man of his social class, William Lovett published an autobiography: *The Life and Struggles of William Lovett in his Pursuit of Bread, Knowledge and Freedom.*[2] He had lived a long and eventful life and throughout it he had meticulously collected copies of his numerous contributions to newspapers in scrapbooks, along with other press cuttings and papers about his activities.[3] But in compiling these scrapbooks, and even more so his autobiography, Lovett was composing a version of himself, trying to make sense of his life and forgetting or discarding what seemed irrelevant or embarrassing. Partly the act of composing would have been subconscious; but it was also only human that Lovett strove to present a picture of himself that readers would recognize and find appealing. He wanted to provide posterity with a detailed understanding of what he thought he was actually like. And he succeeded: as Eileen Janes Yeo observes in her thoughtful analysis of the gender politics of his autobiography, Lovett's *Life* became 'a source which has shaped the views of generations of historians'.[4] It was thrice reprinted, in 1920, 1967 and 1984.[5]

One of the most enduring themes in Chartist historiography is therefore to a considerable extent the consequence of a 76-year-old mid-Victorian suppressing the passion with which he had advocated his political opinions forty years earlier. A great many historians of Chartism (tasked with the need of explaining why it failed) read back from the views of the elderly Lovett, and constructed a fatal flaw within early Chartism where one did not exist. All Chartists in 1839 faced a profound strategic dilemma. If petitioning the political establishment to dissolve itself does not work, what then? By the autumn of 1839, in the weeks either side of the Newport Rising, Lovett was absolved from answering that question because he was in Warwick gaol. Once released in July 1840, he could answer it with the luxury of hindsight. The idea that Lovett was pitched into a battle with 'a few mad advisors' (as he described them), who 'by furious appeals to the passions of the multitude, stirred up the demons of hate, prejudice and discord, to obstruct its [Chartism's] onward progress' – is nonsense. But that is the proposition Lovett made and in case his readers were in any doubt as to whom he was referring, in the next paragraph he helpfully referred specifically to 'the violent ravings about physical force, by O'Connor, Stephens and Oastler'.[6]

However, the 'Lovett versus O'Connor' dichotomy is rooted not only in a particular reading of the empirical data available concerning Chartism, but also in the ideological context in which some early twentieth-century historians worked, especially Mark Hovell, author of the first scholarly history of Chartism to appear in English. Hovell's *The Chartist Movement* was published posthumously by Manchester University Press in 1918 to wide acclaim. A cheap second edition, aimed primarily at the Workers' Educational Association (WEA) was issued in 1925. Manchester reprinted the book in 1943, 1950, 1959 and 1963. The publisher then issued a third edition in 1966 and reprinted it in 1970. A specialist 'revival' publisher re-issued this edition in 1994. This was a volume of remarkable longevity.

Hovell's close acquaintance with Chartism had its origins in 1910, in the WEA classes he had taught in the cotton towns of Ashton-under-Lyne, Colne and Leigh. These, Ashton in particular, were heartlands of Chartism where the memory of the movement was still very much alive. After his death, the secretary of one of his WEA classes wrote to the *Highway*, the Association's journal, that Hovell was 'a man with a large heart, one who sympathized with the sorrows and sufferings of the people. His great desire was to serve his fellows by educating, and so exalting the manhood of the nation.'[7] Although he went on to study and teach for a year (1912-13) at Leipzig's Institute for Cultural and Universal History, Hovell's approach to Chartism was rooted in a close reading of contemporary sources, especially Lovett and the papers of his metropolitan mentor Francis Place, with limited engagement with what modern historians often term the 'rank and file' or 'grass roots' of the movement. There is no evidence that he was influenced by any element from the oral tradition that survived of Chartism and which he must surely have encountered through the WEA. For example 'Th' Owld Chartist' William Chadwick (imprisoned for sedition and conspiracy in 1848), had lectured for the Liberal Party in the 1890s and even campaigned in the 1906 General Election: he was buried in Stockport in 1908. And in the same year that Hovell's *History* appeared the Leeds academic Frederic Moorman published a dialect poem, 'The Hungry Forties', in a volume dedicated to the Yorkshire members of the WEA: it clearly draws on direct accounts of the decade, including the 1842 strikes.[8]

What mattered above all to Hovell were issues of leadership. His lectureship at Manchester was in military history and much of the book was written in intervals during officer training in 1915.[9] Leadership preoccupied him, both for its intrinsic importance in understanding why Chartism failed, but also because leadership style offered practical pointers to the conduct of contemporary politics. In Hovell's text the essential division in the leadership of Chartism is not between physical force and moral force: a division he presciently saw was superficial, throwing only limited light on what he termed 'the fundamental problem of the Chartist ideal'. The essential difference was a class one. On the one hand there were the 'leaders of higher social position', who taught Chartism 'little that conduced to moderation, business method, or practical wisdom'; and on the other hand there was 'a better type of Chartist leader', personified in Lovett but also in Thomas Cooper, and distinguished by 'steady honesty of purpose, their power of learning through experience to govern themselves and others, their burning hatred of injustice and their passion for the righting of wrongs'. Feargus O'Connor, of course, personified the first category. But not coincidentally, O'Connor also personified the first category of the 'clearest way of dividing the Chartists'. This was into 'a reactionary and a progressive section', a divide between those who viewed society as 'so hopelessly bad as to be incapable of improvement' and therefore 'to be ended as soon as practicable', and 'the school of Lovett and Cooper [which] accepted the Industrial Revolution and tried to make the best of it'.[10]

There is a paradox here: none of the words quoted in the preceding paragraph were Hovell's. Tragically Second Lieutenant Mark Hovell had died on 12 August 1916 attempting the rescue of a member of his platoon overcome by fumes in a shaft in which a mine had just been detonated beneath a German trench. The book's long concluding chapter was the work of the medievalist Thomas Frederick Tout, head of History at Manchester. This was explained by Tout in a short preface that few probably bothered to read (and which was omitted completely from the third edition).[11] How Hovell would have completed his history had he lived is an issue too complex to explore here. Furthermore successive generations approached 'Hovell' as an organic whole and it was as such that it exercised an enduring influence on the historiography of Chartism. As a text it derived considerable emotional force from the circumstances of Hovell's death. This was boosted by the inclusion of his photograph, in the uniform of his regiment the Sherwood Foresters, as the frontispiece of the book (its only illustration in fact). An explicit claim of moral authority was to be found in Tout's emotional introductory chapter. He observed that 'the problems of fourteenth-century administration … under ordinary circumstances would have had a first claim upon my time'; but 'a veteran can hardly have a more acceptable war task than doing what in him lies to fill up a void in scholarship which the sacrifice of battle has occasioned.' Tout quoted verbatim the Foresters' chaplain's account of how Hovell had asked to receive Holy Communion before going into the trenches for the last time. 'He has', the chaplain concluded, 'as the soldiers say, "gone West" in a blaze of glory. He has fought and died in the noblest of all causes.' Tout himself added that the author of *The Chartist Movement* had 'made the supreme sacrifice, and the cannon still roar round the British burial ground … where he lies at rest … the enemy's guns still rain shell round his unquiet tomb'.[12]

This added moral authority, un-anticipated by Hovell when he put aside his manuscript in July 1915, was emphasized by contemporary reviewers. Almost all referred to the circumstances of the author's death, several referring to him by his military rank throughout.[13] No less significantly, many reviewers saw the book as a contribution to post-war political discourse and understanding as much as to historical scholarship, 'full of lessons to be learnt by the Chartist failure'. The *Contemporary Review* predicted Hovell would henceforth 'be known to fame as the historian of a great industrial movement and an indicator of the sound lines of social progress'. The *Saturday Review* praised the book for being 'packed tightly with the strong meat of history and political economy', adding that 'there can be no better preparation for the understanding of the terrible events which enfold the nation than tracing through the chapters of this careful work the stream of Socialism to its source in Chartism'.[14] In the *Manchester Guardian*, the Fabian R. C. K. Ensor (subsequently author of one of the most successful volumes in the *Oxford History of England*) emphasized the value of Hovell's 'fidelity to truth' in delineating the issue of leadership. Few histories could assist the modern labour movement more than that of Chartism, argued Ensor, 'in showing it what to avoid … those who were honourable were men, like Lovett, of insufficient calibre; those who had the capacity for leadership on a large scale were either unmitigated charlatans like Feargus O'Connor or doctrinaire revolutionaries like Bronterre O'Brien'.[15]

It is Lovett's modernizing tendencies that most commended him to his twentieth-century posterity, a perspective heavily influenced by the Fabian Society (a formative influence on the British Labour Party that emphasized calm reflection and rational planning over direct confrontation as the ideal approach to political action). Very few reviewers took issue with Hovell's stringent criticism of O'Connor.[16] For several the book's depiction of 'the evil spirit of an excellent movement', as one newspaper summarized it, was a conspicuous virtue.[17] Lovett was effectively reconstituted for an early twentieth-century readership as a Fabian *avant la lettre*. The credit for this – if credit it be – was not Hovell's alone. A range of earlier authors had anticipated this line of argument, but did so mainly polemically within the context of contemporary political debate. Thus George Bernard Shaw, in the famous 1889 *Fabian Essays in Socialism*, surveyed the Social Democratic Federation under the leadership of Hyndman and commented it was 'as if Chartism and Fergus O'Connor had risen from the dead'.[18] In 1900 the Independent Labour Party activist Ramsden Balmforth presented a compelling pen-portrait of O'Connor (whom Balmforth's father had known). 'Possessing lungs of brass and a voice like a trumpet, he was the most effective out-door orator of his time … Unfortunately, both for the movement and for himself, he was a man of unbounded conceit and egotism.' Characterizing O'Connor as the leading figure in 'a "physical force" party … sprung up in the movement in opposition to the "moral force" party led by Lovett', Balmforth judged him the Chartist leader 'most culpable' for the movement's failure.[19] Missing from polemic and Hovell alike was any sense of the Lovett who wrote the *Manifesto* of the 1839 Chartist Convention with its unambiguous statement of ulterior measures and his portrait prominent on its title page; or of the Lovett who wrote this explicit assertion that Whig government policy was a breach of the contract that required from the governed the duty of obedience:

> When the liberties of a million people are prostrated to the dust at the will of a grasping, despicable minority – when an attempt is made to destroy their representative rights, the only existing bond of allegiance, the only power through which laws can be justly enforced, is broken. Then has the time arrived when society is dissolved into its original elements.[20]

However, from these observations about late-Victorian treatments of Chartism Gammage's *History of the Chartist Movement* must be exempted. Much though he detested him, Gammage presented O'Connor as the near-constant presence around which the movement evolved and declined. In the quite extensive revisions made to the 1854 edition for its republication in 1894, no attempt was made to redress the balance in Lovett's favour. Indeed, in the concluding chapter a parallel was actually added comparing O'Connor's slump in popularity in 1852 with Christ on the eve of crucifixion. In the 438 pages of Gammage's *History*, there are but ten references to Lovett and only eight to the LWMA compared to sixty to O'Connor.[21]

Spotlighting Lovett in Whiggish historiographical light continued after

Hovell with the publication in 1920 of *A History of the Chartist Movement* by Julius West. This too was a posthumous publication, though West had died rather more prosaically of influenza in 1919. Hovell had the advantage over West of being published by his university's press; West, on the other hand, was published by a commercial house (Constable) with a weak list in modern history. The book was never reprinted and is far less well known as a result. However, it has the distinct merit of having been conceptualized and completed by its author as a history extending to what West termed Chartism's 'passing' in the 1850s. Despite this the narrative is still largely in thrall to a Lovettite teleology. West praised Lovett's National Association (the organization he founded after his release from prison in 1840) for its educational objectives: its proposal for circulating libraries, thought West, was 'reduced to practical dimensions' by the book box scheme of the Fabian Society. West had worked at the Fabians' head office before the First World War and in his conclusion explicitly compared the LWMA (of which Lovett was the secretary and presiding genius) with the Fabian Society. 'In many respects', he commented, 'there is, in fact, an analogy between the W.M.A. and the Fabian Society. Both produced ideas, and left the task of forcing them upon the attention of an apathetic country to larger bodies.' Although he praised Ernest Jones for the tenacity with which he dedicated himself to Chartism after 1848, West saw him as little more than a pale imitation of O'Connor whose 'dictatorship' he sought to continue.[22]

So by 1920 the interpretive framework of Chartism was largely set. Almost everywhere one looks in the inter-war period, Chartism is presented with Lovett versus O'Connor very much as the over-arching explanatory device. The Fabian and Christian Socialist R. H. Tawney, introducing his 1920 edition of Lovett's autobiography, drew almost exclusively upon Hovell for his citations, albeit varying the diet to reference the Fabian Graham Wallas's biography of Francis Place, 'to whom Lovett owed much'. Tawney drew a sharp contrast between Lovett and O'Connor, portraying the latter as having 'snatched the Chartist movement after 1839 out of the hands of London, and carried it forward on a wave of misery and violence to its ignominious collapse'.[23] Sometimes the history of the movement was virtually reduced to a Lovett *versus* O'Connor narrative. Thus in *The Encyclopedia of the Labour Movement* (published 1928 with an introduction by Ramsay McDonald and contributions by seventeen other ministers in the first Labour Government) Lovett was

a thorough-going Social Democrat, basing his belief in Socialism on well-thought-out lines ... he would use neither appeal to physical force nor oratory to get his aims realized. In all this he was a complete contrast to Feargus O'Connor ... an orator of violent description ... He had no original ideas, but caught up whatever was in the wind ... he beat nobler partners out of the ranks ... Lovett's guidance was the nobler and has proved the more beneficial in the long run'.[24]

The future Labour Party leader Hugh Gaitskell, writing for the WEA, similarly stressed that it was 'difficult to find two persons more naturally antipathetic': Lovett 'serious, conscientious, almost painfully honest'; O'Connor 'rebellious and egotistical ... he cared neither for education nor morals, having neither in great measure himself'. Gaitskell argued that the failure to secure an enduring alliance with the middle class was among the Chartists' greatest failings, largely explainable by middle-class reaction against the working classes' 'evil habit of threatening violence and following rash leaders like O'Connor'.[25] The Hammonds, political liberals for whom reconciling working- and middle-class opinion was the fulcrum of history and contemporary politics alike, praised Lovett in their 1930 *The Age of the Chartists*. He 'managed to arrange a working alliance with the left-wing of the Anti-Corn Law League', but the Hammonds then went on to emphasize that that the fruit of this, the Complete Suffrage Union, 'was destroyed by the sinister hand of Feargus O'Connor'.[26] In so doing they cheerfully ignored the fact that the fatal motion passed at the Complete Suffrage conference in December 1842, condemning the Union for failing to accommodate the wishes of the Chartists, was proposed by Lovett and seconded by O'Connor.[27] Bonamy Dobrée's survey of 1937 contrasted the 'notorious ... intellectually weak' O'Connor ('actually in a lunatic asylum for three years before his death') with Lovett, 'a man of steadfast principle'. The spirit of Lovettism, Dobrée suggested, should preside at every meeting of the WEA.[28] Four years later G. D. H. Cole published his *Chartist Portraits*, twelve essays on representative leaders. These offered the most-nuanced interpretation yet of Chartism's leaders. Yet even for Cole, O'Connor 'stole the movement' from Lovett and the LWMA.[29]

The only alternative to this sustained emphasis upon the qualities of Lovett as a radical leader came predictably from a Marxist perspective. Here Theodore Rothstein's 1929 history *From Chartism to Labourism* sought out an alternative leadership figure, to fit an interpretation stressing Chartism's revolutionary potential, and found it in Bronterre O'Brien. It was hardly to be expected that the avowed Leninist Rothstein, a former leading member of the Social Democratic Federation who from 1921 was effectively exiled from Britain in Soviet Russia, would accept as any kind of desirable model the leadership of William Lovett. The section of his book on Chartism was written, Rothstein explained in the preface, 'to demonstrate, by the example of the contest between the 'moral' and 'physical force' schools of the Chartist movement, the futility of the Menshevik policy of compromise and opportunism'. Lovett he therefore described as 'not over shrewd; capable yet unfit for practical political struggle, since he did not possess even a spark of revolutionary temperament.' O'Connor, on the other hand, along with Frost, Jones and O'Brien, was 'the supreme embodiment ... of the genuinely proletarian current in Chartism' that 'gave the movement its historic character'.[30] A certain sleight of hand was necessary, however, to sustain Rothstein's argument that of this group O'Brien was the chief. In parallel to the valorization of Lovett as a prototype Fabian, O'Brien was singled out by Rothstein as being 'one of the first and most direct forerunners of Marx and Engels'.[31] However, Rothstein's work had little impact before the 1950s.[32] Few other Marxist authors accorded O'Brien much notice, though he was the subject of a 1929 Oxford thesis by a young communist historian Alfred Plummer, on which G. D. H. Cole drew heavily for his *Chartist Portraits*. Plummer's work remained unpublished until, shorn of almost all remnants of its political provenance, it was finally published in 1971.[33]

By then, however, the landscape of Chartist studies had changed considerably and Plummer's biography of O'Brien was destined never to be more than a footnote to the historiography. The distinguishing feature of British communist historiography in the mid-twentieth century was its search for continuities – for the establishment of an apostolic succession of labour leadership every bit as teleological as the Fabians. In this respect, stuck as they had been in the smoke-filled back rooms of Soho pubs, O'Brien and the O'Brienites decidedly represented a dead end. Rothstein's interpretation of labour history itself conceded this. In his words, 'Chartism did not disappear without leaving a trace. On the contrary, its mighty spirit remained alive, and in the very changing process of history continued to act as a creative force as long as the conditions which had brought it into being remained substantially the same. When those conditions disappeared, it died; but this death was its greatest triumph! Chartism has become militant and victorious Communism.'[34] A Communist perspective upon British labour history therefore required a leadership figure with both proto-Marxist intellectual credentials, and a plausible claim to constitute a figure that bridged Chartism with later revolutionary labour movements in a way that Lovett, because of his gradualism, and O'Connor because of his untimely death in 1854, could not. By dint of chronology, his indefatigable application to radical politics in one form or another from 1844 until his death in 1869, and his close acquaintance with Marx, Ernest Jones fitted much more comfortably any interpretation of Chartism that emphasized its precursor function to Communism.

As the Labour Party lost its radical political lustre, a move could be discerned to instate Ernest Jones as the ideal type. Two historians, both then active in the Communist Party and both subsequently very influential figures in Victorian historiography, worked on Jones in the years after the Second World War. As discussed in chapter 9 below, the first was John Saville whose book on Jones, published in 1952, rather captured a territory that the second, Dorothy Thompson, had begun to colonize. In the event her own study of Jones was abandoned; meanwhile a chapter on Chartism in Halifax, co-written with her husband Edward and rich in insight into Jones's career, was dropped from the influential 1959 *Chartist Studies* volume edited by Asa Briggs.[35] The historiography of Chartism was thus deprived of work of substance on Jones by one of the movement's most powerful historians. However, the attempt to instate Jones as ideal Chartist leader made limited headway for other reasons. First, the ructions within the Communist Party around 1956 dramatically lessened the appetite of those historians within its orbit to seek out canonical figures. Second, closely following the events of 1956 (and not unrelated to it) there emerged a distinct and enduring element within Chartist historiography, the local study.

At a rough count there are at least 140 local studies of Chartism, only a dozen of which had appeared before the end of the 1950s.[36] Then Asa Briggs edited a collection of essays, *Chartist Studies* which contained six more and the floodgates opened: fifteen further local studies appeared in the 1960s, 44 in the 1970s, and 48 more in the 1980s, slowing to a mere thirteen in the 1990s. How to account for this phenomenon? In part it was driven by the material circumstances in which higher education found itself from the 1960s, an expanding number of institutions and professional historians turning out growing numbers of students who needed dissertation topics at undergraduate, masters' and doctoral level. Chartism also benefited from its location at the convergence of three separate historiographical trends: the broad growth of interest in 'history from below' and similar surges of interest in the pursuit of local history and in the Victorian period generally. In addition the *Chartist Studies* volume was in itself inspirational.

However, one ventures to suggest that something else was also at work here. 'There are not many points in modern British history at which the historian can profitably speculate whether a revolutionary situation might have developed but did not', J. F. C. Harrison once observed, before adding that Chartism in 1839 and the spring and summer of 1848 constituted two such points.[37] Indeed, he might have added the summer of 1842 as a third. What also stimulated the production of local studies of Chartism from the late 1950s was a form of revolutionary antiquarianism – historiography as a form of comradeship with the past, and the writing of history almost as consolation for failure. It was also a historiography which, sometimes overtly and sometimes almost subconsciously, speculated why those revolutionary situations almost developed but did not. Both local and national histories of Chartism have provided a kind of platform from which to interrogate Marxist theories of revolutionary change. A decline of interest in local studies of Chartism from the mid-1980s arguably reflected broader historiographical trends: Britain's avoidance of revolution was no longer the key question it had once seemed; Gareth Stedman Jones's seminal *Rethinking Chartism* (1983) argued, among other things, against the atomization of the movement's history that the local studies boom had unintentionally promoted; the publication soon after of Thompson's *The Chartists*, itself the work of an author critical of the cumulative effect of local studies on the field, served to complete the process.

However, one of the consequences of the local studies boom was firmly to evict Lovett from a place of eminence in the Chartist pantheon. In *Chartist Studies* itself references to O'Connor outnumber those to Lovett by a ratio of more than two to one. This is, admittedly, a crude indicator but it reflects the inevitable consequences of disaggregating the narrative of Chartism. Lovett's writ ran but imperfectly even in London: elsewhere, and especially in northern provincial centres, Chartism and O'Connorism were close to synonymous. O'Connor's *Northern Star*, not *The Charter* of the LWMA, was the journal of choice in the Chartist provinces; and O'Connor, not Lovett (nor indeed, beyond Manchester and Halifax, Ernest Jones) was the leader most likely to have visited a Chartist locality.

There was, however, a second force at work on the historiography of Chartism in the post-war period that also privileged O'Connor over other Chartist leaders. A generation of historians active in (or schooled against the background of) the campaigns for nuclear disarmament and civil rights, and opposing the Vietnam War, were considerably more empathetic concerning the politics of direct action than earlier social democratic historians. They were also much less insistent upon the importance of conventional party organization. This generation (coming to prominence in the late 1970s and '80s) was much less apt to proclaim its political sympathies within its historical writing in the way that Hovell, Rothstein or West did. But flags were clearly planted for those who would see. Norman McCord saw a veritable forest in Dorothy Thompson's *The Chartists* (1984), 'adding a touch of class' he remarked ironically as well as 'a modest boost' to 'O'Connor hagiography'.[38] John Belchem's 1985 biography of *Orator Hunt* (O'Connor's avowed role model and derived from Belchem's comparative doctoral thesis on the two men) bears a quote from the great African-American musicians Otis Redding and Sam Cooke instead of a dedication: 'A Change is Gonna Come'. And James Epstein's 1982 biography of O'Connor, *The Lion of Freedom*, concludes by observing that the Chartists 'fought with a resilience perhaps best captured in O'Connor's words, 'and No Surrender'.[39]

Epstein's biography was a substantial extension of a process evident long before in journal articles, belatedly rounded-out by a further biography covering his final decade.[40] Thompson's *The Chartists* recast the issue of leadership by pointedly incorporating its treatment into a chapter (one of her shortest) titled 'Leaders and Followers'. Meanwhile the most striking feature of Chartist historiography from the mid-1980s was arguably literary scholarship's cultivation of what earlier had been exclusive territory for the discipline of history. In terms of evaluating the leadership of Chartism this promoted a perhaps exaggerated deference to literary figures in the movement. Ernest Jones was the most obvious beneficiary of this process, with the reprinting of a substantial amount of his fiction and poetry and an avowedly unconventional biography by Miles Taylor, *Ernest Jones, Chartism and the Romance of Politics, 1819-69*, the title indicating a book that interrogated both the style and substance of Jones as a leading Chartist, contextualizing Chartism almost as much within late romanticism as in the evolution of mass politics. Taylor's Jones, it goes almost without saying, is very different to Saville's. Most recently, what one is tempted to characterize as Rupert Murdoch's generation has shown increasing interest in G. W. M. Reynolds, whose reputation rested as much upon his sensational journalism and titillating fiction as it did upon conventional political acumen.

Reynolds, a writer of cheap, ephemeral fiction, shot to prominence in the Chartist movement during the heady spring of 1848. His claim to enduring fame is as the founder of the mass-circulation *Reynolds's Weekly Newspaper* (1850-1967). His was a gamey reputation. Marx declared him 'a scoundrel'.[41] W. E. Adams, the Chartist and later prominent radical journalist, claimed 'the rank and file of Chartism' thought Reynolds 'a charlatan and a trader'.[42] It was primarily Reynolds whom Charles Dickens targeted in an assault on popular serial publishers as the 'Bastards of the Mountain, draggled fringe on the Red Cap, Panders to the basest passions of the lowest natures'.[43] That Dickens should have considered him so influential should alert us to take Reynolds seriously. His politics were deeply rooted in the long-established demonization of Old Corruption. Like his novels (especially *Mysteries of London*, 1844-48, and *Mysteries of the Court of London*, 1848-56) they hinged upon the depiction of the state as the tool of a decadent and debased establishment. This establishment was overwhelmingly landed and this strengthened the appeal of his fiction to a Chartist readership. Anne Humpherys suggests that by excluding from his fiction the middle class who so dominated the canonical Victorian novels, Reynolds simultaneously 'constructed his working-class readers' sense of victimization and gave them a sense of vicarious empowerment'.[44] Clearly, Reynolds should be taken seriously as a novelist; and he should be taken seriously as a leading political figure. More-conventional Chartist scholarship has marginalized him due to its absorption with leadership in a quasi-military sense, and with platform oratory and conventional political literature. But as Henry Mayhew discovered during research into the cultural world of London costermongers: 'Reynolds is the most popular man among them … They all say he's "a trump", and Feargus O'Connor's another trump with them'.[45]

There is an important pointer here for how historians should approach the leadership of Chartism. As with the questions of success and failure with which they are integrally bound up, issues around leadership should not be allowed to obscure the no-less significant politics of the everyday that characterized Chartism, and to the further development of which the movement contributed. 'The Chartists' greatest achievement was Chartism, a movement shot through not with despair but with hope.'[46] The multiplicity of small victories that can be credited to this remarkable mobilization of popular political energy owed little to the leaders, the effectiveness and probity of whom so exercised the twentieth-century historians of Chartism. One of the factors that for so long dogged the interpretation of Chartism was that Lovett and the LWMA appeared so much more 'modern' than O'Connor and torchlight demonstrations on Pennine hillsides. The sober and measured addresses on political issues that Lovett penned reached out to the world of parliamentary social democracy in a way that Feargus's *Northern Star* letters (peppered with capitals, italics and exclamation marks) to 'the fustian jackets, blistered hands and unshaven chins' did not. Lovett even lived long enough to get himself photographed, while in O'Connor's case his final years in a mental asylum was an unpromising basis upon which to launch a political rehabilitation. Hovell and his heirs viewed Chartism through a modernizing prism. We at least can now appreciate how much the movement owed to its local activists, to the popular cultures – both printed and oral – that sustained and gave shape to political indignation, and to a belief in the moral legitimacy of direct action in the political sphere.

Notes

1   This essay concentrates on how leadership has been handled by historians of Chartism. For broader historiographical treatments see D. Thompson, 'Chartism and the historians', in her *Outsiders: Class, Gender and Nation* (London, 1993) and J. Allen and M. Chase, 'Britain: 1750-1950', in J. Allen *et al, Histories of Labour: National and International Perspectives* (Pontypool, 2010), pp. 70-76.

2   W. Lovett, *The Life and Struggles of William Lovett in his Pursuit of Bread, Knowledge and Freedom* (London, 1876).

3   British Library, Department of Manuscripts, Add MSS 34245A, 34235B, 37773-6; Birmingham Central Reference Library, Lovett Collection, MS 753.

4   E. J. Yeo, 'Will the real Mary Lovett please stand up?: Chartism, gender and autobiography', in M. Chase and I. Dyck, *Living and Learning: Essays in Honour of J. F. C. Harrison* (Aldershot, 1996), p. 163.

5   With an introduction by R. H. Tawney in two volumes (London, 1920) and one volume (London, 1967); facsimile of 1876 edition (New York, 1984). Lovett's inclusion in the 'Lives of the Left' biographical series (its only wholly nineteenth-century subject) also helped reinforce the notion that he was central to Chartism: J. Wiener, *William Lovett* (Manchester, 1989).

6   Lovett, *Life and Struggles*, pp. 171-2.

7   *Highway* (December 1916), quoted in T. F. Tout, 'Introduction', in M. Hovell, *The Chartist Movement* (Manchester, 1918), p. 57.

8   For Chadwick see *DLB*, vol. 7; F. W. Moorman, *Songs of the Ridings* (London, 1918), pp. 49-50.

9   Manchester, John Rylands Library, Tout Papers TFT/1/545, Hovell (Lichfield Barracks, 11 June 1915) to Tout: 'I am pegging away at the thesis. I wrote for eight hours yesterday'.

10   Hovell, *Chartist Movement*, pp. 305, 306, 309-10.

11   T. F. Tout, 'Preface' in Hovell, *Chartist Movement*, p. vii.

12   T. F. Tout, 'Preface' and 'Introduction', in Hovell, *Chartist Movement*, pp. vii, xxxvi.

13   E.g. *American Historical Review* 24: 1 (24 Jan. 1918), *Common Cause* (19 Apr. 1918) and *Political Science Quarterly* 1: 34 (Mar. 1919).

14   *Liverpool Courier* 12 Feb. 1918; *Contemporary Review* April 1918; *Saturday Review* 9 Feb. 1918. See also *Spectator* 9 Feb. 1918.

15   *Manchester Guardian* 25 Feb. 1918.

16   The exceptions were *Times Literary Supplement* 31 Jan., *New Statesman* 23 Feb. and *Nation,* 9 Mar. 1918.

17   *Liverpool Courier* 12 Feb. 1918. See also *Manchester Guardian* (25 Feb.) and *Athenaeum* (May 1918).

18   'The transition to social democracy', in G. B. Shaw (ed.), *Fabian Essays in Socialism* (London, 1889), p. 229.

19   R. Balmforth, *Some Social and Political Pioneers of the Nineteenth Century* (London, 1902), p. 189.

20   M. Chase, *Chartism: A New History* (Manchester, 2007), pp. 71-2; London

Working Men's Association, *Address to the People of Canada* (1838), quoted in Lovett, *Life and Struggles*, p. 108.

21   R. G. Gammage, *The History of the Chartist Movement, from its commencement down to the present time* (London, 1854); R. G. Gammage, *The History of the Chartist Movement, 1837-1854* (Newcastle, 1894), p. 390.

22   J. West, *A History of the Chartist Movement* (London, 1920), pp. 151, 258-95 (quoting 288).

23   R. H. Tawney, 'Introduction', *The Life and Struggles of Lovett in his Pursuit of Bread, Knowledge and Freedom* (London, 1920), vol. 1, pp. vii, xv.

24   H. B. Lees-Smith (ed.), *Encyclopedia of the Labour Movement* (London, 1928), vol. 1, pp. 91-2.

25   H. T-N. Gaitskell, *Chartism: An Introductory Essay* (London, 1929), p. 32, 86.

26   J. L. and B. Hammond, *The Age of the Chartists* (London, 1930), pp. 271 and 282.

27   Chase, *Chartism*, pp. 227-9.

28   B. Dobrée, *English Revolts* (London, 1937), pp. 160-1.

29   G. D. H. Cole, *Chartist Portraits* (London, 1941), p. 33.

30   T. Rothstein, *From Chartism to Labourism: Historical Sketches of the English Working Class Movement*, (London, 1983; first published 1929), pp. 1, 35, 50.

31   Ibid, p. 105.

32   J. Saville, 'Introduction' to Rothstein, *From Chartism to Labourism*, p. xviii and see below, chapter 9.

33   A. Plummer, *Bronterre: A Political biography of Bronterre O'Brien, 1804-64* (London, 1971). On early Marxist historians of Chartism see chapter 9, below.

34   Rothstein, *From Chartism to Labourism*, p. 92.

35   A copy survives in the Dorothy Thompson Collection at Staffordshire University. It is finally to be published in S. Roberts (ed.), *The Dignity of Chartism* (London, 2015).

36   Figures based on J.F.C. Harrison and D. Thompson, *Bibliography of the Chartist movement* (Hassocks: Harvester, 1978) and Owen Ashton *et al*, *The Chartist movement: a new annotated bibliography* (London, 1995), plus subsequent annual bibliographies in *Labour History Review*.

37   J. F. C. Harrison, *Early Victorian Britain, 1832-51* (London, 1979), pp. 185-6.

38   Review essay in *History*, 70 (October 1985), 411.

39   J. Belchem, *'Orator Hunt': Henry Hunt and English Working-class Radicalism* (Oxford, 1985); J. Epstein, *The Lion of Freedom: Feargus O'Connor and the Chartist Movement, 1832-42* (London, 1982), p. 315.

40   P. A. Pickering, *Feargus O'Connor: A Political Life* (Monmouth, 2008).

41   Quoted in A. Humpherys and L. James (eds), *G. W. M. Reynolds: Nineteenth-Century Fiction, Politics, and the Press* (Aldershot, 2008), p. 8.

42   W. E. Adams, *Memoirs of a Social Atom* (London, 1903), p. 235.

43   Quoted in Humpherys and James (eds), *Reynolds*, p. 8.

44   A. Humpherys, 'An introduction to G. W. M. Reynolds's "Encyclopedia of Tales"', in Humpherys and James (eds), *Reynolds*, p. 126.

45   H. Mayhew, *London Labour and the London Poor*, vol. 1 (London, 1864), 27.

46   E. Royle, *Chartism*, 3rd edn (Harlow, 1996), p. 95.

3

'BROTHERS UNDER OPPRESSION': CHARTISTS AND THE CANADIAN REBELLIONS OF 1837-8

In the autumn of 1837 a rebellion in Lower Canada (the core of the modern province of Quebec) was brutally suppressed. Between 250 and 300 rebels died in a series of bloody confrontations with the British army in November and December; 500 more were imprisoned and eight banished to Bermuda. A second rising the following year led to few fatalities, but another 800 were gaoled, 58 transported to Australia and twelve hanged. In Upper Canada (the core of the modern province of Ontario) radical reformers, partly inspired by the first French-Canadian rebellion, attempted to capture Toronto in 1837; an armed camp was also established on an island in the Niagara River which was only dispersed in January 1838. Violence in Upper Canada was limited to clashes between rebel and loyalist forces and only a handful of rebels were killed. However 95 others were transported, two executed and many more imprisoned.

Back in Britain the Canadian crisis, John Stuart Mill declared, 'sets one portion of the friends of popular institutions at variance with another, and by riveting all attention upon events of immediate urgency and of melancholy interest, interrupts for the time all movements and all discussions tending to the great objects of domestic policy'.[1] Yet, in *Canada and the British Empire* (2008), a companion volume to the *Oxford History of the British Empire*, there is no chapter on these insurrections. Indeed, they are mentioned a mere nine times in 300 pages. This represents a considerable down-sizing of the insurgencies in the historical consciousness. Specialist literature on the British perspective is also sparse.[2] Yet during Chartism's formative years the rebellions and their causes loomed very large in the British popular imagination. Their repression, pursued in the name of a new Queen by the British government, was widely seen as an ominous stain on the reputation of a monarchy that had still to shake off the taint of the often scandalous behaviour of George IV and William IV. Victoria was not, of course, personally responsible for the Canadian policy of the Whig administration governing in her name, but its handling of unrest in Canada cast a deep shadow. It was widely felt the teenage Queen had too little understanding of public affairs to form any objective assessment of the actions of her Prime Minister, Lord Melbourne. Radical newspapers alleged her uncle Leopold, King of Belgium, carried most authority with Melbourne on the Canadian question.[3] 'The Queen *of new made graves*' had ascended her throne over the blood of the Canadian dead, according to the mordant 'Coronation Ode' that Ebenezer Elliott wrote for the Sheffield Working Men's Association: 'the page that tells the first deeds of thy reign [is] Black, and blood-blotted'.[4]

In 1791 the British government, anxious not to repeat the deterioration of relations that had led to the American Revolution, had established quasi-autonomous legislatures for both Upper and Lower Canada. Executive power, however, remained with senior colonial administrators appointed either from London or by London's chief nominees, the governors in each colony. However, since the early 1800s Canadian thinking around the issue of popular sovereignty had grown increasingly robust. In both provinces radicals increasingly wanted executive power to be fully accountable to the elected assemblies rather than London; additionally, many in Lower Canada wanted the province established as a republic, free of British imperial authority. By the spring of 1837 relations between the overwhelmingly Francophone Quebec assembly and the English cabal that exercised executive power had completely broken down. The British government responded with a series of resolutions, steered through the House of Commons by Lord John Russell (Colonial Secretary at the time) that rejected all the demands of the French-Canadian *Patriotes* and explicitly gave the Lower Canadian executive money raising powers without reference to the assembly.

The response was escalating political defiance that turned into an armed uprising in November 1837. However, for months previously British radicals had been incensed that the fundamental principle of no taxation without representation had been breached. The *London Dispatch* (the stamped radical newspaper that had succeeded the great *Poor Man's Guardian*) compared Melbourne and Russell to British ministers before the American Revolution. 'These nincompoops are not the British Nation', it assured the Canadians, urging them to assert their independence as continued subservience to Britain benefited none but 'the little lords and lordlings'.[5] The radical (later pro-Chartist) and trade union paper *Weekly True Sun* warmed to the same theme: the many were struggling against the few and 'the same aristocratical spirit that drove the United States to rebellion'.

The paper urged working men to remember that 'in supporting the Canadians, they are fighting their own battle ... Colonies are worth nothing commercially ... Colonies are chiefly prized because, like the Church and the Army they are part of the heritage of the Aristocracy'.[6] William Lovett, secretary of the London Working Men's Association (LWMA), was no less passionate in condemning Russell's 'infamous resolutions for the coercion of the Canadians ... proposing to destroy their right of suffrage, and to compel them to be plundered and enslaved by a few officials in the interests of England'.[7]

Unfolding events revealed that the Whigs were prepared to dismiss 'disloyal' public servants, suspend freedom of assembly and Habeus Corpus, impose martial law and deploy substantial numbers of troops in order to suppress opposition. In Britain the impact of this was considerable. Canada was different from any other British colonial possession. The close affinity between the United Kingdom and Canada was evident during the Reform Crisis, when including Canadian MPs in the House of Commons was discussed. Though dismissed as impractical, the fact that the idea was aired at all indicated that British reformers thought differently about Canada than they did Australia or New Zealand.[8] There were especially strong ties between Upper Canada and Scotland, deriving from a steady stream of migrants, with many radicals among the latter subsequently contributing to Canadian reform movements.[9] British papers routinely noted that William Lyon Mackenzie, the leading rebel in Upper Canada, was a native of Dundee and his close colleague David Gibson of Forfar. The latter's father still farmed near Kerriemuir.[10] Mackenzie had visited London in May-June 1832 where his *Sketches of Canada and the United States* (1833) was published by the noted radical house of Effingham Wilson.

However, until the Lower Canadian Assembly responded to a LWMA address to the Canadian people in August 1837, there is no evidence that any leading insurgent bothered to cultivate British popular opinion. Louis-Joseph Papineau, leader of the French-Canadian rebellion, had visited London in 1823 but only to lobby Parliament. Mackenzie did the same, and so too Charles Duncombe, leader of the rebellion in western Upper Canada during a visit in 1836. None of these men had either the time or need to cultivate non-electors. Mackenzie did hear Feargus O'Connor speak in the Commons (and a decade later spoke very warmly of him);[11] and on one occasion dined with William Cobbett. However the latter was dismissive of Mackenzie's *Sketches*; meanwhile a letter on the unstamped press sent by Mackenzie to the *Weekly True Sun* was never published.[12] This underlines that British popular radical sympathy for the situation in Canada was spontaneous rather than influenced by any preceding propaganda campaign by the Canadians. It emerged instead out of a common perception that colonial rule in Canada exhibited exactly the characteristics of undisguised venality and self-interest that British radicals dubbed 'Old Corruption' at home. 'Canada too is … trampled down and degraded, to secure her tyrants the booty of Downing Street', wrote a Tyneside radical pamphleteer.[13] 'Witness the treachery and tyranny of the Whigs towards the people of Canada', declared a Manchester powerloom weaver, 'witness their abominable conduct at home'.[14] For *London Dispatch*

> The Canadians and ourselves, especially the working classes of this country are engaged in a common cause, that of democracy and liberty against aristocracy and despotism, and in aiding them, we but serve ourselves, and show the misery creating few that the many are at last beginning to unite for their common interests.[15]

In November 1837 the Lower Canadian executive ordered the arrests of leading *Patriotes* and armed insurgency rapidly followed. The picture of the idealistic *Patriote* force, crushed by British troops at the Battle of Saint-Charles on 25 November was calculated to win the hearts of British radicals; but the sacking of the town of Saint-Denis after it had surrendered, in revenge for the first battle of the rebellion where rebels beat-off regular troops, was deeply disturbing; so too was the widespread burning and looting of other French-Canadian settlements that followed the decisive British victory at the Battle of Saint-Eustache on 14 December. British radicals drew little distinction between French-Canadian rebels and the protagonists of the rising in Upper Canada, or between the two risings in military terms. Those who supported the emerging Chartist movement saw both rebellions as authentic assertions of popular political feeling in the face of the same despotic rule that British working people faced at home. *Northern Star* proclaimed that 'every blow struck in Canada is a blow at your liberties'.[16]

This stance was powerfully reinforced when the government appointed Lord Durham (son-in-law of the Whig grandee Earl Grey) as Lord High Commissioner of the Canadas with special responsibility for handling the emergency. In retrospect Durham emerged from the crisis well, his famous *Report on the Affairs of British North America* widely credited as both putting forward a framework for the peaceable government of Canada and forming one of the constitutional cornerstones of the British Commonwealth. But at the time future Chartists (and also some middle-class radicals) were horrified when Durham's appointment was made. He epitomized the aristocratic fiscal-military state that Chartists implacably opposed. In 1820 he had spent the staggering sum of £30,000, bribing and glad-handing his way to become the MP for County Durham.[17] The coal owner could easily afford it: he once remarked that a man might manage to 'jog along on with' £40,000 a year.[18] His entourage when he left for Canada in April 1838 was 'a dangerous blend of aristocratic jobbery, amateurism, and political bias',[19] stuffed with cronies, some of dubious reputation. Chief among them was Edward Gibbon Wakefield, a convicted child abductor and energetic promoter of British emigration to the colonies (scarcely reassuring to French-Canadians).[20] Durham appointed his own brother-in-law as a military *aide de camp*. A longstanding friend (once found guilty of adultery with his wife's sister) acted as a legal adviser and as one diarist commented acerbically, 'it appears his law is not a jot better than his morals'. Another friend and adviser even had property interests in Lower Canada.[21]

All this was public knowledge. Feargus O'Connor witheringly tagged Lord Durham 'King of Canada'.[22] *London Dispatch* alleged his appointment had been engineered by the King of Belgium (Durham had once been a guest for several weeks at his palace in Brussels).[23] The peer's fondness for what would now be called 'bling' also attracted critical comment. For the *Northern Liberator* Durham was 'a kind of public jackdaw'. In the 1839 Chartist novel *The Political Pilgrim's Progress*, he was portrayed as 'the Yellow Dwarf' and his entourage a menagerie of exotic but repulsive reptiles – Durham being of short stature and yellow the colour of Whig rosettes. 'The dwarf had cost a great deal of money … he required nice and expensive keeping.'[24] Carmarthen's Working Men's Association was confident that 'the Canadians were not the people to be caught by the vapid dignity, the chicanery, and chaff of aristocracy'.[25] But instead they were caught up by Durham's peremptory handling of the risings – widespread arrests, detention without trial, banishment by diktat. Durham's actions were 'treason against the people', O'Connor declared; 'Rash, petulant, overbearing, and ignorant', 'he is accuser, judge, jury, and executioner in his own person. This he delights in,' declared *Northern Liberator*.[26]

If all this seems somewhat hysterical, we should bear in mind that Durham's behaviour in banishing leading rebels on pain of death forced the government hastily to pass an indemnity act to decriminalize the actions of the civil servants who had to implement the bans. Durham's brief flirtation with radical reform in the early thirties made radical contempt for his actions even more-bitter. 'Lord Durham is a "lost mutton"', declared the veteran London radical Francis Place. (*Lost mutton*, a borrowing from

Shakespeare, denoted a prostitute.) 'He had a chance such as few men have had', continued Place, 'but he was all a Lord and none a man.'[27] Durham resigned, engulfed in controversy, after only eight months. His attempts to pacify Lower Canada led directly to the second French-Canadian rebellion in 1838.

Popular British reactions to the Canadian crisis were also conditioned by the manner in which news was mediated. 'Death and conflagration are the order of the day', was a typical headline.[28] It would be another two decades before the Atlantic telegraph: Canadian news therefore unfolded episodically and often sensationally. Both national and regional press relied on North American papers, published up to six weeks before, for their news coverage. It was several weeks into the New Year before British readers learnt of the battle of Saint-Eustache and of the peremptory destruction of civilian property. British radicals therefore dared to hope that the Canadians might yet be successful for some time after the 1837 rebellions had been crushed. 'The Canadian revolution is assuming a new, and to lovers of freedom a more cheering, aspect', thought the *Leeds Times* in mid-February the following year.[29] 'The war is only now begun in real earnest', *London Dispatch* had declared at the end of January. Its report, 'Atrocities committed in Lower Canada', was adapted from the *Montreal Herald* of 16 December:

> St Eustache presented a heart-rending appearance, the whole of the lower portion being one sheet of lurid flame ... about fifty houses have been burnt, and nothing now is left of them but stone walls or solitary chimneys ... It is conjectured that from 150 to 200 were killed by the military, or perished in the flames. The stench from the burning of the bodies was very offensive. The village having been surrounded, there was no possibility of escape; and the prisoners say that numbers retreated into the vaults of the church and the cellars, where they must have perished miserably ... Our informant also visited the scene of the action at St Charles, and represents the spectacle as most revolting. The dead were yet unburied, and their corpses mangled and mutilated in a shocking manner by swine.[30]

This report was reasonably accurate, though modern estimates put the fatalities rather lower, while conceding 'there is no way of knowing how many patriots died at St Eustache'.[31] But of course 'from 150 to 200' were the figures that gripped the British public. It is important to bear in mind that fatalities from military actions to suppress political dissent in early nineteenth-century Britain were far fewer than even 100. At 'Peterloo' in Manchester (1819) eighteen had died in the most notorious of these incidents. More recently between twelve and twenty protesters had been killed at Rathcormac in 1834, during the Irish tithe war. One would have needed to look back to Ireland in 1798 for carnage exceeding that in the Canadas. The scale of the casualties in Canada, unprecedented in the memory of two generations, therefore seized the attention of the British public.

However, it was not just the extent of the casualties and the circumstances of their deaths, horrific though they were, that exercised British radicals. 'The same tyrants who oppressed the people of Canada also oppressed the people of Great Britain', Robert Knox, a roof slater and leading Tyneside radical, told a 'Female Democratic Festival' in Newcastle to vocal applause.[32] As radical frustration at the post-1832 Parliament's failure to deliver further reform grew, the belief that the Whigs were not merely indifferent to the interests of working people but intent upon distressing them further grew with it. The *True Scotsman* grouped the American Revolution, Canada's rebellions and the plight of working-class Scots as gross examples of taxation without representation.[33] Small wonder Chartist meetings toasted 'The patriots of Canada and may success crown their noble exertions in the cause of freedom' and deplored the government's 'tyrannical conduct to our brave and patriotic brethren'.[34]

Sentiments expressed at a public meeting devoted to Canada in Bradford in early January 1838 perfectly capture the belief that Whig policy, be it in Canada or England, was all of one piece. O'Connor 'entered into a most detailed account of the effect which our foreign policy had upon our domestic concerns. He showed most clearly and ingeniously the relevance which the Canadian question had to the Poor Law Amendment Act and the whole system of machinery.' Peter Bussey, a local beershop keeper and militant weaver trade unionist, spoke admiringly of 'the spirit which fired the Canadians with the love of liberty'. He then moved a resolution that the demands of the Canadians ought to be conceded because it would also relieve 'this country from heavy pecuniary charges annually sustained in consequence of its connexion with that Colony'.[35] O'Connor's family had been deeply committed to the cause of independence for Ireland but he was now carving out a career as a leading figure in British radicalism. Ireland, however, was the optic through which he viewed events in Canada. In the summer of 1838 he told a rally in Barrhead (nine miles south-west of Glasgow) that it was futile to look for anything resembling justice from the Whigs: their first act had been the coercion of Ireland and their most recent the coercion of Canada.[36] (The Irish Coercion Act of 1833 had severely curtailed freedom of political expression and assembly in Ireland.[37]) In Glasgow a few days later O'Connor widened the agenda further. Referring to the bill then before the Commons to create a national network of police forces, he declared there was little to distinguish it from the government's suppression of Canadian radicals.[38]

Nor was O'Connor alone in making this kind of connection. Rochdale Chartists linked Whig tyranny in Canada to the sentences of transportation for life passed on trade union leaders in rural Dorset and in the Glasgow cotton industry.[39] Warming to the same theme a speaker at a protest meeting in Huddersfield linked the persecuted trade unionists and Canadian rebels with the Rathcormac protesters. All would 'rise in awful accusation against these bloodstained myrmidons of hell ... her Majesty's Ministers'.[40] LWMA missionary John Cleave urged workmen in the Essex garrison town of Colchester not to enlist in the army: 'I entreat you not to lift a murderous arm against the Canadians; they only ask what we ask for ... No, do not take the shilling; there is murder, there is slavery in the offer'.[41] *Northern Star* branded Whig policy a 'crusade of despotism'.[42] Henry Vincent used his *Western Vindicator* to argue that the Whigs would not 'trample upon our liberty as they have upon that of Canada ... were the people installed into political power'.[43]

Concern was most-sustained in London where the LWMA had taken a lead in supporting Canadian 'Brothers under Oppression' as soon as Russell's 'infamous resolutions' were put to Parliament. A petition, written by the highly regarded unstamped pressman Henry Hetherington and sent to Parliament in March 1837, prayed that the Canadians should elect their own legislative council, have control over the collection and dispersal of taxation and be responsible for the Canadian judiciary. It was prefaced by frank criticism of Whig conduct, variously described as 'aristocratic domination', 'fraught with tyranny and injustice', and 'pregnant with evil'. The LWMA petition was just one of 74 presented to Parliament during the 1837-8 session against Whig policy in Canada. Collectively their 12,000 signatures were only 25 per cent fewer than those petitioning for universal suffrage that session, and they exceeded in number those petitioning for factory reform. Although Canada paled beside the biggest issues of the day (the New Poor Law and the condition of ex-slaves in British colonies following abolition), it was nonetheless among those topics that most exercised the petitioning public at this time.[44]

As the parliamentary session wore on, a number of petitions also criticized the conduct of the war. The LWMA sent a second in March 1838 doing just that, but as Lovett wearily commented, 'our prayer for impeachment was very much like appealing to culprits for a judgment against themselves'.[45] The LWMA was the hub of a corresponding network with some 140 like-minded groups across the British Isles. It added Montreal to its network via an open letter in August 1837 to the French-Canadian rebels. Their response, written by Papineau and elaborately copied onto parchment, was burnt in a loyalist arson attack on the offices of the main *Patriote* newspaper. Fortunately Papineau's text did make it across the Atlantic where it became the principal *Patriote* statement circulating among British radicals. The LWMA published both texts as a pamphlet: 'These are noble documents, and ought to be most extensively circulated', commented a review in the pro-Chartist *Leeds Times*.[46]

—O—

This chapter has so far summarized in broadly descriptive terms what popular radical responses in Britain to the Canadian rebellions were. Had the episode, though, any lasting significance? At the risk of stating the obvious, it made not an iota of difference to the predicament of the Canadian rebels. Indeed, the second French-Canadian rebellion of November 1838 had been briskly suppressed before news that it had even begun reached Britain. But by that time something truly remarkable had happened to British radicalism: the emergence of the Chartist movement. While it would be ridiculous to claim that the Canadian rebellions had a direct causal impact on Chartism, it is not exaggerating to say that they had a formative influence on the Chartists. Histories of Chartism, however, have failed to register this.[47] Whig policy in Canada was more than just another chapter in the history of betrayal traced by Chartists since the Reform Act – the blunt refusal to widen the electorate further, Irish Coercion, the New Poor Law, the Rural Police Bill, the transportation of trade unionists. The treatment of the Canadian rebels was widely seen as foreshadowing what might happen to a British reform movement. In May 1838 troops killed twelve farm workers during a riot at Bossenden Wood, three miles north-west of Canterbury, giving 'the men of Kent a taste of Canada' according to 'Republican', writing in the *London Dispatch*.[48] 'The conduct which ministers were pursuing in Canada would be imitated here if they had only the opportunity', James Osbourne, a leather worker, told Brighton Chartists. 'They saw sufficient in the blood-thirsty practices in Canada to assure them that the same fate would attend the unsuccessful asserters of freedom in this country' claimed another south coast Chartist.[49] Canada had been forced into revolt, according to one

London carpenter and trade unionist, and the government 'would shortly force this country into revolution' as well.[50]

Three things followed from such close comparisons. First, while the outcome of the rebellions was unclear, radicals dared to hope that Canada might strike the first heavy blow against Whig misrule. As the *Patriotes* in Lower Canada regrouped prior to their second rebellion, the printer James Watson widened the comparison further: Haiti 'had once been governed by France, but the people of that country got rid of their rulers as Canada, he hoped, was soon likely to do with regard to England.'[51] Second, as Chartism coalesced into a nationwide popular crusade, the example of Canada stiffened the resolve of the Chartist leadership to act decisively. 'The Whigs shall never violate the Constitution of this country, as they have done in Canada', George Julian Harney told the Derby rally that elected him to Chartism's National Convention in January 1839:

> They charge us with being physical-force men; I fling the charge back in the teeth of these canting Liberals. Let them call to mind their own words and deeds ... above all let them look to Canada – have they not sent forth the women and children to perish in the snow? Have they not fired the cottages and desolated the hearths of the Canadians? Have they not burnt the temples of the living God and the bodies of the dead?[52]

'The country is on the edge of a frightful precipice and is in danger of being hurried over it', commented the *True Scotsman*. 'If the middle and upper classes do not open their eyes to the real state and sentiments of the people', the paper continued, the people would be 'driven to extremities' by their indifference. Chief among the complaints it listed were 'domestic turmoil in abundance', the state of Ireland and Canada 'under a military despotism'.[53] In the weeks after news from Saint-Eustache reached Britain, the phrase *military despotism* was frequently applied to the trajectory that Whig government was taking, for example by Thomas Doubleday at Felling, Peter McDouall at Manchester, Bronterre O'Brien at a West Riding rally on Hartshead Moor and again (with O'Connor and Reginald Richardson) in the Convention.[54] 'This is what our foul Aristocracy calls "British Justice"', a Tyneside Chartist observed: 'would you put an end forever to such villainy? ... hurl down the blood-stained Oligarchs and take the position of men in the government of your own country'.[55] Rebels in the gaols of Canada should be freed, the tailor Robert Lowery told Carlisle Chartists, and government ministers hanged by the head in their place.[56] In September 1838, speaking at the rally outside the Houses of Parliament that formally launched the

Chartist movement in the capital, William Lovett vividly captured this mood of defiance:

> The People's Charter contained all that they now contended for, because it would give the people the means of remedying all their wrongs. (Cheers.) ... We shall be told of the unreasonableness of our demand – (Hear) – of the necessity of taking our rights just as our lords and masters please to give them, by instalments – (Hear). But we have been listening to those proposals for the last six years, and we have gained as instalments a coercion law for Ireland – several oppressive measures for England – revolution and despotism for Canada – (Hear, hear). We want no more such instalments.[57]

The third issue that followed from British radicals' empathy with the Canadian rebels concerned a rapidly evolving belief in the legitimacy of violent resistance to tyranny. Even before Lower Canada rose, the radical *Weekly True Sun* had predicted that the Canadians would not 'for a moment entertain any other thought than that of physical resistance'.[58] The disproportionate response meted out by the state against them helped to justify Chartist belligerence. Augustus Beaumont, *Northern Liberator's* proprietor until January 1838, reportedly even contemplated leading a private army of 500 Tynesiders to Canada to assist the rebels.[59] What was happening in Canada, simultaneously with the emergence of Chartism, infused a profound sense of immediacy and urgency into the hitherto theoretical discussion around the constitutional right of Britons to bear arms and, if necessary, to use them to resist tyranny. Knox declared to a cheering rally in Sunderland that,

> There was no way to get their rights but by making the Government afraid ... In Canada they [the Whigs] had taught the people a dreadful lesson of flame and blood, and it recoiled upon their own heads ... There was a crisis approaching, and perhaps millions would meet on the ruin that would gloom over what was once happy and smiling England.[60]

This point about Canadian events accelerating the tendency to militancy among Chartists is also important because it exposes how prevalent support for direct action and physical force was in early Chartism. The historiography of the movement has been dogged by a spurious dichotomy between so-called moral force and physical force Chartism. However, before 1840 hardly any Chartist (certainly no English or Welsh one) unequivocally rejected the use of force for political ends. This was true even of Lovett, held up by early historians of Chartism as an exemplary leader in contrast to allegedly hot-headed mob orators, O'Connor conspicuous among them.[61] As has been shown above, William Lovett was as forthright as any in his condemnation of Whig Canadian policy and as vocal in his insistence that it presaged a need for democratic resistance in Britain. Henry Hetherington was another so-called moral force Chartist whose view of the rebellions was bleak: 'If working men would know what state of things the Whigs are preparing for this country, they have only to consider what is going on in Canada', he wrote when news of the sacking of French Canadian villages reached England. Even more scathing was Thomas Perronet Thompson, labelled by a recent biographer the 'principal advocate of "sensible Chartism" ... by which he meant that Chartists had to employ moral rather than physical force'.[62] Thompson invoked the execution of Charles I at Whitehall in a speech that speedily acquired notoriety:

> Treason in England was treason in Canada, and he stood there to avow and to maintain that the ministers of the crown ... had committed an act of treason, which the British people, if they were not unwise, would not fail to punish when they had the power. (Great cheering.) Whitehall had already witnessed an execution; that scene might be repeated. (Cheers.)[63]

'He would stand on no nice fence as to what precise quantum of grievance might justify resistance,' Thompson reiterated the following week when he spoke with Henry Vincent at another meeting in Canada's support.[64] A similar perspective was offered by a group dedicated to keeping alive the illustrious memory of William Cobbett. Members of Lower Canada's legislative assembly, the Cobbett Club noted, had petitioned Westminster 'without any more attention being paid to them than if they had been so many jack-asses'; they had rightly resolved to resort to arms. However, 'another means, too, they used to assist in the same cause, namely "*moral force*" (a very good thing if well seconded and backed by physical force, but, without *that*, not of half the value of one *single rifle ball*)'.[65] This is a particularly revealing indication of the symbiosis between moral and physical force positions in early Chartism, especially noteworthy since these were the words of an otherwise moderate body within English radicalism.[66]

The significance of the Canadian Question for British radicals was therefore multi-faceted. In explaining Chartists' jaundiced view of Whig government, Canada is an important factor. It revealed the Whigs not just as the architects of policies that were widely perceived as discriminatory, unjust and divisive, but as fully prepared to close down such constitutional channels of political representation as existed and to use extreme force against subjects of the British crown. No other issue (not even Irish coercion) illustrated so vividly the likely government response to a reinvigorated radical reform movement in Britain. The rebellions also provided a litmus test by which to assess the long-held argument that the Tory Party constituted the true enemy to democratic progress, and that the Whigs (who were allied with a growing tranche of middle-class liberal reformers) were therefore the logical party with whom Chartists should make common cause. This was the argument advanced by Daniel O'Connell, the great Irish nationalist leader, whose tactical alliance with the Whigs in Parliament infuriated British radicals. O'Connor attacked O'Connell for deluding Ireland with talk of 'Canadian liberty' and for failing to oppose Whig Canadian policy in Parliament as he had once promised. Oldham's Radical Association claimed O'Connell could have exerted influence over the Whigs to prevent 'the violence, the bloodshed, and civil wars' in Canada; instead for personal short-term political advantage he 'suffered the miseries of civil war to be inflicted upon an injured and oppressed people'.[67] Even after the lapse of five years, Harney rounded on O'Connell: he 'BETRAYED THE CAUSE OF THE CANADIANS FOR THE FILTHY PATRONAGE OF THE "BASE, BLOODY AND BRUTAL WHIGS" – the remorseless despots who ravaged Canada with fire and sword'.[68] Lovett was the most scathing Chartist to comment on O'Connell's stance on Canada:

There are no acts or atrocities which the Tories have inflicted on England or Ireland, that can match those deeds which the perfidious Whigs have inflicted on our Canadian brethren ... Talk of what the Tories did in America, match their deeds if you can with what the Whigs have inflicted on Canada. They have not scrupled to destroy every vestige of their constitutional rights – their selfish and arrogant myrmidons were the first to provoke Canadian resistance to their unparalleled despotism – they then imprisoned their legislators and proscribed and hunted down the best men of the country, they have brutally encouraged ignorant savages to glut their thirst for blood, they have destroyed the freedom of the press, suspended the Habeus Corpus Act, proclaimed martial law, burned their churches, sacked their villages, laid the country in ashes at the fiat of one man, and confiscation and plunder have been the warwhoop of their brutal soldiers. Gracious creator of human beings! Talk of the crimes of Toryism! Match Whiggery with Nicholas [i.e. old Nick, the Devil] instead.[69]

The Canadian rebellion was therefore one of the issues that drove a wedge between the emerging Chartist movement and Irish radicalism under O'Connell's direction. This was a matter of considerable importance in terms of the concerted threat the British government faced from radicals at home and in Ireland. In 1839 and 1842, the peak years of Chartist mobilization, there simply was no concerted threat. It would take the death of O'Connell in 1847 to make it possible for British Chartists and Irish nationalists to co-operate. Events in the year of European revolution, 1848, suggested how potent the intersection of Irish and British radicalism might be, but by then Chartism was already a movement in decline.

Relations with Ireland were of course not the only fracture in radicalism. There were profound and irreconcilable differences between the vast majority on each side of working-class and middle-class radicals and reformers. When in January 1838 the London newspaper proprietor John Bell tried to move an amendment at a radical meeting, 'for postponing the consideration of Canadian grievances until those of the working classes were redressed', he was fiercely shouted down by the *workmen* present. Amidst scenes of uproar Bell's amendment was put, but only one person supported it.[70] The government's oppression of Canada was linked explicitly to its attitude to the working classes at home. Prominence in the agitation to support Canada was a defining feature among many who led the early phase of Chartism. The pro-Canada movement was overwhelmingly one of working men: almost all those quoted in this chapter were manual workers or journalists of working-class origin. There were exceptions: O'Connor of course; Ebenezer Elliott was an iron merchant and Perronet Thompson a retired army officer; but Elliott's economic security was parlous, having almost been bankrupted in 1837, while Thompson's stance on Canada was uncharacteristically extreme and alienated most other middle-class reformers.[71] From its inception, views of the Canadian crisis cleaved along class lines, a situation acutely summarized by John Stuart Mill: Russell's resolutions had passed through the Commons 'with about fifty dissentients, and (except from the brave Working Men) hardly a whisper of public disapprobation'. Middle-class liberals, he added, 'consider this a trifling matter, a thing which may be softly remonstrated against, but which is no "practical grievance".'[72]

These same class lines would soon be reflected in the Chartist experience. East London Chartists collecting signatures for a pro-Canadian petition in November 1838 among shopkeepers and small tradesmen found that none 'attempted to deny any of the allegations contained in the petition; on the contrary, they entirely approved of it, but they were so situated that they could not affix their signatures with safety to their own interests'.[73] In January 1839 Chartist workmen surged into a middle-class liberal meeting in Newcastle Guildhall, to heckle a speech by a Whig MP. 'You'll soon lose Canada' was yelled repeatedly to loud cheers. The purpose of the meeting was completely subverted: instead of passing its promoters' resolution in favour of tax reform, the meeting concluded 'with three cheers for Canada and ... three groans' for the local liberal newspaper.[74]

—O—

It would be fallacious to claim Canada remained at the forefront of Chartists' minds as it had done in 1838. During the movement's formative period Chartists had nurtured the very real hope that their 'brothers under oppression' would succeed. The rebellions' failure thwarted their hopes while Parliament's dismissal of the 1839 Petition, the Newport Rising and the treatment of Chartist prisoners, cumulatively eclipsed the Canadian question. Meanwhile Chartism rapidly generated its own heroes, martyrs and *causes célèbres*. Furthermore, apprehension that the United States was seeking to profit from the destabilization of its neighbour introduced a note of ambiguity to some Chartist comments on Canada.[75] In addition, government treatment of the Canadian rebel leaders in the mid-1840s compared highly favourably to that of Frost, Williams and Jones.[76] This understandably diminished Chartist attachment to the Canadian cause.

However, the Canadian rebels remained green in the Chartist memory. When he visited North America in 1843, the veteran Huddersfield Chartist Lawrence Pitkethly sought out William Lyon Mackenzie and wrote an account of their two meetings for *Northern Star*. (The two men discussed the Newport and Upper Canada risings, John Frost, O'Connor and Sir Robert Peel.[77]) Early in 1848, as the revolutionary crisis in France took shape, Harney serialized reminiscences by Mackenzie.[78] The costs of the rebellions and the bravery and subsequent treatment of the rebels were a frequent point of reference: 'We speak of them with that reverence and respect in which we shall ever hold the brave, who openly arm, and boldly defend, themselves against oppression'.[79] The Canadian rebellions of 1837-8 are a significant part of the explanation for the militancy of early Chartism and for the preparedness of the overwhelming majority of active Chartists both to countenance the use of force against authority and to do so in language that was uncompromising and explicit.

Reference was made in the introduction to this chapter to amnesia among historians regarding the rebellions. This partly stems from a

Canadian historiography that habitually stressed the local circumstances in their causation and argued for the autonomy of events in Lower and Upper Canada from each other. Groundbreaking work by current Canadian historians, however, has stressed the roots of these rebellions in an 'Atlantic' republican tradition.[80] This was a perspective that many Chartists, especially those who esteemed Paine and the memory of the American and French Revolutions, shared. An influential historian of the Canadian rebellions, Michel Ducharme, has recently observed that 'with the military defeat of the Patriotes and radicals in 1837-38, the British [government] succeeded not only in liquidating the republican opposition in the colonies but also in putting an end to the cycle of the Atlantic revolutions begun in the empire's own defeat in 1783'.[81] One way of interpreting Chartism is that it constituted a coda to that cycle. A Parliament elected on the principles of the People's Charter would, Chartists emphasized, move quickly to implement democracy in Britain's colonies. As the *Address of the London Working Men's Association to the People of Canada* declared:

> When the voice of the millions shall be heard in the senate house, when *they* shall possess power to decree justice, our colonies will cease to be regarded as nurseries for despots, where industry is robbed to pamper vice.[82]

Notes

1   J. S. Mill, 'The Canadian Portfolio', *London and Westminster Review*, 6:2 (Jan. 1838), 502-533 (p. 504).

2   The exceptions (though neither examine Canada's implications for Chartism) are W. Thomas, *The Philosophic Radicals: Nine Studies in Theory and Practice, 1817-41* (Oxford, 1979), pp. 338-405 ('Durham, the radicals, and the Canada mission') and M. J. Turner, 'Radical agitation and the Canada question in British politics, 1837-41', *Historical Research* 79:203 (Feb. 2006), 90-114. M. Brook offers a purely narrative account of a post-rebellion encounter in his article 'Lawrence Pitkethly, Dr Smyles, and Canadian revolutionaries in the United States, 1842', *Ontario History* 57 (1965), 79-84.

3   E. g. *LD* 15 Apr. 1838.

4   *Poetical Works of Ebenezer Elliott, the Corn-Law Rhymer* (Edinburgh, 1840), p. 163, reprinted in *NL* 30 June 1838.

5   *LD* 30 Apr. 1837.

6   *Weekly True Sun* 12 and 19 Mar. 1837.

7   W. Lovett, *Life and Struggles of William Lovett in Pursuit of Bread, Knowledge and Freedom* (London, 1876), p. 103.

8   B. Hilton, *A Mad, Bad, and Dangerous People? England, 1783-1846* (Oxford, 2006), p. 560.

9   A. M. M. Evans, 'The Scot as politician', in W. S. Reid, *The Scottish Tradition in Canada*' (Toronto, 1976), p. 287; M. E. Vance, 'Scottish Chartism in Canada west? An examination of the "clear grit" reformers', *Scottish Tradition* 22 (1997), 56-102.

10   *LD* 4 Feb. 1838.

11   *NS* 24 June 1843.

12   M. Fairley (ed.), *Selected Writings of William Lyon Mackenzie, 1824-37* (Toronto, 1960), pp. 134-40, 157-70, 247-60, 312-30; *Cobbett's Magazine* 6 (July 1833), 587. Mackenzie's letter subsequently appeared in his *Colonial Advocate* 21 Feb. 1833, see C. Read and R. J. Stagg (eds), *The Rebellion of 1837 in Upper Canada* (Toronto, 1985), p. 28. Mackenzie's papers in the Archives of Ontario include a file of cuttings from *Chartist Circular*, *Northern Liberator* and Beaumont's *Radical*, grouped under a heading 'Chartism, or White-slavery – labourers – workmen': see Vance, p. 87.

13   A. H. B[eaumont], *Whig Nullities: or, A Review of a Pamphlet Attributed to the Right Hon. John Cam Hobhouse, M.P. for Nottingham* (London, 1837), p. 8.

14   *LD* 30 Apr. 1837.

15   *LD* 19 Mar. 1837.

16   *NS* 6 Jan. 1838.

17   *The History of Parliament: the House of Commons, 1820-1832, Volume 2: Constituencies Part 1*, ed. D. R. Fisher, (Cambridge, 2009), p. 335.

18   H. Maxwell (ed.), *Creevey Papers* (3rd edn, 1905), pp. 373-4, quoted in Thomas, *Philosophic Radicals*, p. 339.

19   Thomas, *Philosophic Radicals*, p. 387.

20   D. J. Moss, 'Edward Gibbon Wakefield', *Oxford Dictionary of National Biography*, Oxford University Press, 2004; online edn, May 2007 [http://0-www.oxforddnb.com.wam.leeds.ac.uk/view/article/28415, accessed 11 Nov 2014].

21   Charles Greville, quoted in G. Martin, *The Durham Report and British Policy* (Cambridge: 1972), p. 24.

22   *NS* 28 July 1838.

23   *LD* 15 Apr. 1838; Thomas, *Philosophic Radicals*, p. 348.

24   *The Political Pilgrim's Progress* (Newcastle upon Tyne, 1839), p. 32.

25   *NL* 11 Aug. 1838; *NS* 21 Apr. 1838.

26   *NS* 21 July 1838; *NL* 11 and 18 Aug. 1838.

27   Place to Harriet Grote, 2 Jan. 1839, quoted by Thomas, *Philosophic Radicals*, p. 401.

28   *NL* 3 Feb. 1838.

29   *Leeds Times* 10 February 1838.

30   *LD* 28 Jan. 1838.

31   A. Greer, *The Patriots and the People: The Rebellion of 1837 in Rural Lower Canada* (Toronto, 1993), p. 327.

32   *NL* 8 June 1839.

33   *True Scotsman*, 15 and 22 Dec. 1838.

34   Examples from Halifax, Leeds and Rochdale, *NS* 6 Jan, 13 Jan and 17 Mar. 1838.

35 *NS* 13 Jan. 1838.

36 *NS* 21 July 1838. Others had already drawn similar conclusions, e.g. *Weekly True Sun*, 12 Mar. 1837, 'The Canada Coercion Bill will be every whit as atrocious as the Irish Coercion Bill'.

37 D. Thompson, *The Chartists: Popular Politics in the Industrial Revolution* (London, 1984), pp. 18-19.

38 *NS* 28 July 1838.

39 *NS* 17 Mar. 1838.

40 *NS* 27 Jan. 1838.

41 Quoted in A. F. J. Brown, *Chartism in Essex and Suffolk* (Chelmsford, 1982), p. 49.

42 *NS* 6 Jan. 1838.

43 Publicola, 'Politics for the People', *Western Vindicator* 23 Feb. 1839.

44 Calculations based on *Companion to the Almanac; or Year-book of General Information for 1839* (London, 1838), pp. 216-18.

45 Lovett, *Life and Struggles*, p. 150.

46 'The Permanent and Central Committee of the County of Montreal, to the Working Men's Association of London', *Weekly True Sun* 3 Dec., *Leeds Times* 9 Dec. 1837; *An Address to the People of Canada: with their Reply to the Working Men's Association* (London: 1838); *Operative* 23 Dec. 1838.

47 Canada's impact on Chartism is restricted to the LWMA even in Richard Brown's collective history *Three Rebellions: Canada 1837-8, South Wales 1839 and Victoria, Australia 1854* (Southampton, 2010), pp. 630-3.

48 *LD* 10 June 1838.

49 *Brighton Patriot* 22 Jan., 16 July 1839.

50 *LD* 14 Jan. 1838.

51 *LD* 28 Oct. 1838.

52 *NS* 9 Feb. 1839.

53 *Brighton Patriot* 23 Apr. 1839, quoting *True Scotsman*.

54 *NS* 24 March, *NL* 30 March, *Charter* 14 April, *Liverpool Mercury* 26 April, *Champion* 5 May, *Bradford Observer* 23 May.

55 *The Way to Universal Suffrage. By a Tyne Chartist*, (Newcastle, 1839), pp. 27-8

56 *Carlisle Journal* 27 Oct. 1838.

57 *NS* 22 Sept. 1838, *LD* 23 Sept. 1838.

58 *Weekly True Sun* 26 Mar. 1837.

59 T. A. Devyr, *Odd Book of the Nineteenth Century* (Greenpoint, NY, 1882), p. 159; W. H. Maehl, 'Augustus Hardin Beaumont: Anglo-American radical (1798–1838)', *International Review of Social History*, 14:2 (Aug. 1969), 237-50.

60 *NL* 2 Feb. 1839.

61 See chapter 2 above and chapter 6 on Brewster, the Scottish Chartist.

62 M. J. Turner, 'Thomas Perronet Thompson, "sensible Chartism" and the chimera of radical unity', *Albion* 33:1 (2001) 51-74 (p. 52).

63 *LD* 7 Jan. 1838; Turner, 'Radical agitation', pp. 99-101.

64 *Weekly True Sun* 14. Jan. 1838.

65 *A political tract by the Cobbett Club of London: addressed to the people of the United Kingdom* (London, 1839), p. 29.

66   For the Cobbett Club see M. Chase, 'Cobbett, his children and Chartism', in J. Grande and J. Stevenson (eds), *William Cobbett, Romanticism and the Enlightenment: Contexts and Legacy* (London, 2015).

67   *Operative* 2 Dec. 1838; *NS* 24 Feb. 1838; *LD* 20 Jan. 1839.

68   *NS* 4 Nov. 1843.

69   'The Working Men's Association to the Irish People' (1838), quoted in Lovett, *Life and Struggles*, pp. 191-2.

70   *LD* 7 Jan. 1838.

71   Turner, 'Radical agitation'.

72   Mill, 'Canadian Portfolio', *London and Westminster Review*, p. 514.

73   *LD* 11 Nov. 1838.

74   *NL* 2 Feb. 1839.

75   M. J. Turner, *Liberty and Liberticide: The Role of America in Nineteenth-Century British Radicalism* (Lanham, MD, 2014), pp. 40-1.

76   A point argued forcefully in Parliament by Duncombe. See Hansard, House of Commons Debates vol. 84, c880 (10 Mar. 1846).

77   *NS* 24 June 1843.

78   *NS* 29 Jan. and 5 Feb. 1848.

79   *NS* 2 Feb. 1839. See also 15 June and 20 July 1839, 18 Jan., 29 Feb., 24 Oct. 1840, 12 June 1841, 4 June 1842; *Political Almanac for 1840; and the Annual Black Book* (Manchester, 1839), pp. 6, 56, 61; *English Chartist Circular* 5 [March 1841] p. 20, 7 [March 1841], 11 [April 1841] p. 44, 42 [Nov. 1841], p. 168, 59 [March 1842], p. 28.

80   A. Greer, '1837-38: rebellion reconsidered', *Canadian Historical Review* 76:1 (March 1995), 1-18; M. Ducharme, 'Closing the last chapter of the Atlantic Revolution: the 1837-1838 Rebellions in Upper and Lower Canada', in David S Shields et al (eds), *Liberty! Égalité! Independencia!: Print Culture, Enlightenment, and Revolution in the Americas, 1776-1826* (Worcester MA, 2007), pp. 193-210; A. Schrauwers, *'Union is strength': W. L. Mackenzie, the Children of Peace, and the Emergence of Joint Stock Democracy in Upper Canada* (Toronto, 2009); M. Ducharme, *The Idea of Liberty in Canada during the Age of Atlantic Revolutions, 1776-1838* (Montreal, 2014).

81   Ducharme, *Idea of Liberty*, p. 13. See also Greer, *Patriots and the People*, p. 131.

82   LWMA, *Address to the People of Canada* (1838), quoted in Lovett, *Life and Struggles*, p. 109.

4

'WE WISH ONLY TO WORK FOR OURSELVES': THE CHARTIST LAND PLAN[1]

The Chartist Land Plan ought to have attracted more attention from historians before the 1990s. Even those largely responsible for what might be termed the rehabilitation of its promoter, Feargus O'Connor, as a serious politician fought shy of close engagement with the Land Plan. Epstein's biography significantly stopped short of it, though its section on O'Connor's agrarian ideas was nonetheless a notable exception in a historiographical pattern that had generally alternated between condescension and hostility. *The Chartist Experience* (1982) virtually ignored the Plan, even though the collection was consciously cast as the successor to the pioneering *Chartist Studies* of 1959. It was still to McAskill's essay in the latter that a reader requiring a broad and dispassionate treatment of the Chartist Land Plan had to turn.[2]

The treatment accorded the Land Plan until recently by historians derived directly from its contemporary reception at the hands of critics of O'Connor. For Robert Gammage, himself a Chartist, the scheme was patently a 'fallacy', 'illegal in its very foundation' and a 'great folly which was to contribute to the disgrace of the Chartist movement'.[3] The historiography of Chartism has been conditioned by a need to frame an explanation for the movement's failure; at the same time generations of historians, habituated to seeing the history of the labour movement almost as an apostolic succession, were quick to dismiss the Chartist Land Plan as an irrelevance. Hovell's verdict that it was 'not a real Chartist scheme' is the most conspicuous example of this tendency, persisting long after the main tenets of his interpretation had been revised.[4] 'Absurd and doomed to failure from the start', wrote A. L. Morton (from a very different perspective to Hovell's), 'it took up energy that might have been better spent'.[5] There was a striking degree of unanimity across historical treatments of the Land Plan. It was dismissed as 'unquestionably reactionary', 'crack-brained', and 'harebrained';[6] as 'utopian' and 'nostalgic' (as if these terms precluded need for further analysis);[7] and in influential textbooks as 'the greatest distraction of all' and 'the most ambitious deviation of all'.[8] Even work of substance on Chartism generally could disappoint by the paucity of attention paid to the scheme,[9] while fuller and more sympathetic accounts were on the whole either descriptive narratives, or preoccupied with the topography of the Chartist settlements.[10] For a more considered approach it was necessary to look beyond Britain to some neglected reaches of Chartist historiography: for many decades the cumulative portrait within Edouard Dolléans' *Le Chartisme* (1912-13) remained the lengthiest of the Land Plan available, while Bachmann's *Die Agrarreform in der Chartistenbewegung* (1928) still remains the only book-length treatment of its subject.[11]

It is helpful to recount this historiography in order to appreciate how understanding the Land Plan has been impeded by a tendency to 'Whig interpretation', inclined to dismiss it as a wrong turning and in extreme cases condemn it for impeding the forward march of labour. Even so, how is it that, at the heart of the earliest mass movement of industrial workers, an agrarian analysis of social problems – and an agrarian prescription for them – could exercise so persuasive an appeal?

'We seek not to be rich in this world's goods – we wish only to work for ourselves so that we may enjoy the fruit of our toil, without being subject to a tyrant master.' So wrote William Loveless to his brother George, the Tolpuddle Martyr, in December 1847, concerning his membership of the Chartist Land Plan. We are afforded this glimpse of William, anticipating 'an opportunity for a brief sojourn in this world before passing on to "a better land"', in John Harrison's *The Second Coming*.[12] An agricultural labourer, Loveless had recently joined the branch of the National Land Company (its official title at this time) in the Dorset town of Bridport. 'Mr O'Connor ... anticipates locating 30 thousand in 7 years from the commencement', he wrote to his brother: but in common with thousands of other members, William Loveless was not among those that O'Connor had managed to settle before the National Land Company was wound up in 1851. By then the whole enterprise reeked of futility: with more efficient management the Company might have located some 300 further members within its life span, but no more. The actuary to the National Debt calculated that 115 years would have been necessary to settle the full membership. Mortgages had been miscalculated, an almost millennial plenitude of agricultural produce envisaged and thus revenue from rentals had been grossly overestimated.[13]

In its almost limitless vision and heedless enthusiasm, the Chartist Land Plan seems almost at one with the millenarian speculations of William Loveless and his contemporaries. Loveless did not however equate the

Land Plan with the millennium, and neither did his contemporaries; but if there is one thing above all that the work of John Harrison teaches us, it is to listen to that which is unfamiliar. 'It is not easy for the historian to hear the voices of the people, for they have left relatively few records, and their views and opinions are drowned or crowded out by the louder and more insistent voices of the educated classes.'[14] In the case of the Land Plan, the drowning and crowding out was done not only by condescending and frequently hostile contemporaries, but also by Feargus O'Connor himself. O'Connor has somehow to be disentangled from those who supported the Plan. The current state of Chartist historiography differs markedly from the situation until the 1970s, in that O'Connor is now taken seriously and his words heeded instead of being dismissed as demagoguery and bluster. However, the Land Plan presents a particular problem of interpretation: here more than on any other facet of Chartism, O'Connor's personality is stamped comprehensively. It may well be that, had the term Chartism not been coined, historians would have termed the movement O'Connorite radicalism, yet it is none the less possible to envisage Chartism without him. Without O'Connor, however, the Land Plan would be inconceivable.

This is not to suggest that there would have been no interest among Chartists in getting 'back to the land' without O'Connor: radical agrarianism had a long pedigree. Furthermore, from the 1820s there was a multitude of land schemes of one kind or another, part of a general proliferation of 'self-made social institutions' among British wage-earners.[15] The Land Plan has to be seen in this social context, as well as within the political context of Chartism, if it is to be properly understood. What marks it out is firstly its size, with at least 70,000 weekly subscribers making payments towards shares which entitled them to a place in the regular ballots for allotments of land. Each cottage smallholding was to be one of hundreds, on estates bought on behalf of the Plan; and each was to pay an economic rent into a fund from which further estates would be purchased. The scheme's huge success, in terms of the support that it attracted, had never been anticipated. 'The number of names over-came us,' said the hapless legal clerk detailed to compile the register of shareholders.[16] The second distinguishing feature of the Land Plan is a function of its size and of its association with Chartism and *Northern Star* in particular. There is a wealth of information, still yet to be fully fathomed, particularly in the newspaper's weekly reports from branches, in the shareholders' register with its 20,000-odd entries,[17] and in the evidence of the Parliamentary Select Committee appointed to investigate it. Over them all resound the very substantial echoes of that voice like a trumpet, Feargus O'Connor's weekly letters in the *Northern Star*, his polemics against the Plan's detractors and his only book of substance, *A Practical Work on the Management of Small Farms.*

How far can – or should – we seek to discount the voice of O'Connor in studying the Land Plan? The relationship between the radical platform and its audience was a complex one, and to summarize it as demagoguery is both lazy and patronizing. As historians become more critically aware of language and communication (both verbal and non-verbal), there is an increasing appreciation of the subtleties of platform rhetoric. It was two-way: it reflected as much as it directed the aspirations of the audience. The notion of audience is itself problematic: those who attended the mass rallies and meetings at which O'Connor spoke were participants in a drama rather than passive recipients of a message. Standing before them clad in the fustian cloth of the manual worker, O'Connor made heavy usage of the first person and of rhetorical questions, which are intrusive on the printed page but which were essential elements in his success as a platform leader. 'I have brought you out of the land of Egypt, and out of the house of bondage,' he told a meeting in the schoolhouse at O'Connorville on Mayday 1847:

And must I not have a cold and flinty heart if I could survey the scene before me without emotion? Who can look upon those mothers, accustomed to be dragged by the waking light of morn from those little babes now nestling to their breasts? (Here the speaker was so overcome that he was obliged to sit down, his face covered with large tears, and we never beheld such a scene in our life; not an eye in the building that did not weep.) After a pause Mr. O'Connor resumed: Yes, this is a portion of a great feature of my plan to give the fond wife back to her husband, and the innocent babe back to its fond mother. (Here the speaker was again compelled to pause, and delivered the remainder of his address sitting down.)

See what a different race I will make – see what a noble edifice for the education of your children. (Cheers.) While a sectarian government is endeavouring to preserve its dominion, and fostering sectarian strife, I open the sanctuary of free instruction for the unbiased training of youth, and woe to the firebrand parson who shall dare to frighten the susceptible mind of infancy by the hobgoblin of religious preference. (Tremendous cheering and waving of hats.) Let the father nourish, and the fond mother nurture, their own offspring (cheers) and then we shall have a generation of FREE CHRISTIANS. (Loud cheers.)[18]

Modern secularization still does not completely blunt the opening biblical imagery. Yet this was more than just imagery: it cast the 'you' of the address in the role of Israel, a chosen people against whom are contrasted, in an inversion of the establishment view of Chartism, the fire-brand parson and a narrow sectarian government. Robust anticlericalism of this kind was deep-seated among those who became Chartists. The focus upon familial, especially maternal, relationships draws on other deep-seated popular emotions, identifying factories with the reversal of the natural order of labour and home life. It is the role of fathers to nourish (that is, provide sustaining food for), and of mothers to nurture, their children. O'Connor made explicit on many other occasions that 'this system of hiring women, to the rejection of men must naturally debase the character of both, by reversing their natural positions and making the husband a dependant upon the labour of his wife, while his creditable support of her and the family should constitute his greatest pride'.[19]

The O'Connorville speech hinged upon Feargus' attack on industrialism's 'house of bondage' (which for males also involved independence in direct economic terms from women). Patrick Joyce has observed how the cluster of ideas around the notion of the cottage economy – 'ideas of independence, of what was "natural", and of what were the proper social relations between master and worker' – served mill hands and domestic workers alike as 'a powerful critique of the factory system'. Joyce rightly sees O'Connor as a particularly powerful advocate of those ideas.[20] He may have been more articulate than his audiences; his delivery was certainly highly personal and theatrical (even melodramatic, but therein lies a further clue to his appeal); yet in a real sense his words were their own.[21] In effect O'Connor gave them a new voice, literally so when his weekly letters in the *Northern Star*, themselves largely dictated, were read out aloud in Chartist pubs and halls.

The Land Plan was itself a bold non-verbal statement – the most visible and powerful means of communicating the cottage economy ideal conceivable. The sheer fact of the Land Plan, its estates and O'Connor's energetic promotion of it, were the most powerful embodiment of the independence argument of all. When this was amplified through events such as 'The People's Jubilee' (the significant title of the official opening of the first Chartist estate), and by engravings showing the estates in sylvan settings after the manner of topographical views prepared for aristocratic patrons, the result was a powerful and intoxicating statement about Chartism's potential potency as an agent for change.[22] Aspects of Chartism's history that at first sight appear mildly risible, have to be understood in this context where actions could and often did speak louder than words:

The first object that met our view, was a huge tri-coloured banner floating, high above an immense chestnut tree, bearing the inscription 'O'Connorville'; and secondly, Rebecca, the Chartist Cow, like the sacred cows of old, clothed in her vesture of tri-colour, rendered holy by the popular voice, which is the voice of God.[23]

The extensive literature generated by the Land Plan allows us to listen further to this popular voice, not necessarily only as O'Connor articulated it, though inevitably he looms large. By introducing the Land Plan into the Chartist movement O'Connor, rather than imposing upon it a maverick of his own devising, was developing aspects of the legacy of ideas which Chartism had naturally inherited from early radical policies. The institutional origins of the Chartist movement in campaigns concerning factory reform, the New Poor Law, and parliamentary reform reinforced an overall tone that was stridently anti-establishment; and that establishment, overwhelmingly, was landed. Furthermore the thrust of Chartism's economic critique was primarily against excessive wealth. This, rather than industrial capitalism per se, was the target, and hence the principal source of oppression was perceived as the landed aristocracy, its powers and privileges. Of course Chartism, including the Land Plan, did criticize and interrogate developments in industrial production. But Chartists' perceptions of the process of industrialization were subjective and untutored by hindsight. It was experienced as a threat to workers' independence and status, defined at the workplace by skill (a concept extending well beyond the conventionally defined skilled trades), and in the domestic sphere by a moderately comfortable subsistence. Participation in the Chartist Land Plan seemed capable both of restoring discretion over the process of work while securing the material basis of domestic comfort through the acquisition of a cottage holding.

Chartism's criticism of excessive wealth was thus more than merely a moral critique of society, but one which embraced the roots of economic and political inequalities as well. Since the movement's inception, land redistribution had been widely seen as among the most immediate and pressing issues a democratic parliament would need to confront.[24] Correspondingly, there was a lively interest in land schemes which might achieve locally what parliamentary legislation would eventually achieve nationally. The decaying textile centre of Cirencester was probably the first Chartist locality to consider the formation of an 'Agrarian Company' in August 1840, following a call by O'Connor to establish 'Chartist Agricultural Associations – Five-Acre Associations – or Landed Labour Associations'.[25]

Indeed much of the initial momentum behind the Chartist Land Plan came from key local activists, often steeped in the radical agrarian tradition of the pre-Chartist years: in Manchester James Leach; in London's East End the veteran Spencean and socialist Allen Davenport; in Cheltenham Thomas Sidaway; in Bradford James Arran, and in north Lancashire William Beesley. The advice of two such figures – both of them Owenites – Joshua Hobson of Leeds and Thomas Martin Wheeler of west London, was critical to O'Connor at the formative stage of the Land Plan, and to Wheeler should probably go the credit for the lion's share of the *Practical Work on the Management of Small Farms*.[26]

It was provincial support of this nature that largely secured approval for the Land Plan at the Birmingham Convention of 1843; but we should note too the consistency before then with which both the *Northern Star* and other Chartist newspapers covered 'The People's Question – The Land! The Land!'[27] Indeed, so strong was the interest in agrarianism among Chartists that the Land Plan can be credited with sustaining the movement as a whole during the doldrums years of the mid-1840s. It is not surprising to find O'Connor demanding 'where Chartism would be but for the Land? I may ask you where it was from 1842 to 1845, when the breath of Landism was breathed into its nostrils and gave it fresh vitality?' But the Middleton Chartist who wrote of 'The Resurrection of Chartism' spoke for many communities, as successive local studies have shown.[28] Chartism's success in mobilizing in 1848 owed much to an underlying infrastructure largely derived from the Plan which had taken off nationally the year before. In ensuring that the 1848 Petition was borne on a wagon constructed from timber felled on the company's estates, O'Connor once again revealed his grasp of non-verbal communication.[29]

The Land Question was central to Chartism, then, politically as the fulcrum for the distribution of wealth and power in society, and organizationally as an issue that gave it renewed momentum after the frustrations of 1842. Yet this only goes part way towards understanding the function of agrarian issues in Chartism. What was the intellectual substance that lay beneath rhetoric such as, 'the accomplishment of the political and social emancipation of the enslaved and degraded working classes being the peculiar object of the Society'? Central to the Plan was a sense of a widening division in society which, with increasing momentum, was propelling it to the verge of disaster. Such a perception was, of course, far from unique to Chartism in the 1830s and 1840s. It was most obvious in Owenism, the influence of which was manifest in the literature of the Land Plan, and in Chartist thinking on land generally: 'We know of nothing but such a system of co-operative unity as is involved in home colonization, that is capable of preserving the country from inevitable destruction. Let the people be drawn from the manufacturing districts, and located upon the land.'[30] *The Practical Work on the Management of Small Farms* drew conspicuously on contemporary Owenite and phrenological theories of the formation of human character:

> The system which I propose would at once develope [sic] all the virtues of our nature, while I defy the devil himself to invent one so calculated to foster and encourage all those vices to which man is heir, as that which I labour to destroy. Never lose sight of this one irrefutable fact, that man is born with propensities which may be nourished into virtues, or thwarted into vices, according to his training. That system which I propose would nourish those propensities into virtues.[31]

However, even a cursory glance at the contrasting layout of the Chartist and Owenite communities confirms that their underlying ideologies were sharply divergent. It was the central function of the family as the socializing force that dictated the topography of Land Plan settlements: two-, three- or four-acre individual holdings, with a cottage at the centre of each – the diametrical opposite of the Owenite geography of settlement, the communitarian basis of which reflected Robert Owen's antipathy to the family, 'the main bastion of private property and the guardian of all those qualities of individualism and self-interest to which he was opposed'.[32] Different, too, was the place of women in the two systems: Owenism committed to equality and domestic emancipation, and the Land Plan emphatic as to the domestic, 'natural' role of the mother. The design of the Chartist cottages, with the kitchen the largest of the domestic rooms, is itself eloquent on this issue, expressive of both the traditional pattern of home life and of woman's place at its centre. For O'Connor, and for many of his followers, the crisis of the 1840s was as much a crisis of the family and male authority as anything else, and 'sexual difference was intimately bound up in notions of labour, property and kin in popular radical thought'. The Land Plan can be seen as a key part of the rolling back of that autonomous female participation in politics which was as notable at the beginning of the Chartist movement as it was absent at its close.[33]

Idealization of the family and of the domestic sphere was just one aspect, albeit crucial, of the socio-economic vision of the Chartist Land Plan. That vision, as has already been suggested, turned on the perception of the 1840s as a period of crisis and deepening division in society. One of the principal means through which that division was conceptualized was in the dichotomy of the *natural* versus the *artificial*. This vocabulary was deeply rooted within radicalism, and agrarian radicalism in particular.[34] It achieved its widest currency in the Chartist Land Plan. For example one of its directors, the Mancunian Irishman Christopher Doyle, argued that state intervention could alleviate the mass unemployment caused by 'the artificial state of the labour market' by enforcing the cultivation of waste lands. When the first Land Plan members from Preston secured their allotments, the local branch celebrated their being 'taken from the miseries naturally attendant upon the present artificial labour market, and placed in a position for a fair development of their capabilities of labour when applied to the cultivation of the natural resources of this country'. 'God gave you the land, and told you to cultivate it,' added O'Connor, 'and to make you labourers he made natural labour, but the devil made you artificial labour. (Cheers).'[35]

This usage of *natural* and *artificial* links the Land Plan to the long-established radical agrarian strategy of promoting labour's relative scarcity, as O'Connor crisply put it to 'thin the artificial labour market by employing thousands who are now destitute, and constituting an idle reserve to enable the capitalists to live and make fortunes upon the reduction of wages'. Capitalism created an artificial market in which labour was suppressed through its inability to command an adequate and thus natural wage. The connotations of the natural wage, however, extended well beyond mere adequacy. The artificial market depended on the divorce of workers from the land, whereon they would otherwise be able to secure a living through natural labour – that is labour that is independent, God-given and in community with nature. The age-old concept of the innate dignity of agricultural labour reinforced this analysis of contemporary market conditions. A man digging his own land, O'Connor declaimed, was 'the image of his God ... A MAN STANDING ON HIS OWN RESOURCES ... In his own little holding he recognises the miniature of nature'.[36]

The artificial market was not simply that of factory labour: it extended to every sector of the economy where an 'idle reserve' needed to be eliminated before labour could command its natural wage. The standard for the latter was a decent subsistence, honestly derived from work on the land. A 'natural' wage was not, therefore, incompatible with even factory employment, and all industrial workers stood to gain if an exodus onto the land were to drive up wages. This is the key to the exalted predictions made for the Land Plan: 'The capitalists who make fortunes by other men's labour shall henceforth hire that labour in the free labour market, wherein every man will have arrived at a knowledge of its full value.'[37]

Thus, in the words of Thomas Frost of Croydon, 'the Land Question resolves itself into a unity of interests among all men whether they are shareholders or not'.[38] Furthermore it was claimed that workers in the artificial market would purchase the surplus produce of the Chartist allottees, deriving improvements in the quality of provisions along with the elimination of profiteering farmers and middlemen, drawing from O'Connor the gleeful observation, 'I NEVER EXPECTED THE BLOOD-SUCKERS WOULD LIKE THE NATURAL STATE OF MAN'.[39] Yet it was precisely the isolation of the Chartist colonies from market centres, and the inability of the colonists to generate surpluses beyond their subsistence needs, that attracted contemporary ridicule; but we need to understand that the roots of the illusory fecundity of the colonies were sustained by more than simply O'Connor's rhetoric alone. 'The potentiality of material abundance', noted by John Harrison as fundamental to the Owenite case, was also central to radical agrarianism and to the Chartist Land Plan, and for the same reasons.[40] It was seen as a stinging rebuttal of Malthus; it provided grounds for an acceptance of mechanized production; and it constituted a focus for the cross-fertilization of the Land Plan with millennial expectations. Closely related to it was the assertion of the efficacy of spade husbandry.

The general advantages that contemporary supporters anticipated from the Plan were, therefore, the gradual decline of the artificial labour market, the restitution of a balance in the relations between the sexes and the restoration of the family as the fulcrum of social life, all these in the context of an improved standard of living. The latter, though, was defined in more than simply material terms, important though the anticipated fertility of land under smallholder cultivation was. The inevitable corollary to a view of deepening crisis in society was a degree of nostalgia: 'What was England then? A great national family, the several branches consisting of agricultural weavers and weaving agriculturalists: of producers and consumers regulating demand and supply, and living united in hand and heart in *small agricultural communities*'.[41] The specific appeal here to the memory of weaver-farmers reflects the base of O'Connor's support in the Pennine textile districts. No less significant, however, are the underlying preoccupations: the scale of society, its setting and the status of those within it. That the setting should be rural is self-evident, but this was more subtle than simple escapism. First the countryside was clearly associated with a natural society. Secondly, the view that independence and self-determination were more readily secured in a pastoral context was a pervasive one, in Britain as well as America (where, of course, it was central to Jeffersonian thinking). Thirdly, 'the grand principle of self-reliance' was a key attraction of the Plan to those whose sense of self-reliance at the workplace was rapidly being eroded not only by factory production but more generally by changes in working practices and in the scope for exercising their independent judgement. O'Connor refined this outlook in a consistent advocacy of what he termed 'the principle of individualism against that of centralization'. 'I tell you that no other channel to secure individualism is open but the Land.' The ideas at work here need 'unpacking' carefully.[42]

It has already been pointed out that the topography of the Chartist estates diametrically opposed that of Owenite communities. This reflected not only the perceived centrality of the family as a productive and socializing force, but also Chartist suspicions of centralizing tendencies generally. The emphasis on individualism against centralization, paralleling as it did that on the natural against the artificial, can be seen as part of that abiding suspicion of forces controlling economy and society which were centralized and, therefore, unaccountable – the twin evils of state power and monopoly. O'Connor went so far as to claim that 'the present Labour system of England is one huge system of Communism'.[43] The phraseology may be inimitable, but O'Connor was reflecting a widespread perception among Chartists that the contemporary crisis was contingent upon centralizing tendencies in politics and economy. Thus the concept was extendable to urbanization, to the aggregation of labour in ever-larger units of production; to the concentration of land ownership, and to the exclusive appropriation of legislative power by the propertied. The Charter itself, which would have effectively established a system of democracy through mandated delegates (re-elected annually and thereby wholly accountable to their constituencies), embodied this perception politically, just as the Chartist Land Plan – by devolving control of production – was to have done so economically.

The collapse of the Chartist Land Plan has been well rehearsed. It has been linked to the collapse of O'Connor's personal health and finances, to his diminishing political authority after 1848 and by implication to the decline of the Chartist movement as a whole. However, Chartism was in the grip of secular political and economic trends and it is implausible to ascribe its demise directly, or even partially, to the Land Plan. The death of Chartism in 1848 has in any case been greatly exaggerated. Furthermore continued interest in the land question during the 1850s derived in part from the Plan, and from the discussion of reforms to the system of landed property which it had stimulated. Acceptance of land nationalization as a prominent part of the programme adopted by the Chartist Convention of

1851 should be seen in this context; so too should the espousal of agrarian schemes, in opposition to emigration, by Ernest Jones and his supporters at the Labour Parliament of 1853-4. At least 300 land societies, George Harrison of Nottingham claimed there, had emerged since the winding up of the Chartist Land Plan: 'around Nottingham there were half-a-dozen … that proved that land schemes properly conducted had not failed. (Hear, Hear)'. 'The wish to improve their condition by the possession of land is taking root in the universal heart of the working classes,' claimed Thomas Cooper in 1850, a claim which has considerable force if the take-off around the same time of freehold land and building societies is borne in mind.[44]

The collapse of the Chartist Land Plan did not, then, mark the collapse of popular interest in 'back to the land' schemes. What it did constitute, however, was a watershed in the evolution of working-class associational forms, the need for sound financial and actuarial management being among the most obvious of the lessons learnt from it. The conclusion that the Plan's chances of success were impeded by the attitude of the state was also widespread, which led to a greater realism in framing mutual societies either to operate within the parameters of the law or, if not seeking legal registration, to derive relative security through modest scope and size. From the well-known figure of Thomas Martin Wheeler, once secretary of the Land Company and subsequently manager of the Friend-in-Need Life and Sick Assurance Society, to unheeded grass-roots leaders such as James Maw of Middlesbrough, a founding trustee of the town's Equitable Permanent Benefit Building Society, the active participation of former Land Plan supporters in mutual organizations after 1850 is striking.[45]

Where the Chartist Land Plan did mark a closure was in the demise of popular belief in the potentiality of material abundance. It can be seen also as ending literal acceptance of a reclaimable natural state, derived from the paradigms of Locke and the popular enlightenment. Though the appeal of 'back to the land' remained powerful, the Chartist Land Plan marked the effective end of agrarian fundamentalism. On the other hand it was part of a rapidly evolving popular culture of home-centredness, a culture which sought in the home a compensatory sphere for diminishing control and status at the workplace: 'the ideal of domesticity as an idyllic ending to the melodrama of the working-class struggle', as Anna Clark characterizes it.[46] It is not too fanciful to see in the growth of home ownership, and in working-class home-centredness generally, a vestigial agrarianism, no longer intent on subverting the wider economic and social system but rather on creating spaces within that system that would be insulated from its worst effects. For all its intentions to destroy the artificial economy, therefore, the Chartist

Land Plan cannot be completely disaggregated from the contemporary growth of building societies. The rhetoric of domesticity was a key element in its promotion. Although, as we have seen, William Loveless sought 'a brief sojourn in this world before passing on to "a better land"', the motives of others for joining the Land Plan may have been more mundane. As will be shown in chapter 12, the chance simply of owning their own home is likely to have motivated some shareholders.

In this we can detect a shift that parallels the outlook of the labour movement as a whole after 1850 as, in Edward Thompson's vivid phrase, 'the workers having failed to overthrow capitalist society proceed to warren it from end to end'. As a historical process it went back much earlier than the final defeat of Chartism, but the later 1840s marked the take-off of a wide range of workers' self-made social institutions, building societies not least among them. Ultimately the Land Plan must be seen in this context: situated on the cusp of the warrening process, melding the ethos and practical procedures of the new mutualism, along with the transcendent ambitions of both the wider Chartist movement and the agrarian tradition of which it was part. Therein lay both its uniqueness and the conditions for its downfall.[47]

Notes

1   The tangled nomenclature of the Land Plan is explained in the first note of chapter 5.

2   J. Epstein, *The Lion of Freedom: Feargus O'Connor and the Chartist Movement, 1832-1842* (London, 1982), pp. 249-62; J. Epstein and D. Thompson (eds), *The Chartist Experience* (London, 1982); J. MacAskill, 'The Chartist Land Plan', in A. Briggs (ed.), *Chartist Studies* (London, 1959), pp. 304-341. On the later historiography of the Plan see below, chapter 5.

3   R. G. Gammage, *History of the Chartist Movement, 1837-1854* (Newcastle, 1894; first issued in parts, 1854), pp. 268, 249.

4   M. Hovell, *The Chartist Movement* (Manchester, 1918), p. 32; see also B. Dobrée, 'not really Chartism at all', *English Revolts* (London, 1937), p. 156.

5   A. L. Morton, *A People's History of England* (London, 1938), p. 425.

6   J. Saville, *Ernest Jones, Chartist* (London, 1952), p. 24; Morton, *People's History*, p. 424; R. K. Webb, *Modern England* (London, 1980 edn), p. 262.

7   N. Gash, *Aristocracy and People* (London, 1979), p. 212; H. Perkin, *Origins of Modern English Society* (London, 1969), pp. 237, 390; M. Thomis, *The Town Labourer and the Industrial Revolution* (London, 1974), p. 99.

8   E. Royle, *Chartism* (London, 1980), p. 37; E.H. Hunt, *British Labour History* (London, 1981), p. 226.

9   Dorothy Thompson, *The Chartists* (London, 1984), pp. 294-306.

10   The main estate-centred histories are W. H. G. Armytage, *Heavens Below*

(London, 1961), pp. 224-37; P. Searby, 'Great Dodford and the last days of the Chartist Land Company', *Agricultural History Review*, 16 (1968); A. M. Hadfield, *The Chartist Land Company* (Newton Abbot, 1970); D. Hardy, *Alternative Communities* (London, 1979), pp. 75-105; K. Tiller, 'Charterville and Chartist Land Company', *Oxoniensia*, 50, (1985). Important exceptions to this pattern should, however, be noted: D.J.V. Jones, *Chartism and the Chartists* (London, 1975), especially its analysis of Land Plan shareholders, pp. 134-7; J. Saville's introduction to the 1969 Cass reprint of Gammage's *History*, pp. 48-62; E. Yeo, 'Some Practices and Problems of Chartist Democracy', in Epstein and Thompson (eds), *The Chartist Experience*, pp. 345-80.

11 E. Dolléans, *Le Chartisme*, 2 vols (Paris, 1912-13), vol. 2, pp. 278-301, 328-36, 348-54, 367-86; F. Bachmann, *Die Agrarreform in der Chartistenbewegung: eine historisch-kritische Studie uber die doktrinen des englischen Sozialismus von 1820-50* (Bern, 1928); see also H. Niehuus, *Geschicte der englischen Bodenreformtheorien* (Leipzig, 1910).

12 J.F.C. Harrison, *The Second Coming: Popular Millenarianism, 1780-1850*, (London, 1979), pp. 224-5; on the Land Plan in Dorset see R. A. E. Wells, 'Southern Chartism', *Rural History*, 2:1 (1991), 51-5.

13 *PP* (Reports from Committees) Session 1847-48 (398), XIX, SC on the National Land Company, evidence of Finlaison, q. 4541.

14 Harrison, *The Second Coming*, p. xiii.

15 M. Chase, *'The People's Farm': English Radical Agrarianism, 1775-1840* (Oxford, 1988). The useful phrase 'self-made social institutions of British wage-earners' is J.H. Clapham's, *An Economic History of Modern Britain: The Railway Age, 1820-1850* (Cambridge, 1939).

16 SC National Land Company, evidence of Chinery, q. 186.

17 Provisional registration documents for the National Land Company, and lists of shareholders, TNA, BT/41/474-6.

18 *NS* 8 May 1847.

19 F. O'Connor, *A Practical Work on the Management of Small Farms*, (London, 2nd edn, 1845), p. 19.

20 P. Joyce, *Visions of the People: Industrial England and the Question of Class, c. 1848-1914* (Cambridge, 1991), pp. 32-4, 97-101, quotation from p. 32.

21 For a suggestive reading of English popular politics in terms of the melodramatic forms of political imagination, see J. Vernon, *Politics and the People: A Study in English Political Culture, c. 1815-1867* (Cambridge, 1993).

22 For jubilee see M. Chase, 'The Concept of Jubilee in Late-eighteenth and Nineteenth-century England', *Past & Present*, 129 (1990), 132-47, esp. n31; *O'Connorville: The First Estate Purchased by the Chartist Co-operative Land Company*, British Library (Bloomsbury). Map Library, MAPS 162.S.1.

23 'Chartist Jubilee: Grand Demonstration to the People's First Estate, "O'Connorville" ', *NS*, 22 Aug. 1846.

24 *NS* 19 Oct. 1839; *English Chartist Circular* 128 [July 1843]); *London Democrat*, 18 May 1839.

25 *NS* 16 May, 29 Aug. 1840.

26 *NS* 31 Oct. and 21 Nov. 1840, 29 Oct. and 5 Nov. 1842, 30 Sept. 1843; A.

Davenport, 'The Social Sun', *Reasoner*, 1, (1846), 158; W. Stevens, *A Memoir of Thomas Martin Wheeler* (London, 1862), p. 25; T. Frost, *Forty Years' Recollections* (London, 1880), p. 96; 'Thomas Martin Wheeler', *DLB*, vol. 6; O. R. Ashton, 'Chartism in Gloucestershire: The Contribution of the Chartist Land Plan, 1843-50', *Transactions of the Bristol and Gloucestershire Archaeological Society*, 104, (1986), 205. See also A. Davenport, *The Life and Literary Pursuits of Allen Davenport: With a Further Selection of the Author's Work* (M. Chase, ed., Aldershot, 1994; first pub. 1845), pp. 45-6, 53-4, 61.

27   The title of an article by 'A Working Agriculturalist of West Suffolk', *English Chartist Circular*, 128, (n.d. [1843]).

28   *NS* 23 Aug. 1843; G. J. Barnsby, *The Working-class Movement in the Black Country* (Wolverhampton, 1975), pp. 136-41; R. B. Pugh, 'Chartism in Somerset and Wiltshire', in Briggs (ed.), *Chartist Studies*, p. 212; J. Cannon, *Chartists in Bristol* (Bristol, 1964), p. 12; Frost, *Forty Years*, p. 96; A. J. Brown, *The Chartist Movement in Essex and Suffolk* (Colchester, 1979), p. 10 - cf. 'Essex and Suffolk Land and Chartist Union', *NS* 8 Apr. 1848; G. Crossick, *An Artisan Elite in Victorian Society: Kentish London, 1840-1880* (London, 1978), pp. 201, 203, 208; K. Wilson, 'Chartism in Sunderland', *North East Labour History*, 16, (1982); M. Chase, 'Chartism, 1838-1858: Responses in Two Teesside Towns', *Northern History*, 24, (1988), p. 163.

29   *NS* 11 Mar. 1848.

30   Editorial (by Hobson?), *NS* 1 Jan. 1842.

31   O'Connor, *Practical Work*, p. 20.

32   J. F. C. Harrison, *Robert Owen and the Owenites in Britain and America: the Quest for the New Moral World* (London, 1969), pp. 59-60.

33   S. Alexander, 'Women, Class and Sexual Differences in the 1830s and 1840s: Some Reflections on the Writing of Feminist History', *History Workshop*, 17 (Spring 1984), 136; D. Thompson, 'Women and Nineteenth-century Radical Politics: A Lost Dimension', in J. Mitchell and A. Oakley (eds), *The Rights and Wrongs of Women* (London, 1976), pp. 112-38. See also chapter 10 below and A. Clark, 'The Rhetoric of Chartist Domesticity: Gender, Language and Class in the 1830s and 1840s', *Journal of British Studies*, 31 (Jan. 1992), 62-88.

34   Chase, *People's Farm*, pp. 143-4.

35   *Preston Chronicle* quoted in *NS*, 18 Mar. 1848.

36   O'Connor, *Practical Work*, p. 40.

37   *Idem*, p. 149.

38   *NS* 24 July 1847.

39   *NS* 30 Jan. 1847.

40   Harrison, *Robert Owen*, p. 68. The implications of material abundance for radical thought are further explored by N. W. Thompson, *The People's Science* Cambridge, 1984), pp. 181ff., and in Chase, *The People's Farm*, esp. pp. 134-43.

41   F. O'Connor, *'The Land', the Only Remedy for National Poverty and Impending National Ruin: How to Get it; and How to Use it* (Leeds, Labourers' Library, nos 2 and 3, 1841), p. 14.

42   'The Land and the Charter', *Labourer*, I (1847), 81; *NS* 9 Nov. 1844, 11 Nov.

1848.

43   *NS* 18 Nov. 1848.

44   See chapter 12 below; *People's Paper* 18 Mar. 1854; *Cooper's Journal* 17 Jan. 1850.

45   Saville, 'Thomas Martin Wheeler', p. 268; M. Chase, 'Chartism and the "Prehistory" of Middlesbrough Politics', *Bulletin of the Cleveland and Teesside Local History Society* 55 (Autumn 1988), 24 and 29.

46   Clark, 'The Rhetoric of Chartist Domesticity', 87.

47   E. P. Thompson, 'The Peculiarities of the English', *Socialist Register* (1965), pp. 310-62; revised version in *The Poverty of Theory* (1978); cf. J. Saville, *1848: The British State and the Chartist Movement* (Cambridge, 1987), pp. 208-10.

5

'WHOLESOME OBJECT LESSONS':
THE CHARTIST LAND PLAN IN RETROSPECT

With 20,000 shareholders (and at its peak 70,000 weekly subscribers), some 600 local branches and five estates, the Chartist Land Plan is among the most extraordinary organizations of the early-Victorian period.[1] Though originally intended as a relatively small-scale enterprise demonstrating the economic and social benefits of a movement back to the land by industrial workers, its objective was little short of fundamental:

> To purchase land on which to locate such of its members as may be selected for that purpose, in order to demonstrate to the working classes of the kingdom, firstly the value of the land, as a means of making them independent of the grinding capitalist; and, secondly, to show them the necessity of securing the speedy enactment of the 'People's Charter', which would do for them nationally what this society proposes to do sectionally; the accomplishment of the political and social emancipation of the enslaved and degraded working classes being the prominent object of the society.[2]

Such was the extent of contemporary agrarian enthusiasm that the Plan effectively spiralled out of control and its history bears more than passing similarity to that of the contemporary railway mania. Even John Stuart Mill, in *Principles of Political Economy* (1848), praised the scheme's 'well-conceived arrangements', adding that they offered a model for Irish land reform.[3] However, far from being well-conceived, its capacity to function with any degree of administrative efficiency was simply swamped by the size of its membership. This peaked at around 70,000 weekly subscribers, each making payments towards shares which entitled them to a place in regular ballots for allotments of land. Yet the Plan never generated subscription income sufficient to purchase enough land to divide among all its shareholders. Efforts to raise additional finance through a specially created

Land and Labour Bank were insufficient, while attempts to raise revenue by imposing rent payments on those shareholders who had been granted an allotment were ineffective and politically embarrassing. Following a parliamentary enquiry, the scheme was wound up in 1851. A further five years were needed to straighten out its affairs in Chancery.

This lamentable history dogged the reputation of Chartism (and especially its promoter, Feargus O'Connor) among contemporaries and historians alike. Historiographically, the recent revival of interest in the Chartist Land Plan owes much to the rehabilitation of O'Connor's reputation and to the recognition of the importance of the agrarian tradition in earlier English radical politics.[4] Earlier estimates of O'Connor largely took their cue from Robert Gammage, the first historian of the movement in which he had himself played a part. Gammage's cumulative portrait of 'the Land Company... going to wreck more and more every day' was not calculated to promote its memory and this was the interpretation that prevailed in the historiography of Chartism for more than a century.[5]

However, the 1990s were kind to O'Connor's 'bold plan for national regeneration'. It is now generally agreed that it was a central element in the Chartist movement. There has been a modest flurry of publications,[6] and four of its five colonies – O'Connorville (Heronsgate, Hertfordshire), Lowbands and Snigs End (Gloucestershire) and Dodford (Worcestershire) – have been designated conservation areas. Some eighty Chartist cottages are now scheduled historic buildings. More than a quarter of these are at Charterville (the fifth settlement near Minster Lovell, Oxfordshire), dismissed a century ago as 'a hideous colony of small square-cut cottages'.[7] Symbolic assimilation to the national heritage was completed in 1997 when the National Trust purchased the last remaining 'unimproved' Chartist cottage, with its four-acre holding, at Dodford. The acquisition of a property whose importance lies in its links with the labour movement was an innovation for the Trust and, consciously or not, surely a response to changes in the contemporary political climate: 'It was acquired because of its national importance and historical significance and will help to deepen the interest and broaden the appeal of the charity'.[8] Given the power of the built environment in shaping popular understandings of the national past, this may come to be seen as a pivotal point in the development of ideas about English heritage.

It is not perhaps too fanciful to see this renaissance of interest in the Land Plan as a reflection of current sensitivity to the problematics of large-scale commercial agriculture. As will be seen below, previous attitudes to it have closely reflected changes in the way the land question has been formulated.

During the 1850s, the protracted and humiliating manner of the Plan's demise rendered its many supporters largely silent. The Plan, however, was simply too substantial an enterprise to be ignored in subsequent debates about allotments and smallholdings. While historians of Chartism were, at least until recently, damning or dismissive, there was another tradition of looking at the Plan which, even when critical, was much less inclined to dismiss it. This tradition lay outside conventional historiography in a rich but now largely unregarded literature investigating the case for land redistribution through allotments and smallholdings. Many of its authors were close to – and sometimes consciously sought to continue – the popular tradition of agrarian individualism of which the Land Plan was in many senses a climax. Since it signally disappointed those who invested their hopes and savings in it, the extent and causes of its failure were widely debated among those still seeking a resolution to social and economic problems through and on the land. This article traces the Land Plan's 'posthumous' career and explores how attitudes to it evolved during the century after its demise.

Although recent scholarship has increased our awareness of the intersection of Chartism with later Victorian popular politics,[9] there has been little recognition of the extent to which it remained a reference point in debates about land. The exception to this concerns the evolution of arguments in favour of land nationalization.[10] Until endorsed by the NCA in 1851, however, land nationalization had been tangential to Chartist thinking. Centred as it was on establishing popular access to the land through privately acquired smallholdings, the Land Plan had been criticized from its inception by those Chartists (notably Bronterre O'Brien) who favoured state-led and collectivist policies. Its collapse was not unwelcome to such critics but they were a minority within Chartism. At the time a more potent source of criticism derived from the burgeoning freehold land societies, a movement closely associated with Cobdenite liberalism and mostly drawing on the same popular aspirations as the Chartist scheme.[11] It thus brought together both many of those opposed to O'Connor's plan on political principle and moderate Chartists who, for reasons of simple expediency, wanted to distance freehold land societies from it. Though the aim of many of these societies was little different to that of building societies, they were widely seen as a potential medium for the promotion of peasant proprietorship. When he expunged all reference to the Chartist Land Plan from the third edition of *Principles of Political Economy* (1852), Mill retained mention of freehold land societies as a potentially effective engine for land redistribution.[12] However, 'trace all these societies to their fountain head and you will find in them the impress of the mind of Mr. O'Connor', claimed one Chartist paper, whilst *The Times* linked them to O'Connor's 'well-meant utopia'. It was hardly surprising, then, that 'in some parts societies have not flourished, in consequence of their being confounded with O'Connor's Land Scheme'.[13] Freehold land movement publications therefore drew careful attention to O'Connor's insanity and dismissed the Plan as 'a swindle' and 'a failure'.[14] 'The principle of wholesale purchase and retail subdivision … could not have failed to have been advantageous to all concerned', claimed the movement's newspaper the *Freeholder*, 'excepting in the hands of an inveterate bungler'. It went on to compare O'Connor to the disgraced 'railway king', George Hudson.[15]

Once the freehold land movement consolidated around the provision of suburban plots primarily for building purposes, the use of the Chartist Land Plan as a comparator dwindled.[16] Harriet Martineau, however, wrote warmly about 'the great extension of Freehold Land Societies [which] affords to a multitude of townsmen in England the means of leaving town-industry for rural independence'. In support of her argument that 'a future generation may see a revival of the order of peasant proprietors', she quoted Cobbett and the spade husbandry authority John Sillett. But that Sillett had once been among O'Connor's warmest supporters there was no hint.[17]

John Sillett and his practical works on the cultivation of small farms in themselves constitute an essay in miniature on the ambiguous reputation of the Land Plan. Sillett, a Chartist and small shopkeeper, had been inspired by what he described as O'Connor's 'excellent work on *Small Farms*' to take up a smallholding in the early 1840s. From his Suffolk farm he wrote several books concerning the efficacy of spade husbandry, pitched at the Chartist market. Having written to O'Connor in 1846 'acknowledging my gratitude to him for the great service his work had rendered me', Sillett was naturally enlisted in the front rank of Land Plan supporters. His works were reviewed and quoted extensively in the Chartist weekly *Northern Star*, whose commendation Sillett added to the title page of his *New Practical System of Fork and Spade Husbandry*.[18] When Parliament set up its Select Committee on the Chartist Land Plan in 1848, he gave detailed technical evidence in O'Connor's support. It is an interesting reflection of how little damaged initially the scheme was by the Committee's proceedings, that the veteran radical publishers James Watson and Abel Heywood should have published Sillett's evidence as a separate pamphlet 'clearly proving that a man may live well and save money on two acres of land'.[19] However, Sillett's 1850 edition of *Fork and Spade Husbandry* deleted all reference to O'Connor and the Land Plan.[20] This was the edition to which Martineau referred (and which was republished as a practical agricultural handbook as late as 1906, along with her *Farm of Two Acres*).[21] Sillett went on to design a model cottage for the smallholder, exhibited at the 1851 Great Exhibition, which bore more than a passing resemblance to the designs used on the Chartist estates.[22]

As O'Connor sank into insanity and the 1851 winding-up act took effect, it became increasingly difficult to defend the Plan. 'One of the hugest delusions to which the working men of this country ever lent themselves under demagogue leadership', was one early verdict; 'being unaccustomed to husbandry [the colonists] were speedily reduced to the condition of ruined paupers'.[23] Gammage's *History*, appearing in instalments soon after O'Connor's death, offered scant consolation. A few of the latter's staunchest supporters did seek to counter Gammage, notably Thomas Martin Wheeler, formerly secretary of the National Land Company. 'Instead of being a failure, it has proved a signal success': the Plan had 'rekindled the ancient flame' of interest in the land question. Wheeler's earliest attempt to retrieve the reputation of the Plan had been made even before it was wound up, in instalments of his novel *Sunshine and Shadow* which appeared in *Northern Star*, 1849-50: 'never did a Company, established for any sectional or commercial purpose, ever affect such a revolution in public opinion', Wheeler had written there.[24] In a vestigial form this view was reflected in the origins of the Co-operative Wholesale Society, which lay in meetings held at a co-operative farm dubbed Lowbands by the Lancashire working men who led this new phase of the co-operative movement.[25] Such gestures, however, were insufficient to rescue an enterprise which by the mid-1850s seemed poised to fall into obscurity. A telling illustration occurred in 1855 when the distribution of its remaining assets to shareholders by order of Chancery appears to have escaped all notice.[26] In the 1860s, the most heated invective launched against the Plan hardly circulated in Britain. This was a recapitulation of criticisms first made in 1847 by the 'whistler at the plough' Alexander Somerville. Somerville's account, published in Montreal, was mostly self-serving and his claim that the Plan was 'directed at the ultimate subversion of all the territorial property of Britain and Ireland' melodramatic and implausible.[27] More damaging was evidence concerning Charterville, published in 1868 by one of the parliamentary commissioners on the employment of women and children in agriculture. This included an interview with John Bennett, a Chartist sail-cloth weaver from Stockton-on-Tees and, it was claimed, one of only two surviving original allottees at the Oxfordshire colony. Initially awarded two acres, Bennett had acquired two more. Despite this his experience was not, he insisted, a happy one:

Those that paid up a whole share got the first choice of an allotment. I paid up mine, £1. 7s. 6d. I got one in six months. I never would have if I had known what I do now. It has taken me 20 years to learn how a man can live without victuals, and I've just about come to it. Thousands paid up part of their share and lost it all, and I believe they were best off.

Bennett's holding, on which there was a rent charge of £9 10s, had just been sold under him. Another interviewee, who had bought up no less than twenty-six allotments to rent out, believed that ten acres was the minimum viable holding if held at a fair rent. Though a subsistence could be scraped by owners of two, 'none of those who have these allotments singly at a rent are able to live off them'.[28]

This argument was directly contradicted in an account of O'Connorville published the same year by the veteran west London Chartist and land reform enthusiast H. D. Griffiths.[29] Griffiths, however, was something of a political maverick: in general the Land Plan in the late 1860s was a source of embarrassment to those who directed the revival of interest in land reform, whether through the free-trade agitation of the Land Tenure Reform Association, or the Land and Labour League whose objective was land nationalization. 'The reform I advocate', wrote the proposer of an English Land League in 1865, 'has immensely suffered through the blundering of Feargus O'Connor.'[30]

Only in the 1870s, as radical interest in the land question quickened and a surge of agricultural trade unionism (the 'Revolt of the Field') repoliticized the promotion of smallholdings, did the Chartist Land Plan's 'posthumous' political career begin. The relative ineffectiveness of attempts to promote allotments and smallholdings in the mid-Victorian period has been ascribed to an ambivalence towards legislation on the part of the allotment movement itself.[31] While it is certainly the case that, from the 1870s, there was greater willingness to countenance legislative intervention, it could also be argued the movement was benefiting from the chronological distance now opening up between it and Chartism. Several land reformers sought to restore the reputation of the Land Plan as a practical model for economic and social reconstruction. It was held up as a flawed but honourable exemplar, whose colonies offered a glimpse of the disaggregation of landed estates which, it was anticipated, would follow the implementation of land reform.

The first account of the Chartist Land Plan to advance such arguments was compiled in 1875 for the *Newcastle Daily Chronicle*, a radical liberal paper owned by Joseph Cowen MP, one of very few Englishmen elected to the executive of the Irish Land and Labour League. 'The relationship of the labourers to the land is coming to the front as a great national question', a special editorial explained. 'The Chartist effort of 1845 was an attempt to solve the difficulty in the then condition of England. We propose to give the history of that movement as a contribution to the settlement of that problem.' The author, William Longstaffe, did not spare O'Connor from criticism, arguing in particular that his mismanagement of the internal procedures of the scheme was primarily responsible for its 'hopeless collapse'; yet 'the failure was far more attributable to faults of the head than the heart'.[32] Longstaffe visited four of the estates and claimed to have found viable independent communities, living out their lives largely as O'Connor had predicted colonists would. He interviewed four original allottees and the son of a fifth, noting that 'none whatever' of the original residents of Charterville survived. At O'Connorville, the elderly Worcester Chartist Thomas Merrick and his wife Ann were surprisingly 'fresh, hearty and jovial'. Philip Ford, originally a carpenter from Gloucestershire, was a living vindication of the political and practical benefits of smallholding: that autumn he had harvested ten bushels of wheat from forty poles of land, 'his potatoes are "like bags of flour"', 'his cabbages, turnips and mangolds are invariably large and good', his pears 'fine and luscious' and his apples 'perfect pictures'. Mrs Ford, meanwhile, had grown 340 quarts of strawberries, for which there was 'a regular custom amongst the wealthy people of the neighbourhood'. In all, the holding had earned the couple 'over £40 in hard cash' above and beyond what was taken for family consumption. 'Philip Ford is not a man who needs much sympathy', concluded Longstaffe, 'he is still as hale and hearty a specimen of the English yeoman as can be found in a long day's march … A prettier little homestead it would be impossible to enter; and the old man, with a newspaper for his leisure, is as contented and happy as most human beings may be.'[33]

The fecundity of nature under the spade was somewhat less evident at Snigs End. Yet even here James Greenwood, once a Stalybridge handloom weaver, reported wheat yields between forty-five and fifty bushels an acre. Longstaffe scarcely disguised his glee on discovering 'the prosperous farmer' John Lee. In 1848, the experience of 'the poor fellow Lee', a cabinetmaker from Exeter, had been held up as a prime example of the futility of the Plan in evidence presented to the Select Committee on the National Land Company. Longstaffe found him 'in possession of more money and more land than when he started; we find every rood of ground cultivated as carefully as a garden … and what is more important, the produce yielded is said to be actually larger and better than that of any other person in the district'.[34] Meanwhile a Lowbands resident claimed O'Connor had come close to making the colony 'a perfect Eden'. Longstaffe's consistent message, and that of those he interviewed, was that only the first year's operations were hazardous. Thereafter, smallholding offered an honourable and independent, though never easy, means of living. The son of an original allottee, a Sunderland tallow chandler, stressed that 'no man could be expected to succeed without he has strength, endurance, determination and a sufficiency of funds to make him entirely independent of the first year's hardships and hazards'.[35] Gilding the lily somewhat (and seeking to refute a common criticism of the venture that industrial workers made poor farmers), Longstaffe concluded that allottees from urban communities 'speedily make better cultivators than the agricultural labourers', on account of the latter being 'too ignorant to make the best use of their advantages' and unable 'to work hard without supervision'.[36]

However, at the point Longstaffe was writing, renewed interest in the Plan came mainly from the rural rather than urban labour movement.[37] Among the significant features of the 'Revolt of the Field' was an adjunct agitation for peasant proprietorship drawing explicitly on the Chartist Land Plan for inspiration. At the inaugural meeting of the National Agricultural Labourers' Union, the platform party even included Arthur O'Neill, the former pastor of the Birmingham Chartist Church imprisoned for his part in the 1842 disturbances. 'With four acres of land upon one of the O'Connor allotments', a Gloucestershire Chartist colonist told a union rally in 1873, he 'could and did make a living for his family, and was better off than when he worked for a farmer at 12s. per week'.[38] 'A lot of the men were craving for the land ... properly "land mad"', the Union's leader Joseph Arch later recollected.[39] Its newspaper gave prominence to a biography of a long-standing Charterville allottee, John Jacob. Raised 'in the hardest of circumstances', Jacob epitomized the redemptive capacity of the land: he had first rented a two-acre plot around 1850, one of many taking a chance when holdings became cheaply available as the Land Plan descended into chaos. 'He is now a thoroughly hard-working man, always turning his hand to something', whose 'buildings are a picture of neatness ... the pigsties, especially, are perfect.'[40] In Louth, Lincolnshire, the Amalgamated Labour League marched under the banner 'The Land for the People' and the branch was one of several to initiate its own allotment scheme. Arch's union split in 1875 largely because of dissent on the issue of smallholding provision. The break-away National Farm Labourers' Union established a 'Land and Cottage Fund', similar in conception to the Chartist scheme, likewise floated as a separate company to surmount legal obstacles to the union holding property and likewise also short-lived.[41]

Partly because of its associated agrarian schemes, but also because of the general tenor of its rhetoric on landed property, the 'Revolt of the Field' was closely associated in the public mind with land redistribution.[42] This was abundantly evident in the deliberations of the 1879-82 Royal Commission on Agriculture, chaired by the Tory Duke of Richmond. Evidence gathered by the Richmond Commission described the Chartist Land Plan as 'a mischievous delusion' and its estates as populated by ineffective cultivators, universally shackled by debt. Horace Ripley, the vicar of Minster Lovell since 1872, discoursed at length on Charterville, declaring that its 'present condition is very bad'.[43] Ripley provided much of the data used by one of the Assistant Commissioners, Andrew Doyle, to compile a substantial attack on the Land Plan, 'all of it conclusive as to the hopeless and pitiable failure of this attempt to convert "tradesmen, artizans and weavers" into small farmers'. 'Thousands of simple people' had been duped by O'Connor's very vague and unpractical inducements'. Subsequent occupiers had faired no better: 'the general effect of the O'Connor allotments has been to draw great numbers of people from both town and country ... to complete ruin'.[44] Doyle trumped Longstaffe's failure to trace any original Charterville settler with an interview with Thomas Holland (originally a Manchester bricklayer). Holland was the last surviving allottee and he was languishing in Witney Workhouse. He was one of three allottees imprisoned in 1850-51, having failed to meet the costs awarded against them when they contested O'Connor's move to evict them.[45] Not unexpectedly, Holland had nothing to say in the Plan's favour. Doyle's report then went on to paint a lurid picture of an immiserated French peasantry, their precarious freeholds in the clutches of Jewish money lenders, before concluding that 'indebtedness is apparently inseparable from any extensive system of small ownership'.[46]

The surge in farmworkers' trade unionism had done much to undermine the social confidence of the rural establishment. This was clearly uppermost in Ripley's mind when he deviated from the Land Plan to attack Arch, for 'abusing the Church ... gentry, nobility and landed proprietary'.[47] There were, though, broader political issues of which the commissioners were clearly mindful. As memories of the 'thirty golden years' of English farming receded in the depression, the economic influence of landowners was once again a political issue. Demands for free trade in land, relatively quiescent in the 1860s, were once again foregrounded by Liberal politicians. Free trade in land was Andrew Doyle's *bête noire*. He also freely criticized J. S. Mill and William Thornton who, like Mill, was widely cited on the viability of smallholdings at this time. Doyle placed particular emphasis upon the historical tendency for small farms ('obstacles to scientific agriculture') to disappear: 'the consolidation of holdings is the result not of the English system of land-tenure, but of an economic law wholly independent of it'.[48]

It had been a commonplace of land reform arguments since the late eighteenth century that English land law strongly favoured the aggregation of property. The limited number of owners, because of the economic power vested in their hands, profited from unearned increments in the value of their land; because they overwhelmingly preferred capitalist farmers as tenants, they also withheld land from potential smallholders and allotment cultivators. This in turn depressed wages and the living conditions of labourers. Of the two strands within agrarian reform advanced to counter this, the most radical and potentially disturbing, land nationalization, was making only limited headway in the 1870s and early 1880s. (Doyle's one compliment to the Land Plan was that it was 'at least distinguished by the absence of any trace of communistic doctrine or design'.) Far more popular at this time were proposals for legislative intervention in the land market to promote the gradual dispersal of landed property. Arguments that a proliferation of small farms would depress output were met by claims for the high productivity of allotments and smallholdings. It was here that the Chartist Plan assumed a pivotal place in contemporary debate. 'No fairer opportunity', insisted Doyle, 'could be presented of testing by experiment the practicability of locating labouring men upon small plots of land.' However:

> these 'estates' have come to assume a character wholly different from what was originally contemplated; their history and present condition furnish striking illustrations of the tendency of small properties of this description to fall into the hands of mere speculators – to involve the tenants in debt – to become amalgamated.[49]

For those who opposed free trade in land, the political significance of the Chartist Land Plan thus outlasted the movement to which it had belonged, a calamitous portent of the fate awaiting attempts to demonstrate the supposed benefits of free trade through direct intervention in the land market. On the other hand, as interest in land redistribution burgeoned in the 1870s and early 1880s, the Chartist example was frequently enlisted by agrarian radicals. In Scotland its adoption was suggested as a means of rescuing crofting through the purchase of Highland estates: 'the people are not free as long as the land is tied up in the hands of the few'.[50] The Magna Charta Association, heart of the populist crusade to support the Tichborne Claimant, contemplated developing a land scheme explicitly modelled on

Chartism's.[51] Meanwhile, the formative ideas behind the Freehold Land Movement were revived by the National Liberal Land Company, founded in 1880 with a prospectus declaring 'the reform of land tenure [is] the best promise of national prosperity'; legislation to this end being stifled, its promoters called for 'social and commercial efforts as instruments of reform'. The Richmond Commission annexed this document to its report on the Chartist Land Plan, and drew direct comparison between the two.[52]

The Company was essentially a commercial operation run with an eye to benefiting from the co-operation of Liberal municipalities. The Commission's fire might have been better directed at the Allotments and Small Holdings Association, which had taken up the cause of the Chartist colonies with particular enthusiasm. Arch was among its leading supporters, whose greatest luminary was Joseph Chamberlain, then a minister in Gladstone's cabinet. The Association's secretary, Frederick Impey, wrote extensively on the Chartist estates, arguing that their history strengthened rather than weakened the case for the redistribution of land.[53] Impey conceded that 'broadly speaking, the history of the O'Connor estates is a melancholy story of high hopes destined to be inevitably blasted'. It was the inexperience of the allottees ('mostly Chartist artisans from the great towns') that mainly accounted for their failure: but the success of the Dodford colonists once they commenced specialization in strawberries and other market garden crops vindicated the principle of the scheme.[54] Impey claimed twenty original allottees or their children still resided at Dodford, stating this with some emphasis because length and continuity of holding was an important issue in arguments about the social and economic viability of smallholdings.

Like almost all advocates of allotment and smallholding schemes at this time, Impey grounded his argument in a broader discussion about the condition of rural England and the flight from the land. The election of the Association's president, Jesse Collings, as Liberal MP for Ipswich in 1880 stimulated the *Suffolk Chronicle* to compile a lengthy critique of the Chartist scheme. Its 'special commissioner' visited all five estates and interviewed the remaining original allottees. Among them was a Snigs End colonist who still adhered to the complex crop rotation originally advocated by O'Connor in his *Practical Work on the Management of Small Farms* (1843). This cultivator thought, however, that smallholding offered little prospect for the future of rural society. The last surviving Charterville allottee was portrayed 'hunted to earth by the late bad seasons ... an inmate of the Union Workhouse', bearing out the evidence to the Richmond Commission.[55] Frederick Impey took issue with the paper, asserting that the economic principle of peasant cultivation exemplified at Snigs End and Dodford, 'notwithstanding its apparent failure' was 'unassailable'. The *Chronicle* was complimented, however, by Horace Ripley who warned that to implement anything like the Chartist scheme would 'simply turn England into another Ireland'.[56] The early 1880s marked the high point of land reform agitation in Victorian Britain, which the Richmond Commission did nothing to dent. Indeed, as far as the reputation of the Chartist Land Plan was concerned, by ignoring Dodford (the most successful of the five colonies) the Commission provided the basis upon which supporters of smallholdings could attack its arguments. As a result, Dodford loomed large in smallholdings literature after 1882. The extent to which the reputation of this and the other four colonies became part of the debate around land reform was striking. It was understandable that veteran Chartists might praise the Land Plan as 'before its time' and 'the best illustration ... [of] the practicality of a project of peasant proprietory'; or claim that 'to describe the scheme as a failure is not in any sense correct'.[57] However, the praise lavished on it by those without connection to the movement is more surprising. The social and economic viability of the Chartist colonies, at least once holdings were extended in size, was widely stressed in the mid-1880s. They now found even clerical supporters. Early relations between the Established Church and the colonies had been fraught.[58] However, in 1885 Charles Stubbs, a prominent member of the Christian socialist Guild of St Matthew (and later Bishop of Truro) drew attention to the latter-day success of Charterville. Stubbs was active in promoting relations between the Church and the labour movement; on his appointment in 1884 to the living of Stokenham, Devon, he had established a communitarian 'home colony' on the glebe land. Communities of smallholders worked, Stubbs believed, if appropriate moral and religious leadership was forthcoming from rural social elites. In an appendix, 'The Feargus O'Connor Allotments', in his book *The Land and the Labourers* (1885) Stubbs claimed that godless O'Connorville had, even as late as the mid-1870s, been so bad that it was 'not safe for passing through at night. All had now changed.'[59] Yet there was a tension in Stubbs' account. O'Connor's scheme was unequivocally the most ambitious land redistribution scheme in English history. Stubbs plausibly diagnosed that neither Charterville's soil nor its local market were conducive to self-sufficient cultivation of holdings as small as two or four acres; but these failings could hardly be ascribed specifically to the Chartist origins of the venture.

Stubbs' intervention in the debate around labour and land was made at a crucial point in the months either side of the general election of 1885, in which considerable prominence was given to the land question by radical Liberals.[60] The Chamberlainite *Radical Programme*, developed over the previous two years and published as a whole in July 1885, was firmly committed to land reform and peasant proprietorship: 'the object of all land reform must be the multiplication of landowners'.[61] Jesse Collings, who wrote the land reform sections of the Programme, went so far as to call on 'the working classes ... [to] assist in securing ... three or four thousand Great Dodfords in England'.[62] Dodford's history became a contested issue in West Midland politics. 'How many broken hearts lay buried under that Great Dodford soil?', asked one Tory candidate. Moderate Liberals claimed all five colonies had 'proved signal failures'.[63] Original allottees defended Collings: 'commercially the good old town of Bromsgrove is none the worse for Feargus O'Conner [sic] locating his Chartists within two and a half miles of it', argued Alexander Shaw, originally a carpenter from Scotland. The colonists employed labour in the summer months to harvest their strawberries, they paid all civil rates and taxes and their claims on the Poor Law were minimal.[64]

The most important supporter of the Chartist colonies in this phase was a Birmingham corn merchant and councillor Charles Sturge (brother of Joseph Sturge, leader of the Complete Suffrage Union in the 1840s). Charles was an executive member of the Allotments and Small Holdings Association and succeeded Impey as its secretary.[65] For all the faults of O'Connor's original proposal, Sturge argued that each of the Chartist colonies maintained a population four or five times greater than similar acreages farmed conventionally. Furthermore, the impact of agricultural depression was no more severe than on neighbouring larger farms.[66] In Sturge's view the Plan had 'sufficiently withstood the all proving test of time as to permit us to readily mark the points of its weakness and its strength'. Justifiably describing it as 'the only large or systematic experiment ever made in this country in the purchase of estates for subdivision into small agricultural allotments', Sturge produced a classic account of radical Liberal land reform aspirations, demonstrating *inter alia* why the example of O'Connor's scheme was so central to them. The scheme failed, Sturge suggested, for five reasons. These were financial miscalculation by the promoter; 'the unexampled rapidity with which the popularity of the scheme grew'; the physical locations of the estates, which were particularly unsuited to large-scale cultivation of potatoes (upon which O'Connor's predictions of success largely rested); the lack of co-ordinating managerial influence once the Land Company was wound up and, finally, the small size of allotments. Far from indicating that continental style *petite culture* was unsuited to English soil, the realization of a comfortable subsistence under such difficulties on the Chartist colonies suggested

> the germ of a possibly successful social revolution, which would increase the productive power of the soil, distribute the population over the country, and retain an adequate labour supply in the rural districts; which would create a new demand for home manufactures, and go far to satisfy one portion of the demand for agricultural produce, and which would revivify town and country. The experience gained by a trial of 40 years of O'Connor's scheme would enable any, who may direct their energies to such another enterprise, to avoid the mistakes of the Land Company.[67]

Sturge made a particular study of the Snigs End colony, finding among its forty-eight holdings ten cultivated by original allottees or their children. He asked a Chartist from Banbury, 'whether he had done better than if he had remained a weaver'. He replied that when he came he was considered consumptive, but had enjoyed good health ever since. 'It was a hard struggle at first, but of later years comparatively easy work'. About seven acres were needed to live comfortably, 'the greater part of the people' hiring themselves out to local farmers and their 'wives and daughters working at glovemaking when it could be got'. The heavy clay of Snigs End would never present an easy living but Sturge judged the colony a success on the grounds of the health and contentment of its residents, especially in comparison to 'the dissatisfaction amongst farmers generally'.[68] If its economic and social viability was vulnerable, this was because of the owners' refusal to abate rents paid by colonists, nine of whose farms had fallen in during the bad seasons of 1881-84.[69]

At this point the smallholdings issue took a dramatic turn as it became entangled with the issue of Irish Home Rule. At the general election of 1886 Collings was among the renegade Liberals returned as Liberal Unionists under Chamberlain's leadership. The new Conservative government had no immediate need of their support, but it was happy to give Liberal Unionism its head in seeking to supplant the Liberals as the natural party of rural radicals (Arch was among the Liberal MPs who lost their seat in 1886). The Rural Labourers' League, founded by Collings in 1888, was part of this strategy. So too was a select committee on smallholdings the same year, chaired by Chamberlain and of which Collings was the leading member. There is a certain wry amusement to be gleaned from the evidence presented to it by none other than the Revd Horace Ripley. In a *volte face* (perhaps influenced by Stubbs), Ripley obliged the committee with a glowing picture of life at Charterville. Its residents, despite the contemporary depression, were 'doing fairly well considering the times'; 'they were very prosperous indeed about ten years ago'; 'they have done decidedly better [than] the farmers in the neighbourhood'; 'they are a very industrious and sober set of people, exceedingly so, why the Chief Constable of Oxfordshire had withdrawn the village constable on account of there being no crime there – Do you think that this was due to this experiment? [asked Chamberlain] – Yes, entirely so. 'It is the cure of pauperism', Ripley opined, adding that there is 'no drunkenness' and that residents' children are 'a more intelligent set' than those of their neighbours. 'Then, in a word, the possession of the land is a great stimulus to social and civic virtues?', enquired Chamberlain – 'Exactly so'.[70]

Though Ripley conceded that sources of support in addition to their holdings were needed by almost all the residents of Charterville, the general picture he painted was entirely favourable and strongly reinforced the Liberal Unionist argument that the State should promote allotments and smallholdings. Collings' own evidence to the Committee emphasized the merits and economic viability of the Dodford estate. In an interesting aside he revealed that the form of quit-rent tenure that had evolved at Dodford was the source of his own proposal for the legal basis upon which smallholders should hold land from public authorities. Dodford cultivators enjoyed significant security of tenure through having paid one quarter of the value of their holding on entry, the remainder constituting a permanent mortgage. Earlier that year, Collings had built this form of tenure into his unsuccessful private member's bill promoting smallholdings.[71]

Significantly, Collings' evidence on Dodford failed to mention any connection to O'Connor or Chartism. This contrasted with that of the President of the Institute of Surveyors whose views, one senses, were less welcome to Chamberlain: Charterville 'was distinctly what I consider a failure', the only mitigation being that Robert Owen's socialist Harmony Hall experiment was a 'most absolute and disastrous failure'.[72] What we see here is a process by which Collings sought to uncouple Dodford from Chartism, an act probably influenced by the ambiguities of his position as a Liberal Unionist. The espousal of land reform was an important means by which Chamberlain sought publicly to emphasize the distinctiveness of Liberal Unionism compared to Conservatism. Collings, one of Chamberlain's closest political associates and a veteran advocate of peasant proprietorship, was central to Liberal Unionist tactics precisely for this reason. As we have seen, when a radical Liberal, Collings had explicitly recognized the Chartist pedigree of smallholdings, but as a Liberal Unionist he was rather more circumspect.

Similarly circumspect were the assistant commissioners to the 1894-97 Royal Commission on Agricultural Depression who, in the final report, criticized the first volume of the body's findings for presenting 'too strongly the less-favourable view of small holdings'. This submission conspicuously excluded all mention of Chartism, even though (or perhaps because) the first volume had dwelt at some length on 'the perfect failure of Charterville'.[73] This negative note was, however, discordant with the prevailing view of the Chartist Land Plan in the 1890s. John Stuart Mill contributed posthumously to this situation through an 1891 reprint of *Principles of Political Economy*, wherein the ringing endorsement of the Plan he had removed from all editions after the second was restored by the editor, the Liberal chairman of the London County Council, John Lubbock.[74]

It is unclear if Lubbock consciously sought to resuscitate the reputation of the Plan, but a succession of radical journalists from about the same time were intent on exactly this. The most prominent was George Millin, a journalist whose early interest in the Plan culminated in a book, *The Village Problem* (1903). This included details of an interview he had conducted some years before with – he claimed – the last surviving Charterville allottee, whom he encountered not in the local workhouse but at his allotment gate. In view of the subject's advanced age and the earlier findings of the *Suffolk Chronicle* and the Richmond Commission, one can only conclude that Millin deployed rather more creativity than was consistent with journalistic good practice. His view of 'poor Feargus O'Connor's bold land scheme' emphasized the negligible agricultural experience of the first settlers. However:

> In some respects it was very cleverly planned, and it came much nearer to success than was commonly supposed; but the motley crew of diggers and delvers brought into the scheme foredoomed it to failure ... but I remember being very much impressed by the fact that even by his scheme, which proved a total failure, O'Connor left behind him a really thriving little estate for working men.[75]

Millin's approach was closely echoed in the work of the most enthusiastic Edwardian defender of the Land Plan, Louisa Jebb, a leading member of the Co-operative Small Holdings Society. Her substantial 1907 study of smallholdings commenced with a photographic frontispiece of 'an early attempt to re-establish the smallholder', a Charterville cottage, surrounded by ripening barley. Jebb held that the Plan offered 'wholesome object-lessons' in the promotion of smallholdings and attacked the Richmond

Commission, particularly for its failure to take any account of Dodford. Her case rested heavily on the Dodford settlement. She suggested a third of its original occupiers remained there thirty years after its foundation and that a large number of their children were still resident. She interviewed the head of one of three surviving original families, the son of a railway labourer and Scottish Chartist whose plans to emigrate to America were deflected by the enticements of the Land Plan:

> He was a successful drawer at the ballot for lots, and migrated with his whole family. They found the place such a wilderness on arrival that they all returned to Glasgow next day. Six years later they returned for a final settlement. During the time the father employed another allottee to get his holding into order, while he continued his profession in Glasgow. Most of the settlers were mechanics from the North of England, and in many cases they continued at their trades, employing Irish labourers to dig their holdings.[76]

Jebb was concerned to refute a commonplace argument that the small acreages undermined smallholders' chances of success. Instead, she identified their limited farming experience as the primary cause, compounded by the lack of industrial by-employment. Even so, once established, the Dodford colonists and their families had effectively lived rent free with all the vegetables and bacon they needed, plus a weekly surplus of about 7s 10d. A switch to strawberry growing increased the average surplus per holding to around 17s 6d weekly. 'The general look of Dodford at the present time', observed Jebb, 'is prosperous.' She also interviewed a new occupier, a Birmingham brass foundryman who hawked fruit and vegetables around Kidderminster. 'The place he was on had changed hands many times, and had just been bought by a Birmingham manufacturer ... the competition of Birmingham capitalists is very strong when the holdings change hands. Many of those who are now cultivating the lots for a living are paying high rents to new landlords and have no sense of security.' Jebb judged the Plan to have been 'a marked success in the long run', but observed that this same success forced up the market value of holdings to a point where current or aspiring cultivators could not afford them.[77]

This had been one of the Plan's original dilemmas: the more suited a piece of land for its purposes, the more that land cost. Chamberlain, Collings, Millin and Jebb all argued that state intervention was needed if the land was to be made available to ordinary working people; but Millin and Jebb also adhered to the view that the Chartist holdings were of a viable acreage. A somewhat cooler appraisal appeared in 1909 in a 'Social Service Handbook', *The Land and the Landless*, co-authored by a Quaker social reformer, the younger George Cadbury.[78] Cadbury wrote against the background of the 1908 Small Holdings and Allotments Act which required county councils to satisfy demand for holdings and awarded compulsory powers to effect this.[79] This represented the most extensive intervention to date by the state in the rights of private landed property in England, and can in part be ascribed to the cumulative impact of claims that smallholders, among them those on the former Chartist colonies, needed the security of tenure that state ownership brought. Cadbury supported this view, but believed state involvement needed to be further extended to facilitate closer involvement in the management of smallholdings. Crucially, as far as 'wholesome object-lessons' were concerned, these needed to be larger than the two, three or four acres on which the Chartist holdings were based.

The last substantial case study of a Chartist land colony appeared as late as 1917, compiled by an employee of the Board of Trade, Arthur Ashby. Subsequently head of Oxford University's Institute for Research in Agricultural Economics (and appointed to the Agricultural Wages Board by the first Labour government), Ashby wrote at length on Charterville. In his judgement, too, its failure as an agricultural enterprise stemmed from the holdings being too small. Once adjacent plots were aggregated in the late 1850s, Charterville had been an economic and social success and 'to 1887 the colony settled down to the most prosperous period in its chequered history'.[80] Much of Ashby's information seems to have derived from his father, Joseph, originally an agricultural labourer and for many years a pillar of Methodism and radical liberalism in south Warwickshire. Joseph had spent much of the early 1890s touring the south Midlands with the red vans of the English Land Restoration League, painted with the slogans 'Fair Rents, Fair Wages, The Land for All, Justice to Labour and Abolition of Landlordism'. Though the League's ideology was significantly different to the Chartist Land Plan, these were still slogans to which Chartists would have assented.[81]

The younger Ashby's other main source of information was one of Ripley's successors as vicar of Minster Lovell, who believed Charterville had weathered the depression better than other parts of the parish. He was greatly impressed by the colonists' work ethic: 'I have said to one of them who worked for me, – How is it you work so splendidly? You do too much work, – and he said – "We get into this way of working for ourselves and we cannot stop it".'[82] Ashby concluded that the productive capacity of Charterville, for all its disadvantages of soil and market location, had considerable potential for improvement, but noted most settlers held their allotments on short leases from petty rentiers; this undermined effective co-operation among them. Ironically, in deploring Charterville's 'general looseness and lack of organization', Ashby implicitly drew attention to one positive aspect of the colony in its original Chartist phase.[83]

Ashby's was the last appraisal of the Chartist Land Plan to take seriously its claim to be a model for rural reconstruction. In marked contrast to what had gone before, interest in the Plan during the inter-war period was attenuated. In *The Enclosure and Redistribution of Our Land* (1920), William Curtler provided a somewhat bland account, while the agricultural historian C. S. Orwin, an advocate of land nationalization, made a brief critical appraisal in 1935. In the Chartist colonies themselves, all sense of the original aims was apparently lost: local knowledge relied heavily on secondary sources, notably Hovell's strongly anti-O'Connor history of Chartism.[84]

There was to be, however, one last twist to the posthumous career of the Chartist Land Plan, in which it was enshrined as an alternative version of Englishness by one of the best-selling authors of non-fiction in inter-war Britain, H. J. Massingham. Idealization of English rural life and an organicist view of society drew Massingham into a position of profound antipathy to modernity. He discerned in the Chartist settlements the tragic quintessence of a vanished Englishness, where work meant craftsmanship, production was not commodified and men worked in an organic relationship with each other and the soil. In 1940, bemoaning the sprawl of suburban development and values, Massingham concluded a chapter entitled 'Conquered Country', by deprecating 'the brick wilderness called Heronsgate ... all that is left now is the name of one of the local pubs – "The Land of Liberty"'. He then proceeded to invoke the names of two who 'might almost be called the last not exactly of the Chartists but of those who have borne on their standard the legend for which the Chartists implicitly fought – "For England, Home and Beauty"'. Both had lived and worked nearby in the south-eastern Chilterns. The first was G. K. Chesterton, the poet and critic whose political and cultural writings were suffused with medievalist sentiment. The second was the sculptor and designer Eric Gill, whose own complex engagement with modern aesthetics had strongly medievalist leanings. Massingham believed the artistic colonies Gill founded were potential centres for an anti-capitalist and anti-modernist counterculture. And, he thought, in a different way the Chartist colonies had once been the same.[85]

'For England, Home and Beauty' is a very partial and politically charged abridgement of Chartist ideals. Massingham was no democrat: he described Labour's 1945 election victory as a 'bound forward to despotism unknown since the dictatorships of Henry VIII and Cromwell'.[86] That one so wholly in antipathy to the labour movement could elevate the Chartist Land Plan to a kind of totem, alerts us to its powerful yet contradictory messages. His interpretation was the obverse of that commonplace view among labour historians that condemned the Plan as reactionary and diversionary. It also indicates the extent to which, by the Second World War, interest in the redistribution of landed property had been abandoned by liberalism and the left.[87]

The extent to which the Chartist colonies were read as an effective indictment of the distribution of landed wealth varied remarkably over time. For almost two decades after its winding up, the memory of the Plan was largely seen as distinctly unhelpful to the continuing cause of land reform. Distance, however, lent it some enchantment and reviving interest in the radical press nurtured the argument that, as a practical endeavour, the Chartist Land Plan was less disastrous than generally supposed. From the 1870s, a succession of reformers once more cited the Plan as a benchmark and object lesson. They could do so as long as the essential parameters of the land question remained unchanged. However, the continuing urbanization of politics shifted the way in which the land question was formulated. An important, if not decisive, impulse to this process derived from the American reformer Henry George whose arguments achieved wide currency in late Victorian Britain. George contended that a single tax on land values would enable taxation of all other earned income to be abolished, and establish common property in land without interfering in its legal ownership. As a result, radical politics became increasingly absorbed with the issue of economic appropriation of rent, rather than with land ownership per se. By 1898, Sidney and Beatrice Webb could observe that 'instead of the Chartist cry of "Back to the Land", still adhered to by rural labourers and belated politicians, the town artizan is thinking of his claim to the unearned increment of urban land values'.[88]

Rising interest in George's ideas intersected with the burgeoning campaign for land nationalization, arguments in favour of which stood or fell without reference to smallholdings. Though sympathetic to smallholder cultivation, the President of the Land Nationalization Society, Alfred Russel Wallace (whose introduction to politics had been through artisan London in the mid-1840s), never referred to it. Meanwhile, the Society's secretary presented the Chartist movement as aiming purely at the nationalization of land.[89] In annual debates on the land question at the Trades Union Congress, a majority of delegates favoured land nationalization for the first time in 1887; the following year calls for peasant proprietorship, once a staple feature at the Congress, disappeared altogether from its proceedings.[90]

Though the reputation of the Chartist Land Plan arguably peaked in the 1890s, its 'posthumous' career was therefore drawing to a close from the late 1880s as the land question was substantially reshaped, on the one hand, by nationalizers and single taxers and, on the other, by Liberal Unionism. The centrality of smallholdings to the Liberal Unionist platform increased the tendency for more radical circles to perceive them as merely palliative. On the political left, the relevance of the Chartist Land Plan to contemporary politics diminished accordingly, a trend reinforced by a continuing decline in Feargus O'Connor's reputation: a cheap reissue of Gammage's *History* in 1894 reinforced a growing Fabian influence on the labour movement's view of its past. 'Doomed to failure from the start', O'Connor's Plan was 'one of the wildest and maddest schemes that ever entered into the mind of a rational being', wrote the influential ex-Chartist W E. Adams in his 1903 memoirs. This flatly contradicted both his original support for the Plan and his defence of it (noted above) in the 1880s.[91]

Beyond the labour movement, interest in the Chartist Land Plan was increasingly bound up with contemporary concerns about rural depopulation ('the village problem' of which Millin wrote). As a general economic and social panacea, smallholding was losing its force in the first decade of the twentieth century, though its appeal as a palliative held up in Liberal circles. Even here, its advocates were increasingly apt to marginalize or ignore the Plan. We have seen how Frederick Impey, as secretary of the Small Holdings and Allotments Association, had stoutly defended Dodford in 1880. However, in 1908, having been appointed the Board of Agriculture's special commissioner on smallholdings, Impey produced an historical account of the subject which moved seamlessly from Cobbett and the repeal of the Corn Laws to the 1880s, not once mentioning O'Connor or the Land Plan.[92]

Readings of the Land Plan had always taken divergent forms: it was beset by ambiguities just as it had been at its formation. With the growth of interest in allotments and smallholding (whether as a political palliative, social control or philanthropic endeavour), these ambiguities arguably increased. In 1886 William Morris had acidly observed that 'three acres and a cow, duly reduced to a very humdrum allotment scheme, will not bring about a very great revolution'.[93] It was a Conservative government that passed a Small Holdings Act in 1892 which incorporated a form of Collings' Dodford-inspired quit rent tenure.[94] 'There is no measure with which I am more proud to have been connected than with that giving peasant proprietorship in such large measure to Ireland', the Conservative leader Arthur Balfour declared in 1909, adding 'and I hope to see a great extension of such ownership to England.'[95] In this context the Chartist associations of the widest-known proposal for peasant proprietorship were no recommendation. We have seen how Jesse Collings, who had done much in the early 1880s to retrieve the reputation of the Plan, fudged Dodford's Chartist origins in 1888. In 1906, having served as a Conservative government minister, he produced an otherwise compendious volume, *Land Reform: Occupying Ownership, Peasant Proprietorship and Rural Education*, that mentioned neither the Land Plan, nor even Dodford, at all.[96]

By the time of Liberalism's land campaign under Lloyd George,[97] Liberal enthusiasts for smallholdings were locating them within the wider issue of calls for state management of agriculture, as we saw in George Cadbury's 1909 *The Land and the Landless*. From 1916, close government direction of agriculture in order to meet wartime subsistence needs fundamentally redefined the land question away from issues of ownership, tenure and taxation, towards those of state management of – and support for – farm production. (Ashby's treatment of Charterville in 1917 was itself part of a study of agricultural organization). After the First World War, even the general secretary of the National Union of Agricultural Workers was portraying land reform solely as a means towards tackling 'the problem of land management'. Furthermore, the post-war extension of the principles embodied in the 1908 Small Holdings Act, first by the state to assist the settlement of ex-servicemen on the land and later by the Land Settlement Association to relocate the unemployed, enjoyed very limited success.[98]

The state's retreat from agricultural management during the inter-war period proved only temporary. As the key question in agriculture became increasingly that of maximizing production through the application of mechanical and chemical technologies, issues of ownership and tenure were subjugated to efficiency and management. The agrarian fundamentalism so strikingly evident in the Land Plan pushed it beyond even the margins of contemporary politics. Thus Massingham in 1940 could appropriate it unchallenged for his reactionary ruralism. By the 1950s, with technically advanced large scale farming privileged by the post-war Labour Government's Agriculture Act, the Chartist Land Plan was sufficiently anodyne a subject to be an article in *Country Life*.[99] 'Nowadays', an acerbic piece in the *New Statesman* claimed in 1997, 'the Chartist model town of O'Connorville is a leafy, arcadian village, much sought after by the Mercedes-owning classes.'[100]

Notes

1   'Chartist Land Plan', the commonest contemporary usage, is here used throughout. The scheme passed through a number of official titles: initially an adjunct to the NCA, it was launched as a separate entity as the Chartist Co-operative Land Society in April 1845. To facilitate registration as a Friendly Society, this was changed to National Co-operative Land Society. Refused registration because it was a lottery, the Plan was redesignated the National Co-operative Land Company. Finally, in 1847 registration was sought under the 1846 Joint Stock Companies Act as the National Land Company, a title retained until it was wound up by an Act of Parliament in 1851. For the legal history of the Plan see E. Yeo, 'Practices and problems of Chartist democracy', in J. Epstein and D. Thompson (ed.), *The Chartist Experience* (London, 1982), pp. 345-80.

2   Rules of the Chartist Co-operative Land Society (5845), quoted in *PP* (Reports from Committees) Session 1847-48 (398), XIII: SC on the National Land Company, 2nd Report, p. 49.

3   J. S. Mill, *Principles of Political Economy* [book 2, ch. 10], ed. J. M. Robson (Toronto, 1965), vol. 2, p. 1001. See also D. Martin, *John Stuart Mill and the Land Question* (Hull, 1981), pp. 30-31.

4   For O'Connor see particularly J. Epstein, *The Lion of Freedom: Feargus O'Connor and the Chartist Movement, 1832-1842* (London, 1982) and D. Thompson, *The Chartists* (Aldershot, 1982). On the agrarian tradition within radical politics see J. Bronstein, *Land Reform and Working-Class Experience in Britain and the United States, 1800-1862* (Palo Alto, 1999), pp. 23-51; M. Chase, *'The People's Farm' English Radical Agrarianism, 1775-1840* (Oxford, 1988) and E. Royle, *Robert Owen and the Commencement of the Millennium* (Manchester, 1998), pp. 39-46.

5   R. G. Gammage, *History of the Chartist Movement, 1837-54* (1854, 2nd edn, Newcastle upon Tyne, 1894), pp. 248, 268-69, 376. For a more detailed discussion of the historiography of the Plan see chapter 4 above, and of Chartism generally D. Thompson, 'Chartism and the historians' in her *Outsiders: Class, Gender and Nation* (London, 1993), pp. 19-44.

6   Bronstein, *Land Reform and Working-class Experience*; chapter 4 above (first published 1996); I. Foster, *Heronsgate: Freedom, Happiness and Contentment* (Rickmansworth, 1999); A. M. Hadfield, *The Chartist Land Company* (Aylesbury, 2000 – new edition, first published 1970); A. Janowitz, *Lyric and Labour in the Romantic Tradition* (Cambridge, 1998); A. Messner, 'Communication: land, leadership, culture and emigration: some problems in Chartist historiography', *Historical Journal* 42 (1999), 1093-1109; D. Poole, *The Last Chartist Land Settlement: Great Dodford, 1849* (Dodford, 1999).

7   P. J. Larkham and J. Lodge, 'Testing UK conservation in practice: the case of the Chartist villages in Gloucestershire', *Built Environment* xxiii (1997), 121-36; *The Chartist Land Plan* (leaflet issued by the Conservation Planning Office, Bromsgrove District Council, 2000); C. Oman, 'The lower Windrush valley', *Oxford Magazine* 8 June 1904, cited in J. Orr, *Agriculture in Oxfordshire: A*

Survey (Oxford, 1916), p. 49.

8   The National Trust, *Rosedene: An Appeal for Restoration* (leaflet issued 1999).

9   E. F. Biagini and A. J. Reid, *Currents of Radicalism* (Cambridge, 1991); R. McWilliam, *Popular Politics in Nineteenth-century England* (London, 1998); M. Finn, *After Chartism* (Cambridge, 1983); A. Taylor, 'Commemoration, memorialization and political memory in post-Chartist radicalism', in O. Ashton et al, *The Chartist Legacy* (Rendlesham, 1999), pp. 255-285; M. Taylor, *The Decline of British Radicalism* (Oxford, 1995).

10 E. Eldon Barry, *Land Nationalization in British Politics* (London, 1965), pp. 47-77; Finn, *After Chartism* pp. 132-33, 140, 262-73; R. Harrison, *Before the Socialists: Studies in Labour and Politics, 1861-1881* (London, 1965), pp. 210-50; J. Hyder, *The Case for Land Nationalization* (London, 1913), 319; A. Plummer, *Bronterre: A Political Biography of Bronterre O'Brien, 1804-1864* (London, 1971), pp. 193-260; S. Shipley, *Club Life and Socialism in Mid-Victorian London* (London, 1983), pp. 1-20.

11 For a detailed study of the movement see chapter 12 below.

12 For similar views see for example the influential C. Brodrick, *English and English Landlords* (London, 1881), pp. 154-55 and V. Scully, *Mutual Land Societies: Their Present Position and Future Prospects* (Dublin, 1851), p. 10.

13 *Reynolds's Political Instructor* 2 Mar. 1850, see also 20 Apr. 1850; *The Times* 26 Nov. 1811; J. E. Ritchie, *Freehold Land Societies, Their History, Present Position and Claims* (London: 1853), p. 22.

14 'Mr O'Connor's Incarceration', *Freeholder and Commercial Advertiser*, 12 June 1852; Ritchie, *Freehold Land Societies*, p. 8; T. Beggs, 'Freehold Land Societies', *Journal of the Statistical Society of London* 16 (1855), 339; *Birkbeck Freehold Land Societies Simplified and Explained* (London, 1855), pp. 3-4. See also *Provident Times*, 8 Mar. 1854; *Freeholder*, 1 Nov. 1850 and 1 July 1851; *Freehold Land Times*, 15 Dec. 1854; *Freeholder and Commercial Advertiser*, 12 June 1852. In 1850 the communitarian Leeds Redemption Society was similarly apprehensive lest it be confused with the Chartist Land Plan, see *The Redemption Society: Fourteen Days' Propagandism. What to Say* ([Leeds], 1851), p. 3.

15 Editorial, 'Mr O'Connor's Land Scheme', *Freeholder*, 1 Mar. 1850.

16 See for example the seminal J. M. Ludlow and Lloyd Jones, *Progress of the Working Class, 1832-1867* (London, 1867), pp. 125-311, wherein coverage of land societies is confined to the freehold land movement.

17 'Our Farm of Two Acres', Martineau's articles from *Once a Week* (9, 16, and 30 July 1859) were anthologized in her *Health, Husbandry and Handicraft* (London, 1861), quotation from p. 270.

18 J. Sillett, *A Practical System of Spade Husbandry* (London, 1847) and *A New Practical System of Fork or Spade Husbandry* ('new and enlarged edition', London, 1848), pp. iii-iv, 12.

19 SC National Land Company, 4th Report, qq. 3816-4172; *The Evidence of John Sillett, on his Examination before a Committee of the House of Commons, appointed to enquire into the National Land Company, clearly proving that a man may live well and save money on two acres of land* (London, 1848).

20 J. Sillett, *A New Practical System of Fork and Spade Husbandry* (London, 1850).

21 *John Sillett the Suffolk Draper: Fork and Spade Husbandry or £51 a Year from Two Acres* (London, 1906) – part of the 'Cottage Farm Series' issued by the Peasant Arts Fellowship. See also J. Marsh, *Back to the Land: The Pastoral Impulse in England from 1880-1914* (London, 1982), pp. 119-21.

22 An illustration of this cottage forms the frontispiece of his *Practical Treatise on Feeding and Fattening Pigs* (London, 1851).

23 T. C. Turberville, *Worcestershire in the Nineteenth Century* (London, 1852), p. 308.

24 T. M. Wheeler, leader article, *National Union* 5 (Sept. 1858), 33. This view was reiterated by his biographer, W. Stevens, *A Memoir of Thomas Martin Wheeler* (London, 1862). See also Wheeler, 'Sunshine and Shadow', *NS* 15 Dec. 1849, reprinted in I. Haywood (ed.), *Chartist Fiction* (Aldershot, 1999), p. 175.

25 P. Redfern, *The Story of the CWS: The Jubilee History of the Co-operative Wholesale Society Limited, 1863-193* (Manchester, 1913), pp. 19-21; Royle, *Robert Owen* p. 228. See also the generous treatment of the Plan in the chapter 'The lost communities', in G. J. Holyoake, *History of Co-operation* (revised edn 1906, first published 1875-9), vol. 2, pp. 183-85.

26 Unredeemed certificate awarded to James Knowles, 5 Oct. 1855. Knowles, a vitriol works labourer of Westleigh near Bolton, passed this certificate down through his family rather than redeem it. I am grateful to his great great-grandson, Robert Charleson, for drawing my attention to this document.

27 A. Somerville, *Conservative Science of Nations* (Montreal, 1860), pp. 219-55, quotation from p. 219. The basis for most of this treatment of the Land Plan was the author's earlier *The O'Connor Land Scheme Examined and Described from its formation to the Present Time. By One Who has Whistled at the Plough* (Manchester, 1847), itself based on the articles contributed to the *Manchester Examiner*.

28 *PP* 1868-9 (Reports from Commissioners) XIII, 2nd Report of the Commissioners on the Employment of Children, Young Persons, and Women in Agriculture, appendix part 1 (report of Assistant Commissioner George Cullen), pp. 99-100, 348-9 – quotations from p. 349. For Bennett see Hadfield, *Chartist Land Company*, pp. 228, 230-35 and M. Chase, 'Chartism in two Teesside towns, 1838-58', *Northern History* 24 (1988), 164.

29 H. D. Griffiths, 'The longest day at O'Connorville', *Beehive* 27 June 1868.

30 W. Maccall, *The Land for the People: An Argument for an English Land League* (London, 1865), p. 1.

31 J. Burchardt, 'Land, labour and politics: parliament and allotment provision, 1830-70', in J. R. Wordie (ed.), *Agriculture and Politics in England, 1815-1939* (London, 2000), p. 125.

32 *NDC* 5 Jan. and 5 Feb. 1875. The reports were anonymous but attributed to Longstaffe by Holyoake, *History of Co-operation*, p. 184. For Longstaffe see O. R. Ashton, *W. E. Adams* (Whitley Bay, 1991), p. 133.

33 *NDC*, 30 Jan. 1875. Photographs of Meyrick and Ford appear in Hadfield, *Chartist Land Company* and there are references to them in Foster, *Heronsgate*, *passim*.

34   *NDC*, 5 Feb. 1875; SC National Land Company, 4th Report, qq 3451, 3678, 3763-86, 3810-15. Quotation from q. 3678.

35   *NDC*, 5 Feb. 1875. The interviewee's father, William Howe, had chaired the committee of allottees which had led an attack on O'Connor's mismanagement, see Hadfield, *Chartist Land Company*, p. 146.

36   *NDC*, 5 Feb. 1875.

37   R. Arnold, 'The "Revolt of the Field" in Kent, 1872-79', *Past & Present* lxiv (1973), 71-95; J. P. D. Dunbabin, 'The "Revolt of the Field": the agricultural labourers' movement in the 1870s', *Past & Present* xxvi (1963), 68-108 and id., *Rural Discontent in Nineteenth-Century Britain* (London, 1974), pp. 62-85; Alun Howkins, *Poor Labouring Men: Rural Radicalism in Norfolk, 1879-1923* (London, 1985), pp. 57-79; R. C. Russell, *The 'Revolt of the Field' in Lincolnshire* (Lincoln, 1956).

38   Quoted in N. Scotland, 'The National Agricultural Labourers' Union and the demand for a stake in the soil, 1872-96', in E. F. Biagini (ed.), *Citizenship and Community* (Cambridge, 1996), p. 155. For O'Neill see *DLB*, vol. 6.

39   J. Arch, *The Story of His Life Told by Himself* (London, 1898), p. 278.

40   *Labourers' Union Chronicle: an Independent Advocate of the British Toilers' Rights to Free Land*, 21 Nov. 1874, quoted in C. W. Stubbs, *The Land and the Labourers: a Record of Facts and Experiments in Cottage Farming and Co-operative Agriculture* (2nd edn, London, 1885), pp. 185-6.

41   Dunbabin, *Rural Discontent*, pp. 102, 112-13, 246-67; Russell, *The Revolt of the Field*, pp. 87-8, 113, 119, 124, 129, 141; evidence of Simmons, minutes of evidence taken before H. M. Commissioners on Agriculture in *PP* 1881, qq 59,237; TNA, BT 31/2240, memorandum of association, National Farm Labourers' Union Co-operative Land Company.

42   F. Clifford, *The Agricultural Lock-Out of 1874* (Edinburgh, 1875) devoted two chapters to the issue in which *inter alia* he criticized Sillett and the Chartist Land Plan, see esp. pp. 274-84.

43   Minutes of evidence taken before H. M. Commissioners on Agriculture in 'Reports from Commissioners, Inspectors and Others: 1. Agricultural Interests', *PP* 1882, XIV, evidence of A. Doyle, qq. 65705-710 (quotation from 62705); evidence of H. Ripley, qq. 64445-594, quotation from q. 64461.

44   'Mr Doyle's Report on "The National Land Company" and Small Holdings', RC on Agriculture, Reports of Assistant Commissioners: Mr Doyle's Reports on Wales, *PP* 1882 (c.3375-III) vol. XV, 68-80 (hereafter 'Doyle's Report') – quotations at 68-9, 71, 72-3.

45   'Doyle's Report', 71. See Hadfield, *Chartist Land Company*, pp. 160-69, and K. Tiller, 'Charterville and the Chartist Land Company', *Oxoniensia* 50 (1985), 260 and 264, for accounts of the attempted eviction and imprisonment episode.

46   'Mr Doyle's Report', 79.

47   Minutes of evidence taken before H. M. Commissioners on Agriculture, 1882, q. 64584, cf qq 64585-57 and 64499-500.

48   Minutes of evidence taken before H. M. Commissioners on Agriculture, 1882, q. 65707; 'Doyle's Report', 74. For Thornton see his *Plea for Peasant Proprietors*

(London, 1848) and C. Dewey, 'The rehabilitation of the peasant proprietor in nineteenth-century economic thought', *History of Political Economy* vi (1974), esp. 29-33.

49   'Doyle's Report', 71 and 74.

50   J. Murdoch, in the *Highlander*, 25 Jan. 1879, quoted in J. Hunter (ed.), *For the People's Cause: from the writings of John Murdoch* (Edinburgh, 1986), p. 19. See also pp. 20 and 39.

51   R. McWilliam, 'Radicalism and popular culture: the Tichborne case and the politics of 'fair play', 1867-86', in Biagini and Reid (ed.), *Currents of Radicalism*, p. 61.

52   The National Liberal Land Company, Ltd, Prospectus – appendix to 'Doyle's Report', 80. Streets in company developments frequently bore the names of radical liberal luminaries and its toll-free crossing of the River Itchen at Southampton was named 'Cobden Free Bridge', see TNA, MT 10/383 (Bitterne Bridge Bill). The company was later renamed the National Land Corporation, see Stock Exchange Year Book (London, 1900), p. 1017.

53   For example undated [1880] 'Letter to the editor of the [Birmingham?] *Daily Post*', Sturge Collection vol. I, f. 15; 'The Dodford Freehold Small Farms', *Birmingham Daily Post*, undated cutting (1880?), Birmingham Central Library Local Studies Section [BCL], Cotton Collection vol. 86, f. 7; 'Peasant Farming', *Suffolk Chronicle* [1880?], undated cutting in Sturge Collection vol. I, ff. 131-32; 'La Petite Culture', *Friends' Quarterly Examiner*, Jan. 1883; *La Petite Culture: Thoughts on the Farming of Small Holdings at Home and Abroad* (London, 1883), pp. 15-18. The 'Sturge Collection' cited here comprises two large volumes of annotated papers, ephemera and cuttings on land tenure, compiled by Charles Sturge (for whom see below), deposited after his death in BCL, and now housed in its Social Sciences Library. See also P. Searby, 'Great Dodford and the later history of the Chartist land scheme', *Agricultural History Review* 16 (1968), 32-45.

54   Impey, *La Petite Culture*, p. 16.

55   'Peasant Farming in England. By Our Special Commissioner', *Suffolk Chronicle* [Feb.?] 1883, – undated cuttings in Sturge Collection, vol. 2, ff. 4-14, where Sturge attributes authorship to one Alfred Harwood.

56   F. Impey, 'Peasant farming', *Suffolk Chronicle*, Feb./Mar. 1883, undated cutting in Sturge Collection vol. I, ff. 131-32; H. C.Ripley, 'Peasant farming at Minster Lovell', *Suffolk Chronicle* undated [Mar. 1883] cutting in Sturge Collection vol. 2, f. 14.

57   B. Wilson, *The Struggles of an Old Chartist* (1887), reprinted in D. Vincent (ed.), *Testaments of Radicalism* (London, 1977), p. 210; W. E. Adams, 'Notes & Queries: Feargus O'Connor's Land Scheme', *Newcastle Weekly Chronicle*, 18 Mar. 1882.

58   See for example Hadfield, *Chartist Land Company*, pp. 61-62; Tiller 'Charterville', p. 265; E. P. Baker (ed.), *Bishop Wilberforce's Visitation Returns for the Archdeaconry of Oxford in the year 1854* (Oxford Record Society, xxxv [1954]), 95-6; J. Noake *Guide to Worcestershire* (Worcester, 1868), p. 308; A. Shaw, 'The Dodford Allotments', *Bromsgrove Messenger* undated [May] 1885

cutting in BCL, Cotton Collection vol. 2 f. 279.

59   Stubbs, *Land and the Labourers*, p. 183. Three further editions appeared by 1891. See also C. W. Stubbs, *Glebe Allotments and Co-operative Small Farming* (London, 1880), p. 20. For Stubbs see P. d'A. Jones, *The Christian Socialist Revival, 1877-1894* (Princeton, 1968), pp. 135-6.

60   See R. Winfrey, *Address on Allotments and Small Holdings* (London, 1907), published by the Political Committee of the National Liberal Club, for the emphasis the Party placed on the land question in the 1885 general election.

61   *The Radical Programme: With a Preface by the Right Honourable J. Chamberlain* (London, 1885), p. 54. See also J. Chamberlain, *A Political Memoir, 1880-92*, ed. C. H. D. Howard (London, 1953), pp. 108-10.

62   J. Collings, 'The allotment question – Great Dodford', undated press cutting from the [Birmingham?] *Daily Post*, Feb. 1885, BCL, Cotton Collection vol. 62, f. 168.

63   'A Liberal JP for the County of Hereford', letter to the editor, *The Times* 28 Sept. 1885; 'A Candidate', 'The O'Connor Land Company', letter to the editor, *The Times* 6 Oct. 1885. Some Tories, though still critical, were more sympathetic: for example the Earl of Onslow (secretary of the Land and Glebe Owners' Association for the Extension of the Allotment System). See his *Landlords and Allotments: the History and Present Condition of the Allotment System* (London, 1886), pp. 42-4.

64   A. Shaw, 'The Dodford Allotments', *Bromsgrove Messenger*, undated [May] 1885 cutting in BCL, Cotton Collection, vol. 2, f. 279. The summer labourers employed were mainly Black Country nailers and their families.

65   Information about Sturge taken from F. Impey, *Three Acres and a Cow: Successful Small Holdings and Peasant Proprietors* (London, [1886]), p. 3 and id., *Small Holdings in England* (London, 1909), p. 3. See also obituary, *Birmingham Daily Post*, 2 May 1888 and A. Tyrell, *Joseph Sturge and the Moral Radical Party in Early Victorian Britain* (Bromley, 1987), *passim*.

66   C. D. Sturge, 'The O'Connor Land Company', letter to the editor, *The Times*, 6 Oct. 1885.

67   C. D. Sturge, 'The National Land Company', press cutting for which no publication details are given but endorsed 'about 1882' in the author's hand, Sturge Collection, vol. 2, ff. 120-24.

68   C. D. Sturge, quoted by F. Impey in a letter 'to the editor of the *Daily Post*', undated press cutting [Nov. 1880] in Sturge Collection vol. I, f. 115.

69   Sturge, 'The O'Connor Land Company', *The Times*, 6 Oct. 1885.

70   SC on Small Holdings, Report with the Proceedings of the Committee, *PP* 1888 (358) XVIII, qq. 2233f.

71   Ibid, evidence of Collings, q. 598; R. Douglas, *Land, People and Politics: A History of the Land Question in the United Kingdom, 1878-1952* (London, 1976), p. 104.

72   Evidence of Walter Dalton, SC Small Holdings, qq. 3727 and 3803. On Harmony Hall see Royle, *Robert Owen*.

73   *PP*, 1897, vol. XV (c. 8540), Reports from Commissioners ... Agriculture, 354-62, quotation from p. 354; First report and minutes of evidence, RC on

Agricultural Depression, *PP* 1894, part III (c. 7400-III), qq. 42,061 and cf. 42,064.

74   J. S. Mill, *Principles of Political Economy*, (no. 6 in the series 'Sir John Lubbock's Hundred Books', London, 1891), pp. 234-35.

75   [G. F. Millin], *The Social Problem* (London, 1892), pp. 18-19; [G. F. Millin] *Life in Our Villages. By a Special Commissioner of the 'Daily News'* (London, 1891), p. 192. G. F. Millin, *The Village Problem* (London, 1903), pp. 169-71.

76   L. Jebb, *The Smallholdings of England: A Survey of Various Existing Systems* (London, 1907), pp. 143, 134.

77   Ibid., pp. 136-37, 142. For another contemporary assessment of the importance of the Dodford strawberry crop, see 'The Dodford Settlement. "The Garden of the Midlands"', *Bromsgrove Messenger*, 21 July 1900.

78   G. Cadbury and T. Bryan, *The Land and the Landless* (London, 1908), pp. 136, 157-64.

79   For which see E. J. T. Collins (ed.), *The Agrarian History of England and Wales, Volume VII: 1850-1914* (Cambridge, 2000), pp. 699, 780-82.

80   A. W. Ashby, *Allotments and Smallholdings in Oxfordshire* (Oxford, 1917), pp. 110-18, 134-40, quotation from p. 113.

81   M. K. Ashby, *Joseph Ashby of Tysoe, 1859-1919* (Cambridge, 1961), p. 152.

82   Ashby, *Allotments*, p. 117.

83   Ibid., 179. Ashby's conclusions qualified a somewhat uncritical assessment by another member of the Oxford Institute, Orr, *Agriculture in Oxfordshire*, pp. 49-50.

84   C. S. Orwin and W. F. Darke, *Back to the Land* (London, 1935), pp. 13-14; W. Curtler, *The Enclosure and Redistribution of Our Land* (Oxford, 1920), pp. 278-79; lecture on O'Connor by the vicar of Dodford, reproduced in an undated [1922?] and unsourced local press cutting, BCL, Cotton Collection vol 54, f. 89; 'The Chartist Movement, 1836-48: Dodford and the Land Scheme', *Bromsgrove Messenger*, 25 Aug., 1, 8 and 15 Sept. 1928; Mark Hovell, *The Chartist Movement* (Manchester, 1918) and see chapter 2 above.

85   H. J. Massingham, *Chiltern Country* (London, 1940), p. 108; cf. F. MacCarthy, *Eric Gill* (London, 1989) and on Chesterton J. D. Coates, *Chesterton and the Edwardian Cultural Crisis* (Hull, 1984).

86   H. J. Massingham, *The Small Farmer* (London, 1947), p. 63. For discussions of Massingham's cultural politics see W. J. Keith, *The Rural Tradition* (Toronto, 1975), pp. 233-52; M. Chase, 'This is no claptrap, this is our heritage', in C. Shaw and M. Chase (ed.), *The Imagined Past: History and Nostalgia* (Manchester, 1989), pp. 128-46; D. Matless, *Landscape and Englishness* (London, 1998), *passim*; R. J. Moore-Colyer, 'Back to basics: Rolf Gardiner, H. J. Massingham and "A Kinship in Husbandry"', *Rural History*, 12:1 (Apr. 2001), 85-108.

87   E.g. Hovell, *Chartist Movement*, p. 32; A. L. Morton, *A People's History of England* (London, 1935), pp. 424-25; T. Rothstein, *From Chartism to Labourism* (New York, 1929), pp. 79-80; J. Saville, *Ernest Jones, Chartist* (London, 1952), p. 24; J. West, *A History of the Chartist Movement* (London, 1920), pp. 213-18.

88   S. and B. Webb, *The History of Trade Unionism* (London, 1898), p. 362; see also S. D. Headlam, *Fabianism and Land Values* (London: English League for

the Taxation of Land Values, [1908]), p. 7.

89   E.g. A. R. Wallace, *Land Nationalisation, its Necessity and its Aims* (London, 1882); Hyder, *The Case for Land Nationalisation*, pp. 232 and 319.

90   Webb, *History of Trade Unionism*, p. 376.

91   W. E. Adams, *Memoirs of a Social Atom* (London, 1903), pp. 160, 208. He had been auditor for the Cheltenham branch of the Plan, see Ashton, *W. E. Adams*, pp. 35, 44. See *supra*, n. 57.

92   F. Impey, *Small Holdings in England* (London, 1908): his list of 'small holdings I have visited' actually excluded Dodford. Louisa Jebb's later work similarly ignored the Chartist Land Plan, see Mrs R. Wilkins [L. Jebb], *The Small Holdings Controversy* (London, 1909).

93   W. Morris, 'Notes on passing events' *The Commonweal*, ii (41) (23 Oct. 1886).

94   Collins (ed.), *Agrarian History*, pp. 325-26, 698, 780-82.

95   Quoted in A. Offer, *Property and Politics, 1870-1914* (Cambridge, 1981), p. 357.

96   J. Collings, *Land Reform: Occupying Ownership, Peasant Proprietorship and Rural Education* (London, 1906) and similarly his two-volume *The Colonization of Rural Britain: A Complete Scheme for the Regeneration of British Rural Life* (London, 1914).

97   For which see B. B. Gilbert, 'David Lloyd George: the reform of British land-holding and the budget of 1914', *Historical Journal* 21 (1978), 117-41; B. B. Gilbert, 'David Lloyd George: Land, the Budget and social reform', *American Historical Review* 81 (1976), 1058-66; Offer, *Property and Politics*, pp. 363-400; Douglas, *Land, People and Politics*, pp. 134-68; I. Packer, 'Conservatives and the ideology of land ownership', in M. Francis and I. Zweiniger-Bargielowska (ed.), *The Conservatives and British Society, 1880-1900* (Cardiff, 1996), p. 54; B. Short, *Land and Society in Edwardian Britain* (Cambridge, 1997); M. Tichelar, 'Socialists, Labour and the land: the response of the Labour Party to the Land Campaign of Lloyd George before the First World War', *Twentieth-Century British History* 8 (1997), 127-44.

98   R. B. Walker, *Speed the Plough: A New Policy for Farming* (London, 1922); E. H. Whetham, *The Agrarian History of England and Wales, Volume VIII: 1914-39* (Cambridge, 1978), pp. 136-39, 217, 301, 304.

99   M. Chase, '"Nothing less than a revolution?" Labour's agricultural policy', in J. Fyrth (ed.), *Labour's High Noon: The Government and the Economy, 1945-51* (London, 1993); E. E. Kirby, 'Three acres and a spade', *Country Life*, 22 Dec. 1955.

100 *New Statesman*, 22 July 1995.

6

RETHINKING WELSH CHARTISM

The process of rethinking Welsh Chartism has had a long and not always distinguished history. As early as 1840 the Reverend Evan Jenkins, a Dowlais Church of Wales parson, unequivocally declared that Chartism was 'as diametrically opposed to the doctrines revealed in the eternal word of God, as the North is to the South'. Therefore, he concluded the first of the fallen angels had himself effectively been a Chartist.[1] This chapter does not offer anything like so fundamental a rethink. Nor does it say anything in detail about the South Wales Rising. The events of November 1839 have arguably skewed the way that historians think about Chartism. This is in no way to diminish the significance and poignancy of what happened in Newport, far from it; but among many scholars there has been a tacit assumption that there is little to be said about Welsh Chartism after 1839. There are exceptions to this generalization: in the early 1970s David Jones, Angela John and Owen Ashton, and two other Welsh historians, Ryland Wallace and David Ormond, more recently.[2] However, Welsh Chartism beyond Newport is an issue to which general works on the Chartist movement are largely oblivious. The second part of what follows will argue that Welsh Chartism's decline after November 1839, though palpable, is too easily exaggerated and was not hugely out of step with the rest of the British Isles. But it begins by re-examining aspects of the origins of Welsh Chartism and the events of 1839 in the context of works about the wider movement since the mid-1980s.

Readers with a working knowledge of these general works will have spotted the allusion in this article's title to a seminal essay, published in 1983, by Gareth Stedman Jones.[3] His argument essentially was that to view Chartism as a movement of industrial workers, certainly of class-conscious ones, with economic motives was mistaken; it was rather the last phase of eighteenth-century radicalism, dedicated to the overthrow not of the economic system but of a venal and corrupt state. Historians had mistakenly imposed a conceptual framework of class (derived from Marxism) onto Chartism: they had failed – Stedman Jones claimed – to read attentively the actual language of Chartism. He also argued that the strong tradition of local studies within the historiography had atomized understanding of Chartism and distracted attention from its central ideology. This was almost a death knell for local histories of the movement, and it is salient to understanding why the study of Welsh Chartism, by academic historians at least, declined after the mid-1980s.[4] But the wider consequence was that Stedman Jones was read as effectively de-coupling Chartism from industrial protest and focusing almost exclusively upon one element of what Chartists said: 'Old Corruption'. The consequence of this powerful and influential study was therefore to play down the potency that class analyses brought to the ideology of the movement.

Stedman Jones had little to say about Welsh Chartism, other than observing that the government's commutation of the death sentence on the leaders of the Newport Rising underlined how the state was no longer malignantly predictable. This was important to his overall argument that, because Chartism's ideology rested upon the conviction that the state was inherently corrupt, it was decisively undermined by any government action that was benign, or undertaken in contradiction to the direct economic interests of the party in power. This reading of Chartism requires that we set-aside any lingering suspicion that the treatment of John Frost, Zephaniah Williams and William Jones *was* malignant; it also effaces the mass petitioning campaign for their pardon, which hardly revealed a movement beset by ideological crisis (more people signed the 1840 petition for a pardon than had signed the 1839 Chartist national petition). If the history of nineteenth-century Wales teaches anything, it is surely that an appropriate and necessary part of historical analysis of the years from around 1830 turns on working people's growing awareness of their distinctive situation and common sense of political purpose. This is not to surrender to a metaphysical concept of class, in which 'the working class' becomes almost an historical actor in its own right, and seemingly capable of independent thought and action. Nor is it to suggest that class consciousness was uniform across all occupations and localities. However, it is important to reaffirm that Chartism was a national movement of unprecedented scope, intellectual reach, cultural vitality and political ambition. Reiteration of the traditional radical trope of 'Old Corruption' could not alone have engendered those qualities.

Of course a common understanding of themselves 'as labourers ... opposed to the interests of the other classes of society' was not all that Chartists thought they had in common.[5] They articulated other 'ways of seeing' their situation: as the politically excluded, as unwilling subjects of a corrupt state and its venal administrators, as true patriots and as 'the

People'. And the means through and by which this repertoire of ideas was articulated was not restricted to print alone. There is now a significant literature on non-verbal communication in the Chartist movement, 'class conflict without words'.[6] Yet even if research into Chartism is confined to printed texts alone, it is still clear that its language drew heavily on the vocabulary and conceptual apparatus of class. This was a movement deeply rooted in a shared conviction among wage-earners that their economic and political interests starkly contrasted with those of the rest of society. Too often, however, its history has been written as if this is all that is needed to explain Chartism. Plainly it is not and this largely explains the enduring influence of Stedman Jones' essay.

So as a first effort in rethinking Welsh Chartism I wish to pose this question: to what extent was radical reformism in Wales fuelled by resentment that political power lay with a propertied elite, ruling through English-based institutions? This was certainly the case in Scotland, where visiting English Chartist leaders shrewdly made a pilgrimage to 'the sacred field of Elderslie', birthplace of William Wallace.[7] But was it so in Wales? Ivor Wilks, in his book on the Newport Rising, claimed that it was. However, Wilks asserted rather than proved that the Rising was 'deeply rooted in the centuries-old Welsh experience of repression'.[8] Almost completely eclipsed by David Jones' magisterial work, published a few months later, Wilks' proposition has never received a full airing. Yet even if it can be shown to have real substance, the central fact of South Wales Chartism was that it was overwhelmingly a movement of industrial workers, articulating sentiments like these in the *Address* of the Swansea Working Men's Association:

> We would have you remember that labour creates capital ... In most parts of England, Scotland and Wales, the oppressed multitudes have become sensible of the enormity of the system that has so long ground them into the dust, and are making the most strenuous efforts to recover their rights as human beings.[9]

One ventures to suggest that Welsh Chartism offers a very necessary corrective to the extreme interpretation of Stedman Jones' thesis. To argue that the radical thrust of Chartism derived entirely from its eighteenth-century radical intellectual inheritance is to travesty the evidence that we are dealing with a rich, multi-faceted and intellectually vital movement.

One illustration of the vitality of Welsh Chartism was its links outside Wales. The *People's Charter* itself originated, of course, with the London Working Men's Association (LWMA), and the strategy of petitioning parliament for reform with the Birmingham Political Union (BPU). Both the BPU and LWMA financed what they termed 'missionaries' to raise political awareness beyond their respective cities; and from the autumn of 1837 the LWMA was targeting mid-Wales with considerable success. But it would be a mistake to think that the political traffic was all one way. For example Thomas Powell, the Newtown-born Chartist leader gaoled after the Llanidloes riots, had lived (1821-1832) in London. He made an important contribution to metropolitan radicalism as a notably active member of the London Co-operative Society and the National Union of the Working Classes; he also lectured on currency reform and was secretary of the British Association for the Promotion of Co-operative Knowledge. Furthermore Powell lived with none other than William Lovett who, as secretary of the LWMA, would later write the *People's Charter*. It was Powell who brought another LWMA leader, the veteran unstamped pressman Henry Hetherington, to Wales in the autumn of 1837 to promote Chartism. When Powell was arrested after the Llanidloes riots, the terms for his bail were set punitively high and it took nearly eight weeks before sureties acceptable to the Montgomeryshire magistrates were found (a particularly blatant example of the manipulation of bail procedures, a tactic the authorities commonly used to detain Chartists without trial). One of the sureties was provided by another of Powell's close London friends, LWMA member and leading radical publisher, James Watson.[10] When he was released from gaol in 1841, Powell returned to London, to manage the retail side of Hetherington's printing and publishing business. Hetherington had frequent brushes with the law on account of the content of his publications and at one point sold his business to Powell in order to thwart official confiscation of all his printing equipment. But from where did Powell obtain the money? The answer is from the Carmarthen solicitor and Chartist Hugh Williams.

Another, and more profound, example of the Welsh contribution to English radicalism can be seen in the pre-Rising career of John Frost. Historians (including Welsh ones) have underestimated the extent to which John Frost was a major *British* Chartist leader, and not just a Welsh one. The great Leeds-based Chartist newspaper *Northern Star* bolstered its sales by distributing engraved portraits to regular readers. One of the earliest, and the first depicted in a full-length portrait, was of Frost. Some 20,000 copies were distributed to Chartist homes and meeting rooms across the British Isles. In an elaborate portrayal Frost, frock-coated and highly respectable, was depicted standing against a background of opulent drapes and an Ionic column. The latter were standard features of elite portraiture and had figured prominently in the depiction of the pre-Chartist reformers Sir

Francis Burdett and William Cobbett. But no other member of the Chartist pantheon, up to this point in *Northern Star's* history, had been depicted thus. This portrait was intended to make a profound visual statement about the importance of Frost in the movement nationally, and to claim for him the dignity and status that Burdett and Cobbett (both MPs of course) and countless other statesmen had enjoyed.[11]

So complex ties of political respect, and of interpersonal trust and friendship, sustained Welsh and English Chartism. It may not be too fanciful to suggest that the closeness of these ties helped mislead Frost into supposing that English Chartists would be with him that fateful November. In the spring of 1839, as South Wales Chartists established clubs to facilitate instalment payments for firearms, copies of Francis Macerone's cheap pamphlet on street warfare, *Defensive Instructions for the People*, circulated among them. These almost certainly emanated from London, where *Defensive Instructions* had first appeared during the reform crisis, primarily through extracts in Hetherington's mass-circulation unstamped paper *Poor Man's Guardian*.[12] Simultaneously in mid-Wales, 'a great number of Copies of Colonel Macerone's work' had allegedly been distributed by Thomas Powell.[13] This helps highlight an issue of considerable importance to the study of Welsh Chartism. Of all the misapprehensions that have dogged the historiography of the movement, one of the greatest has been that the LWMA under the benign tutelage of William Lovett espoused only 'moral force' Chartism, while 'physical force' was the creed of desperate workers from the industrial North of England and South Wales, abetted by Celtic hotheads like Feargus O'Connor.

Few things are further from the truth. Before 1840 all Chartists espoused the right to bear arms and the right of just resistance to tyranny. This principle was enshrined in the Manifesto of the 1839 General Convention, which bore on its cover not only the name of William Lovett (who wrote nearly all of it) but his portrait as well. On the same day (9 April 1839) that the General Convention explicitly endorsed arming, Thomas Powell told a rally of more than 2,000 at Newtown:

> I have at all times stood forth as your leader in the warfare and I hope you will not now forsake me if called upon, but oppose force to force if necessary – some of your members want us to employ moral force – what will moral force do for us, what has it done for us? You have groaned enough under tyranny already and know it will not avail you. Be determined and your opponents will not withstand you – your number is sufficient. Be close together and you will march thro' every town and city in the kingdom.[14]

Standing beside Powell on the platform was Henry Hetherington, whose own comments about the preparedness of mid-Wales Chartists to take up arms alarmed authority. His views are perplexing if viewed solely through the conventional moral *versus* physical force prism.[15] One of the few contemporary pieces of evidence directly linking the Newport tragedy with the mercurial Charles Jones concerns his comments anticipating the 'outbreak', made during a visit to Hetherington's shop and subsequently sent to the Home Office by a disaffected employee.[16] No Chartist before 1840, even those in Lovett's orbit, unequivocally ruled out the use of force for political ends. The only exception to that generalization was the Scottish Chartist, Church of Scotland minister and pacifist, Patrick Brewster. In this Brewster ostensibly resembled some Welsh divines who espoused moral force principles, primarily as a tactic to contain and restrain Chartism, for example Aberdare's Independent Minister John Davies. During the summer of 1839, Chartists took to concerted attendance at services for divine worship and Davies wrote a sermon for the occasion which he subsequently published.[17] But Brewster, by contrast, was a committed Chartist activist whose reading of the scriptures led him to passionate advocacy of the religious imperative of passive obedience to civil authority, but also of the right to steal if subsistence depends upon it. It was Brewster, not the LWMA, who first formulated the argument that Chartism should use moral force alone. He had difficulty securing a hearing for his views even in Scotland. In Wales his writ carried no weight at all.[18]

Furthermore, in the government's view there was little to choose between Welsh and English Chartism in terms of militancy. This is evident in the circular sent by the Home Secretary in May 1839 to those towns judged most volatile, offering to arm special constables, suggesting the formation of voluntary associations to keep the peace, and encouraging for the first time the immediate arrest of Chartist speakers 'at the time of committing the offence' at any illegal meeting. A royal proclamation prohibiting arming and drilling accompanied the letter, the circulation of which effectively mapped the geography of Chartism's greatest strength.[19] Thirty-two English centres were circulated. The Welsh towns covered were Monmouth, Newtown, Newport, Merthyr Tydfil and Pontypool (interestingly not Llanidloes – perhaps the government was confident that all unrest there had been neutralized). Scotland was ignored.

So, although the events in Newport in November 1839 were unique and tragic, they were not the product of uniquely Welsh circumstances as Wilks would have us believe, nor David Jones when he concluded that 'some form of local rising is the most satisfactory explanation of what was intended'.[20] Clearly by the last week in October 1839 the geography of the South Wales valleys made it difficult, if not impossible, to call off the rising (Frost said as much at the time); and the nature of industrial society in the region predisposed many who lived there to desperate measures; but there were comparable societies in the industrial north of England – in the Tyne valley, in south-east Lancashire and north-east Cheshire, in West Yorkshire. Why these regions did not erupt says much about the difficulties of cross-regional communication (especially once the Convention had disbanded in late September). This is not to suppose that success would have attended a Chartist rising in November 1839 had events in northern England and South Wales been properly coordinated; nor is it likely that English workers would have risen to the challenge on quite the scale as Monmouthshire's (or with the same poignant determination to *do something* even if they were not exactly sure what that *something* was). But evidence of a serious intent to revolt is apparent in a number of centres in northern England. This is why, in my *Chartism: A New History*, some time is devoted to reconstructing the series of events across Britain that preceded Newport, and to the incidence of rebellion in England after it – in Barnsley, Bradford, Carlisle, Dewsbury, Halifax, Newcastle, Nottingham, Sheffield, the Spen valley and even the East End of London (another of Britain's 'black domains', to borrow a phrase from David Jones).[21] The resilience of Chartism after Newport and especially the scope and energy of the campaign to defend Frost, Williams and Jones, are also telling indicators that there was widespread endorsement among all Chartists of the principle of armed resistance. With it went a tacit admission that the English Chartist leadership was more deeply implicated in the conspiracy than any could safely admit.

—O—

If English Chartism was not wholly out of step with the mood in South Wales in autumn 1839, it may follow that Welsh Chartism conforms more closely to the broader pattern of the movement than has hitherto been supposed. An understandable concentration of historiographical attention on Newport has led to a tendency to overlook the extent and enduring commitment of Welsh Chartists elsewhere. Until David Osmond's admirable article on Newport after 1840, in *Gwent Local History* in 2005, even the dogged persistence of its Chartists was imperfectly understood.[22]

The table accompanying this chapter collates indicators of the extent and persistence of Chartist activity in Wales. It draws on Dorothy Thompson's *The Chartists* (1984), the appendix to which listed all the Chartist localities she had unearthed at six key dates in the chronology of the movement.[23] To this information seventeen more localities have been added and the timeline extended into the early 1850s. Gaps in Thompson's information on the 1840s have been filled out where further evidence exists. This table is not offered as a definitive summary. Yet even with that caveat, it is clear that Welsh Chartism was in more robust health in the 1840s than historians have allowed. Support in some of these localities was ephemeral. Nonetheless, the 67 locations where Chartist activity can be identified constituted a quantum leap compared to Wales' contribution to the Reform agitation of 1830-32, when there was just one Political Union (at Merthyr) in contrast to over 120 in England. There were around 500 centres of identifiable Chartist activity in England, so it is clear that Chartism constituted an exponential growth in political activity there as well, compared to the Reform agitation. However, the extent to which politicization had *increased* since the Reform Crisis was far greater in Wales.[24]

The evidence offered in the table for the extent of Welsh Chartist activity during the 1840s in no way challenges the argument that Newport profoundly impacted on Welsh Chartists' morale. For a while even publicly to espouse Chartist principles in South Wales risked persecution, as the leading Bath Chartist R. K. Philp discovered when he was arrested after addressing the first openly advertised Chartist meeting in Newport since the Rising, a full eleven months later.[25] Subsequently, when Philp and the other full-time lecturers of the National Chartist Association (NCA) embarked on a lecture tour to revive the movement's fortunes, they omitted South Wales completely.[26] However, as the table indicates, once official apprehensions subsided the profile of Welsh activity after 1839 more nearly matched that of England and Scotland (in both of which there was, in any case, a similarly marked diminution of activity in the mid-1840s). Nor was Wales much out of kilter with England (considered as a whole) in its response to the 1842 strike wave. The notion that there was such a thing as 'the general strike of 1842', an argument notably put forward by Mick Jenkins in a book of that title, somewhat stretches the evidence.[27] 1842 was actually a year of strikingly low levels of industrial unrest in London, for example. Co-ordinated and geographically contiguous strike action was limited to north Staffordshire, Cheshire and the Pennine textile districts, with an important outlier in the industrial region of the west of Scotland and, perhaps, in south Wales. And note that I say 'co-ordinated and geographically contiguous' but not simultaneous. From Staffordshire up to Lancashire and across into the West Riding, strikes 'until the charter became the law of the land' were potent, menacing and met mass support; but beyond Manchester few persisted longer than three or four days. These momentous events are better described as a 'strike wave'. Seen from that perspective, the 1842 stoppages on the South Wales coalfield in and around Aberdare and Merthyr Tydfil are consistent with the English pattern of short, sharp strikes. Merthyr's chief constable declared them 'a shadow of the Manchester affair and their object the Charter'.[28]

In dismissing them as merely shadowy he was arguably whistling to keep his spirits up, for throughout the 1840s the energy and vitality of Chartism in Merthyr was considerable. Almost half of the 48,000 Welsh signatures to the 1842 petition came from Merthyr and its vicinity. David John's and Morgan Williams' Merthyr publishing enterprise, and notably their newspaper *Udgorn Cymru* ('Trumpet of Wales'), constituted a major impulse behind a lively new phase in Welsh Chartism. It is, though, one that has largely been neglected.[29] In January 1842 Merthyr Chartists proposed to evangelize virtually all Wales: 'nothing is wanting to complete the good work but a good and active lecturer capable of speaking the two languages. The places most backward are Swansea, Carmarthen, and the shires of Pembroke and Cardigan. They want visiting very much.'[30] It was in Merthyr too that active commitment to insurrection lingered, the central figure being an itinerant haberdasher and NCA activist from Nottingham, George Black. From his base in the town Black sold 'vast quantities' of arms, according to Glamorgan's chief constable, and co-ordinated shadowy preparations for a further rising. In June 1841 bullet moulds and a copy of the booklet *Defensive Instructions*, hidden in a consignment of haberdashery, were intercepted in transit from Birmingham to a Pontypool address used (under an alias) by Black.[31]

Yet elsewhere in south Wales Chartism appeared so quiescent that even leading activists were ignorant of the extent to which the movement endured. The sole Welsh delegate to the 1842 National Convention, exempted only Abergavenny from a picture of decay, frankly doubting (mistakenly) if there even was a viable Chartist association in Newport.[32] Just over a year later the *Northern Star* ran an editorial on the Welsh Chartists. 'Where are they? What are they doing? Are they still alive? ... It would do us good; indeed it would, to hear something from Wales'. The sole response came from Newport, detailing the first Chartist gathering there for some time.[33] In mid-Wales there are no recorded Chartist activities of any kind during 1843, except for a meeting in Newtown to welcome Thomas Powell on his liberation from gaol. It would be a mistake, however, to equate quiescence with political apathy or fear. Chartists themselves recognized that their own *modus operandi* was unequal to the task of spreading the Chartist gospel in parts of Wales. As a Midlands Chartist missionary observed of the coal mines of north Wales in May 1842:

> The men employed in them are at present suffering great oppression; we must be there; a talented lecturer would bring out the whole district in a few weeks; and then hurrah for the propaganda in Denbigh and Merioneth; Snowdon and Plinlimon would soon echo back to the Wrekin, the shout for the Charter! ... [W]hat Bilston is, such might be Mold and Wrexham.[34]

The language barrier was one element that had always constrained Chartist mobilization in Wales. The absence of Welsh-language lecturers was clearly lamented by Chartist activists in 1842 and may well have been an important factor in earlier years. Furnishing radicalism with Welsh-language literature had long been a problem. 'Not ... the least valuable feature in the advantages of the Welsh language' claimed a winning poet at the Denbigh Eisteddfod organized by the Gwyneddigion Society in 1828, is 'that it has been the means of preserving the Welsh peasantry ... from the pestilent contaminations of such writers as Paine, Hone, Carlile, and I will even add Cobbett'.[35] David Jones suggested as long ago as 1973 that David John's and Morgan Williams' efforts to expand the stock of Welsh-language Chartist literature should be seen as a concerted response to this challenge. Yet there has been a dearth of interest in Welsh-language Chartist material, its circulation and impact. Jones speculated that instinctively 'one would expect to find Chartist groups at places like Ruabon' (south of Wrexham).[36]

And so it proves. A June 1848 conference of the National Association of United Trades (NAUT) noted that there was indeed a 'very efficient district' in Ruabon.[37] Very much an adjunct of Chartism at this time, and largely dependent on *Northern Star* as the medium of communication with its branches, the NAUT survived Chartism to within a few years of the formation of the TUC to become an at times strikingly effective parliamentary lobby on trade unionism's behalf.[38] It drew its support overwhelmingly from older craft trade unions, rather than engineering, mining or heavy industry. This was reflected in its principal Welsh affiliates, who comprised calico printers (Ruthven), handloom weavers (Llanidloes), nailmakers (Cardiff and St Ninian's, Merthyr and Newbridge), shoemakers (Denbigh, Mold and Newport) and tinplate workers (Newport). Their numbers were inconsiderable: a rare surviving balance sheet for the Association suggests these affiliated Welsh trades mustered only around 360 members in total. Around a third of them were in Denbigh.[39] Here, in 1846, the NAUT made a decisive contribution to resolving a serious dispute in the town's extensive boot and shoemaking workshops, when its Executive sent the London Chartist William Robson to negotiate on the strikers' behalf.[40] This episode may also help explain occasional interest in Chartism in the Denbigh-based *Baner Cymru* in the late 1850s and early 1860s.[41]

Though fragmented, the NAUT's presence in Wales further underlines the need to re-evaluate Welsh Chartism during the 1840s. It has to be said, however, that the immediate picture of Welsh Chartism on the brink of Europe's year of revolution is not impressive. Only six Welsh localities, for example, contributed to the costs of fighting the 1847 general election (which had seen O'Connor elected as MP for Nottingham); furthermore, of the 22 constituencies where a Chartist candidate went to the polls none was Welsh. Yet the contributions of English localities to the 1847 election campaign were hardly impressive either. Though 270 English localities contributed, few did so significantly. More money was raised by ex-patriot Scottish linen weavers in Boulogne than in the entire Spen Valley of Yorkshire, for example. Sheffield managed only 2s 6d, Trowbridge, Coventry and Sunderland nothing.[42]

Just as in England, the real Welsh Chartist success story of the late 1840s was the Chartist Land Plan. Given the geography of support for the plan across Britain generally (it attracted little interest in rural areas), the 26 Welsh localities that boasted either their own branch or a smaller cluster of members is consistent with support for the initiative in England. Again it was Merthyr that took the initiative, establishing not only Land Plan branches in Newbridge and Cardiff but also heading a district that covered all Wales plus Bridgnorth and Shrewsbury.[43] How far O'Connor's scheme to provide cottage smallholdings for urban workers helped to sustain or to hinder Chartism has been much debated. However, it is now widely accepted that, up to end of 1847, the Land Plan was an entirely positive development for the movement. The failures of 1848 were due to wholly different factors. The first of these was the catastrophic miscalculation by the NCA executive (intoxicated by events in France) in bringing forward the presentation of Chartism's third mass petition. This imposed an impossible burden on localities to collect and collate the signatures in time. Meetings to congratulate the nascent French Republic, however numerous (and they *were* numerous), did not necessarily indicate that petition sheets were being filled, or that Chartism was once again percolating across the British Isles. Indeed, coverage in the *Northern Star* amply revealed it was not. The 18 March 1848 issue, for example, carried reports of just one general Chartist meeting in Wales (Merthyr, unsurprisingly), of only two in Scotland and of 51 in England. Of the latter, a quarter was in London, seat of the NCA's national executive, a situation which surely skewed its members' perspective of the movement's vitality. Even more indicative of Chartism's polarized state, Chartist Land Plan revenues acknowledged in the same issue exceeded £770, while NCA national funds accrued a mere £5 19s 2d.

Two other key factors help explain Chartism's failings in 1848: O'Connor's failure to mount any kind of defence of the alleged irregularities of the third National Petition in Parliament; and government curtailment of political freedom, sufficient to push elements within London's burgeoning Chartist movement into insurrectionary plans. It was once a commonplace of Chartist historiography that the movement collapsed immediately after the 10 April 1848 demonstration in London, as the deficiencies of the third national petition were exposed by the government. Ever since David Goodway's magnificent *London Chartism*, it has been abundantly clear that this view is erroneous.[44] The peak of Chartism in 1848 occurred from June to August, in the teeth of suppressive government measures forbidding freedom of assembly, which had also established a new treasonable crime of open and advised speech, potentially covering almost any radical political utterance. The establishment's mood was far from one of complacent triumphalism after 10 April. Rather it was apprehensive. However, the Chartist insurrection of 1848 lies completely outside this study, because the plans, as far as one can tell, never involved Welsh Chartists. However, some of this sense of political potency was manifested in a resurgence of millenarian speculation, encouraged by the European revolutions. For example, according to one writer in *Seren Cymru* at Whitsun 1848:

This is the time of troubles for kings and generals ... They have had their day ... the angel is preparing to pour out the sixth phial, and its outpouring will 'prepare the way of the kings of the earth' ... Only the throne established in justice is safe. Parliamentary reform is necessary. For it is not the voice of the people that is heard in the House of Commons but the voice of the aristocracy.[45]

However, in a striking contrast to the months after the 1839 Rising, Chartism across the British Isles went into a steep decline after the exposure of insurrectionary plans in August 1848. There was no nationwide campaign to pardon William Cuffay, the black London trade unionist presented by government prosecutors as the ring leader of the aborted insurrection. In November a new NCA executive was elected, comprising eight London members to conduct routine business, and 45 others representing major towns. The map of Chartist strength revealed by the distribution of these delegates was revealingly skewed: four Scottish localities were represented and just Abergavenny and Merthyr from Wales – but then there were only two delegates from West Yorkshire, while some north-west Chartist strongholds, notably Ashton-under-Lyne and Stockport, were missing completely.[46] Hereafter, one mostly glimpses Welsh Chartism fleetingly: 'T. F.', 'J. P.', 'J.M.' and 'W.A.' of Llanelli remit four shillings to the Honesty Fund in March 1850 (the last record of the movement in the town);[47] in November, Mrs Evans, landlady of the King's Head, Pontypridd, announces the birth of her son Kossuth Mazzini Evans;[48] a NCA branch flickers briefly in Chepstow in 1851.[49] The *Northern Star's* readership was also sharply declining: average weekly sales in 1850 hit a low of 5,000, a thousand below the worst previous year of 1846. *Reynolds's Political Instructor* easily outsold it and in some previously solid Chartist centres like Merthyr Tydfil, the *Star* mustered barely a dozen sales a week.[50]

Nor did the return from Australia of John Frost in 1856 constitute the renaissance for the movement that was widely expected. At Newport and London the reception he met was tumultuous. Even *The Times* conceded that traffic in the capital was disrupted 'for several hours' and described how many more people gathered on Primrose Hill than the area set aside for the rally could hold, leading to half an hour of fighting among those fearful they might not witness the proceedings. Frost's speech was brief, measured and unapologetic. 'Forty years ago I became convinced that the miserable state of our country, and of its industrious inhabitants, was occasioned by the lawgiver – the corruption of the House of Commons ... The only remedy, as it then appeared to me, was to recur to the principles of our ancient constitution, which principles are embodied in what is now called the Charter'. So it was still, Frost maintained: 'Let us be cool, but determined, prudent, but fearless; giving up no principle, satisfied with no less than our due'.[51] This is as flawless a statement of the principles on which opposition to Old Corruption rested as one could wish for. Clearly it was designed to cast the Newport Rising in as reasonable a light as possible. And, realistically, could one expect more from a 70-year old man, wearied by prolonged exile?

However, it is likely this was the ideology to which Frost (born 1784 and thus raised in the era of the French Revolution, his political views maturing during the Regency) had always adhered. This gives some measure of support to the arguments of Gareth Stedman Jones. However, Chartist ideology was composed of layers of thinking which, like geological strata, varied in depth according to locality. And there were crucial social and generational differences too. The draper Frost, aged 54 in 1839, had a different perception of what securing the Charter would mean compared to, for example, the 37 year-old Thomas Powell or the 19 year-old Pontypool cabinetmaker's apprentice George Shell, who died a painful, lingering death inside the Westgate Hotel on the morning of 4 November 1839.

Expectations of Frost upon his return were unfeasibly high: 'From you we expect much for the future ... assist us to gather up the scattered elements of our movement', declared 'the Democracy of Stalybridge', a mill town seven miles east of Manchester.[52] Frost's triumphant tour momentarily consolidated the appearance of a national movement; but it had little substance as Frost soon realized. His preparedness to resume an active role in the movement, coupled with the extensive tour he undertook on his return, mean his conclusions command respect. 'In all the mining districts of Wales', he wrote in 1857, 'among the scores of thousands that at one time took an active part in public meetings, it would at present be impossible to get a meeting ... there are at present no Chartists and no Chartist agitation.'[53] He was exaggerating, but allowance should be made for the jaundiced view of a septuagenarian whose fifteen years of exile, it must have seemed, had been for nothing. Representatives from Montgomeryshire and Merthyr Tydfil attended the final Chartist convention in 1858. Llanidloes sent a modest donation and 'the kind assurance of the faithful few'.[54] John Frost, however, held aloof and lent his support to none of the reform organizations of the next twenty years.

However, the common condition of the political activist is optimism and this was the quality that carried most Chartists forward. In chapter 1 above, Chartism was characterized as exhibiting a multiplicity of small victories and small endings. In Greek mythology the robber Procrustes lured weary travellers to his wayside home, promising them a perfect bed for the night. If their length exceeded that of the bed, he cut short their limbs; if the bed proved longer, he stretched them to make them equal to it. Accounts of Chartism tend to define 'the end' of the movement in a not dissimilar fashion, truncating or stretching their narratives to fit the Procrustean bed of the author's interpretation. Thus Chartism has variously been seen as disintegrating by 1842, or in the early 1840s, on 10 April 1848, after August 1848, in 1851 or 1858. History is seldom tidy: events, movements and organizations rarely come neatly packaged. The end of Chartism was especially untidy: a movement that unquestionably failed on its own terms succeeded in empowering many of its adherents to participate, often with marked effect, in a wide range of civic, political, educational and associational activities. Eventually Chartism collapsed, but *Chartists* did not.

The elegiac mode of historical writing has its perils. So it is important to recognize that careerism, political charlatanry and vapid oratory could all be found in Chartism. There were serious systemic flaws too. Chartists remained united around the democratic and egalitarian vision of the People's Charter: yet something was lost as the locus of Chartist mobilization moved down from the hillsides into smoke-filled backrooms and lecture halls. The gradual transition from a movement that emphatically mobilized whole communities, to one that increasingly espoused the ideal of the male breadwinner and the politics of respectability, also closed off opportunities for women's participation. In 1839 in Wales there were four specifically female Charter associations, but none thereafter. This too, however, was not just a Welsh problem, as we have seen in chapter 1.

Chartism was celebrated in the later nineteenth century, however, for its manifest merits rather than deplored for its flaws. Participation in the movement endowed many Chartists with 'cultural capital'. In Wales this 'Chartist endurance' has been explored by Angela John, in an important article in *Morgannwg*.[55] Across Britain from the early 1850s there were ex-Chartist councillors without number – men like William Gould of Merthyr Tydfil. Gould, an iron puddler turned grocer, served on Merthyr's Burial Board, as a Poor Law Guardian and on the Board of Health. Or Alfred Walton, Geordie by birth but Welsh by adoption, a member of the Council of the First International but no less proud of being a Brecon town councillor and the local leader of the Reform League. Morgan Williams' dedication to the improvement of civic life through his career as a civil registrar and benefactor of the Merthyr Free Library is a further example of the Chartist endurance.[56] Of course only a minority of those who called themselves Chartists sought and attained elected office: the conscientious participant in civic life and municipal electoral processes would have been more typical, though this facet of former Chartists' lives is seldom well-documented.

In 1875 a Merthyr Baptist minister and Chartist supporter, T. D. Matthias, resigned his seat on the local Board of Health when he moved to a new ministry in Staffordshire. There he also assumed the editorship of the *Potteries Examiner*. Chartism, Matthias declared in his first Christmas editorial, was 'the noblest enterprise of the nineteenth century'.[57] Its vision of a more equitable society, where substantial gains in the quality of life in its every dimension would be realized, was – as it remains – a reference point of enduring significance for future generations.

Notes

1   E. Jenkins, *Chartism Unmasked* (Merthyr, 1840), p. 37. For Jenkins see H.
     U. Faulkener, *Chartism and the Churches* (New York, 1916), pp. 60f; D. J. V.
     Jones, *The Last Rising: The Newport Insurrection of 1839* (Oxford, 1985), pp.
     26, 199 and 223.

2   O. R. Ashton, 'Chartism in mid-Wales', *Montgomeryshire Collections* 62:1
     (1971); A. John, 'The Chartist endurance: industrial south Wales, 1840-68',
     Morgannwg 15 (1971), 23-49; D. J. V. Jones, 'Chartism in Welsh communities',
     Welsh Historical Review 6 (1972-3); D. Osmond, 'After the Rising: Chartism
     in Newport, 1840-48', *Gwent Local History* 98 (Spring 2005), 8-52; R. Wallace,
     Organise! Organise! Organise! A Study of Reform Agitations in Wales, 1840-80
     (Cardiff, 1991), pp. 34-67; J. England, 'Engaged in righteous cause: Chartism
     in Merthyr Tydfil', *Llafur* 10:3 (2010), 84-4.

3   G. Stedman Jones, 'Rethinking Chartism' in his *Languages of Class: Studies
     in English Working Class History, 1832-1982*, (1983); an abbreviated version
     appears in J. Epstein and D. Thompson, *The Chartist Experience: Studies in
     Working-class Radicalism and Culture, 1830-1860* (1982).

4   On the sharply diminished interest in local studies of Chartism since the mid-
     1980s, see M. Chase, 'Twentieth-century labour histories', in C. Dyer *et al*,
     Local History since Hoskins (Hatfield, 2010).

5   This quotation is taken from the Liberal MP John Roebuck, *Trades' Unions:
     Their Advantages to the Working Classes* (London, 1834), p. 5.

6   P. A. Pickering, 'Class without Words: Symbolic Communication in the
     Chartist Movement,' *Past and Present*, no. 112 (Aug. 1986), pp. 144-62.

7   M. Chase, *Chartism: A New History* (Manchester, 2007), p. 6.

8   Quotation from the dust jacket of I. Wilks, *South Wales and the Rising of 1839*
     (Beckenham, 1984), see also pp. 229-51.

9   Quoted in T. Herbert and G. E. Jones (eds), *People & Protest: Wales, 1815-1880*
     (Cardiff, 1988), p. 156.

10   See E. R. Morris, 'Thomas Powell – Chartist', *Montgomeryshire Collections*
     80:2 (1992), 104-5; Chase, *Chartism*, pp. 87-91, and M. Chase, 'Exporting
     the Owenite Utopia: Thomas Powell and the Tropical Emigration Society', in
     N. Thompson and C. Williams (eds), *Robert Owen and His Legacy* (Cardiff,
     2011).

11   M. Chase, 'Building identity, building circulation: engraved portraiture and
     the *Northern Star*', in J. Allen and O. Ashton (eds), *Papers for the People*
     (London, 2005), pp. 25-53.

12   *Poor Man's Guardian*, 11 Apr. 1831. Manchester-born Macerone (sometime
     aide-de-camp to Napoleon's puppet king of Naples) lived in London at this
     time, see H. M. Chichester, 'Maceroni, Francis (1788–1846)', rev. K. D.
     Reynolds, in *Oxford Dictionary of National Biography*, ed. H. C. G. Matthew
     and B. Harrison (Oxford, 2004).

13   John Owens (Newtown solicitor) to Lord Clive, National Library of Wales Powis
     MSS 200, quoted by E. Parry, '"The Bloodless Wars of Montgomeryshire": law
     and disorder, 1837-41', *Montgomeryshire Collections* 97 (2009), 144.

14   TNA, HO 40/46, 6 May 1839, prosecution brief for R. *v.* Powell; Morris, 'Thomas Powell', p. 113. See also *Northern Star* [*NS*] 20 Apr. 1839 and Ashton, 'Chartism in mid-Wales', pp. 23-4.

15   As does Parry, 'Bloodless Wars', p. 141. See chapters 2 and 3 above for more-detailed consideration of this issue.

16   R. J. Edwards to Normanby, 6 Nov. 1839, HO 40/44, fos 958-9. On Charles Jones see Owen Ashton, 'Chartism in Llanidloes: the 'riot' of 1839 revisited', *Llafur* 10:3 (2010), 84-4, and Chase, *Chartism*, pp. 109-11, 129.

17   J. Davies, (1803-1854), *Y Ffordd Dda; neu, Bregeth, a draddodwyd ar gais, ac yn nghlyw, y breinlenwyr, (Chartists,) Neu y Siartiaid, neu Broffeswyr Hawliau Dynol, yn nghyd ag Amrywiol Eraill ag Oeddynt Wyddfodol ar y Cyfryw Amser, yn Addoldy yr Anymddibyniaid, yn Nghymydogaeth Heol-y-Felin, yn mhlwyf, a cher Tref-lan Aberdare, Morganwg, Ar Nos Lun, Medi y 9 fed, 1839* (Merthyr, 1839).

18   On Brewster see Chase, *Chartism*, pp. 49-56.

19   Copy of the circular in TNA, HO 41/13, fo. 260 (7 May 1839).

20   Jones, *Last Rising* p. 207.

21   Chase, *Chartism*, pp. 106-40; D. J. V. Jones, 'The Scotch Cattle and their black domain', *Welsh History Review* 5 (1971), pp. 220-49.

22   Osmond, 'After the Rising'.

23   D. Thompson, *The Chartists: Popular Politics in the Industrial Revolution* (London, 1984), pp. 341-368.

24   For 1839 Thompson lists 109 female societies (all but five in localities with other recorded activity), 429 non-gender specific associations and 208 localities with other Chartist activity, i.e. 642 places in all. 1830-32 data taken from N. LoPatin, *Political Unions* (Basingstoke, 1999), pp. 103, 174-7, 179 and 182, and C. Flick, *Birmingham Political Union* (Folkestone, 1978), pp. 185-6. LoPatin (p. 182) describes 29 PUs as 'infrequent one-time meeting Unions'. None of these figures are completely accurate but they do permit useful broad comparison.

25   Philp was bailed for £50 plus a surety of £50, *Bristol Mercury* 31 Oct. 1840.

26   *English Chartist Circular* 30 [Aug. 1841], 117. Peter McDouall visited Wrexham, the sole member of the team to go into Wales.

27   M. Jenkins, *The General Strike of 1842* (London, 1980).

28   TNA, HO 45/265, fo. 38.

29   *Y Gofyniad Pabeth yw Siartist?* (Merthyr, 1840) and *Cyfieithad o Lythyr Diweddaf Mr. Feargus O'Connor* (Merthyr, 1840); *Udgorn Cymru* appeared fortnightly (March 1840-October 1842) accompanied by the same publisher's English monthly *Advocate* (July 1840-April 1841).

30   *NS* 29 Jan. 1842.

31   TNA, HO 45/265 fos. 18-26; HO 45/49, fo. 6, letter from T. J. Phillips (Newport), 7 June 1841.

32   *NS* 23 Apr. 1842.

33   *NS* 3 and 17 June 1843.

34   *NS* 28 May 1842.

35   I. G. Jones, *Mid-Victorian Wales: The Observers and the Observed* (Cardiff,

1992), p. 73.

36   D. J. V. Jones, 'Chartism in Welsh communities', 249.

37   *NS* 17 June 1848.

38   The NAUT still awaits its historian. But see M. Chase, *Early Trade Unionism: Fraternity, Skill and the Politics of Labour* (Aldershot, 2000), pp. 207-18 and J. Belchem, 'Chartism and the Trades', *English Historical Review* 98 (July 1983), 559-87.

39   British Library, British & Early Printed Collections, JAFF 157, item 22, *Balance Sheet of the National Association of United Trades for the Protection of Industry: From 28 June to 29 September, 1847.*

40   *NS* 11 and 25 July 1846. Robson, himself a shoemaker, was described as one of 'the leading Radicals amongst the working classes' by the *Charter*, 23 June 1839; see also *NS* 23 May 1840, 14 Aug. and 11 and 18 Dec. 1841.

41   *Baner Cymru* 30 Dec. 1857, 27 Oct. 1858; *Baner ac Amserau Cymru* 19 June and 28 Aug. 1861.

42   *NS* 1 Jan. 1848. See also chapter 8 below.

43   *NS* 14 Aug. and 4 Sept. 1847.

44   D. Goodway, *London Chartism 1838-48* (1982); see also John Saville, *1848: The British State and the Chartist Movement* (1987) and chapter 9 below.

45   *Seren Cymru* [*Star of Wales*] May 1848, cited and translated by I. G. Jones, *Mid-Victorian Wales*, p. 73.

46   *NS* 11 and 18 Nov. 1848.

47   *NS* 2 and 16 Mar. 1850. The Honesty Fund collected donations towards the cost of O'Connor's disastrous libel action against the *Nottingham Journal*, regarding his management of the Chartist Land Plan.

48   *NS* 23 Nov. 1850.

49   *NS* 15 Mar. 1851.

50   J. A. Epstein, 'O'Connor and the Northern Star', *International Review of Social History* 21 (1976), p. 97; J. Ginswick (ed.), *Labour and the Poor in England and Wales, 1849-51*, vol. 2 (London, 1983), pp. 59-60.

51   *The Times* 16 Sept. 1856.

52   *The Democracy of Stalybridge to John Frost, Esq.* [1856], copy in Tameside Local Studies Library, Ashton-under-Lyne, Tameside Broadsheets L322.

53   *People's Paper* 14 Nov. 1857.

54   *People's Paper* 12 and 26 Dec. 1857; Wallace, *Organise*, pp. 94-5.

55   John, 'The Chartist endurance'.

56   Wallace, *Organise*, pp. 97-8; John, 'The Chartist endurance', pp. 36-44; Williams, 'Engaged in a righteous cause', p. 74.

57   Matthias quoted by A. Jones, 'Workmen's Advocates: ideology and class in a mid-Victorian labour newspaper system', in J. Shattock and M. Wolff (eds), *The Victorian periodical press: samplings and soundings* (Leicester, 1982), p. 310.

LOCATIONS OF CHARTIST ACTIVITY IN WALES

	1839	NCA	1842	1844	NAUT	1848	Land	1850s
ABERDARE	●	●	1					
ABERGAVENNY		2	3	4		●	●	
ABERSYCHAN	●F	5					6	
ARGOED	●							
BANGOR	●		7			8		
BLACKWOOD	●F	9	●	●				
BLAINA	●						●	
BRECON							●	
BRIDGEND	●							
BRYMBO	●							
BUCKLEY	●						●	
CAERLEON	●			●				
CARMARTHEN	●			10				
CAERNAVON	●							
CARDIFF		11	12		13	14	●	15
CEFN MAWR						●		
Chepstow			16	17			18	19
CROSPENMAEN	●							
CRUMLIN	●							
CYFARTHA	●							
DOLGELLAU	●							
Denbigh					20			
DOWLAIS	●	21				22	●	
DUKESTOWN	●	23						
EBBW VALE	●		●				●	
Garndiffaith / Gamdiffeth							24	
Holywell	25		26		27			

	1839	NCA	1842	1844	NAUT	1848	Land	1850s
Kerry							28	
LLANELLI	●						●	29
LLANIDLOES	●	●	●		30		●	31
LLANHILLETH	●							
Llanllwchaearn						32		
Llantrisant			33					
LLANTWIT FARDRE						34	●	35
Llanvbban (sic)						36		
Maesteg		37						
MAESYCWMMER	●							
MELINGRIFFITH							●	
MENAI	●					38		
MERTHYR TYDFIL	●	●	●	●		●	●	39
MOLD	●		●		40		●	
MONMOUTH	●F	41	42			43	●	
MONTGOMERY							●	
NANTYGLO	●							
NARBERTH	●							
NEATH			44				●	45
NEWBRIDGE			●	46	47	48	●	
NEWPORT	●F	●	●	●	49	●	●	
New Radnor							50	
NEWTOWN	●	51		52				53
Overton		54	55					
PENNYDAREN	●							
PENYANE (Pen-y-Waun?)		●	●					
PONTILLANFRAITH	●							
PONTYPOOL	●	56	57					

	1839	NCA	1842	1844	NAUT	1848	Land	1850s
PONTYPRIDD	•	58	59				•	
Porthyglo		60	61					
RAGLAN						•		
RHAYADER	•							
RHYMNEY	•							
RISCA	•							
Ruabon						62		
SWANSEA	•		63	64		65	66	67
TREDEGAR	•	68	•	69		70	71	
Welshpool	72							
Wrexham			73					

Key

Place names in capitals are listed in Dorothy Thompson, 'Location and timing of Chartist activity', in her *The Chartists: Popular Politics in the Industrial Revolution* (1984). In all cases Thompson's sources were from *Northern Star* and are represented thus: •

Place names not in capitals, and all footnoted references, indicate information not in Thompson.

F: female Chartist group.

NCA: National Charter Association activities in 1840.

Land: branch or members of the Chartist Land Plan.

NAUT: National Association of United Trades.

Notes

1   *NS* 15 Jan. 1842, bi-lingual meeting and 93 in NCA branch; 23 Apr. 1842 resolution 'to strike until Charter becomes law of the land', noted by R. Wallace, *Organise! Organise! Organise! A Study of Reform Agitations in Wales, 1840-80* (Cardiff, 1991), p. 46.
2   *NS* 24 Dec. 1841 lists branch.
3   Subscribed in first quarter of 1842, *NS* 9 July 1842.
4   Doyle's lecture *NS* 31 Aug. 1844.
5   Activities noted here by D. Williams, 'Chartism in Wales', in A. Briggs (ed.), *Chartist Studies* (London, 1959), p. 243, citing the Bute MSS.
6   *NS* 17 July 1847 – 28 July 1849 *passim*.
7   *NS* 6 Aug. 1842.

8   Meetings at Menai Bridge and Garth Point, *North Wales Chronicle* 28 Mar. and 4 Apr. 1848; see also *NS* 8 Apr. and 1 July 1848.

9   *NS* 24 Dec. 1841 lists branch.

10   Doyle's lecture *NS* 31 Aug. 1844.

11   *NS* 24 Dec. 1841 lists branch; also meeting at Dinas noted by Williams, 'Chartism in Wales', p. 243.

12   *NS* 23 Apr. 1842.

13   British Library, British & Early Printed Collections, JAFF 157, item 22, *Balance Sheet of the National Association of United Trades for the Protection of Industry: From 28 June to 29 September, 1847*.

14   McDouall lecture *NS* 2 Oct., 6 Nov. 1847.

15   Donations cited in *NS* 1 Dec 1849; 28 Feb 1850, 4 Jan. 1841.

16   'Chepstow friends' contribute to funds, NS 2 Apr., 9 July, I Oct. 1842.

17   *NS* 13 Apr., 5 Oct. 1844.

18   *NS* 31 July 1847.

19   NCA branch, *NS* 15 Mar. 1851.

20   *NS* 1 Nov. 1845, 11 and 25 July 1846; see also note 13 above.

21   Noted by Williams, 'Chartism in Wales'.

22   McDouall lecture *NS* 2 Oct., 6 Nov. 1847; 10 Apr. 1848 meeting in the Market Square – *North Wales Chronicle* 18 Apr. 1848.

23   Noted by Williams, 'Chartism in Wales', p. 243; see, in contrast, *NS* 11 Dec. 1841 on the Tredegar NCA branch meeting in the Butchers' Arms, Dukestown.

24   *NS* 31 July 1847.

25   D. J. V. Jones, 'Chartism in Welsh communities', *Welsh Historical Review* 6 (1972-3).

26   NCA branch listed as not having voted in Executive elections, NS 25 June 1842.

27   *NS* 17 Oct. 1846.

28   Gammage lectures in Baptist church, Jones, 'Chartism in Welsh communities', p. 248.

29   Money remitted to the Honesty Fund, 2 and 16 Mar. 1850.

30   See note 13 above.

31   Ernest Jones lecture and meeting to congratulate Kossuth, *NS* 23 Aug. and 1 Nov. 1851; Gammage lectures 1852 (*Reminiscences of a Chartist*, 1983 [first published 1883], pp. 29-30, 34-5).

32   I. G. Jones, *Mid-Victorian Wales* (1992), p. 144 citing Bishop of St David's Charge of 1848, p. 144.

33   1843 donations listed in *NS* 18 Mar. 1843.

34   Money remitted, *NS* 24 June 1848.

35   Money remitted to various funds, 1850-51.

36   South Wales coalfield, Wild and Taylor lecture *NS* 1 June 1844.

37   Noted by Williams, 'Chartism in Wales', p. 243.

38   *NS* 30 Sept. 1848.

39   Gammage addresses meeting in Market Place, 1852 (*Reminiscences*, pp. 29-30).

40   See note 13 above.

41   *NS* 24 Dec. 1841 lists branch.

42   *NS* 23 Apr. 1842.

43 Noted by Wallace, *Organise!*, p. 53.
44 Money remitted, NS 30 Apr. 1842.
45 Gammage lecture in 1852 (*Reminiscences*, p. 30).
46 Wild and Taylor lecture, *NS* 1 June 1844.
47 See note 13 above.
48 McDouall lecture, *NS* 2 Oct., 6 Nov. 1847.
49 See note 13 above.
50 *NS* 31 July 1847.
51 *NS* 9 Jan. 1841, 25 June 1842.
52 Meeting to welcome Powell from gaol, *NS* 28 Oct. 1843.
53 *NS* 23 Aug. 1851; Gammage lectures 1852 (*Reminiscences*, pp. 34-5).
54 Jones, 'Chartism in Welsh communities'.
55 Jones, 'Chartism in Welsh communities'.
56 Sole Welsh delegate to NCA foundation conference specified he represented this community, *NS* 25 July 1840.
57 Subscribed in first quarter of 1842, *NS* 9 July 1842.
58 Noted by Williams, 'Chartism in Wales', p. 243.
59 1843 donations listed in *NS* 18 Mar. 1843
60 NCA branch, *NS* 24 Dec. 1841.
61 Subscribed in first quarter of 1842, *NS* 9 July 1842.
62 *NS* 17 June 1848 – existence of a 'very efficient district' reported to NAUT conference.
63 Subscribed in first quarter of 1842, *NS* 9 July 1842.
64 Doyle's lecture, *NS* 31 Aug. 1844.
65 Noted by Wallace, *Organise!*, p. 53; 'A few friends' donation *NS* 2 Dec. 1848.
66 *NS* 31 July 1847.
67 'A few friends' donation, *NS* 4 Jan. 1851.
68 *NS* 11 Dec. 1841.
69 Wild and Taylor lecture, *NS* 1 June 1844; Doyle's lecture *NS* 31 Aug. 1844.
70 McDouall lecture, *NS* 2 Oct. 1847.
71 *NS* 31 July 1847.
72 Meetings organised by Powell.
73 Peter McDouall visit on behalf of NCA Executive, *English Chartist Circular* 30 [Aug. 1841], p. 117.

7

THE CHARTIST PENNY ALMANACK

Before the advent of broadcasting, cheap daily newspapers, pocket diaries or large printed calendars, almanacs were an essential household item. These annual publications contained not only the calendar for the year, noting significant dates and anniversaries but also the phases of the moon and, typically, weather and astrological predictions. Housekeeping tips, recipes and seasonal gardening notes were also commonplace. Almost as old as printing itself, the format finally all but disappeared in the later nineteenth century. Millions were produced, but these little periodicals were heavily used and then discarded the following year. Very few survive. As Bernard Capp comments in the standard work, 'the word "almanac" became a synonym for transitoriness. They were utilitarian even as they passed into oblivion, used as lavatory paper, for putting under pies, lighting tobacco or "stopping mustard pots".'[1]

The discovery of a hitherto unknown almanac is therefore worthy of note. *The Chartist Penny Almanack, for the Year 1844* was published in Darlington, County Durham by William Oliver and, judging by its content, it circulated widely both in Durham and Cleveland (the adjacent part of North Yorkshire) and beyond. It appears to be the only surviving popular almanac produced by a printer in the region, and one of only five surviving almanacs directly linked to the Chartist movement. Chartism had a lively, and at times considerable, following in the Cleveland and Teesside region.[2] However, the fortunes of Chartism were uneven and its fortunes were at a low ebb in 1843-44, giving this almanac additional interest.

William J. Oliver (1810/11-?) was a printer and bookseller. He was Darlington's main newsagent and also ran a circulating (commercial lending) library. When the *Darlington & Stockton Times* was launched in 1847, Oliver was its agent and distributor in the town, for the paper itself was produced in Barnard Castle until the following year.[3] Oliver was also agent for the Chartist weekly *Northern Star*, from its earliest issues in 1837-8.[4] This is indicative of some political nerve: though *Northern Star* was the biggest-selling newspaper of the late 1830s, it was militantly radical and unlikely to have been popular with Oliver's more prosperous customers. Still more confrontational were broadsides Oliver published for Darlington's Chartists. 'You ARE now on the brink of a CIVIL WAR at HOME ... OH FOOLISH AND INFATUATED MEN!' declared one 1839 *Address to the Middle Classes of Darlington and its Neighbourhood*.[5]

It is therefore unsurprising he produced the *Chartist Penny Almanack*. But the publication also suggests some business acumen, for the title page indicates that it was joint venture with the publisher of the *Stokesley News and Cleveland Reporter* and with the three of the greatest radical pressmen of the 1840s: London's John Cleave, Leeds' Joshua Hobson (printer and publisher of *Northern Star*) and Manchester's Abel Heywood. All three are extensively documented in histories of nineteenth-century radical politics.[6] The *Stokesley News and Cleveland Reporter* was an early venture of the prolific Cleveland author George Tweddell, a figure whose contribution to Chartism in the region has hitherto not received the recognition it deserves.

George Markham Tweddell (1823-1903) came from a long-established Stokesley family. Their respectability was evident in his being named after George Markham, the Rector of Stokesley who was also Dean of York during the archbishopric of his father – one of the more blatant examples of nepotism and pluralism in the Hanoverian church. Tweddell served an apprenticeship with the Stokesley printer William Braithwaite, celebrated as the publisher of John Walker Ord's *History and Antiquities of Cleveland* (1846). However, by the time Ord's pioneering history appeared, Tweddell had been dismissed from Braithwaite's service because of the forthright political tone the younger man had adopted as editor of the monthly *Stokesley News*, the 1842 issues of which Braithwaite printed and published. Tweddell attacked the Corn Laws, claiming tenant farmers were intimidated by local landowners into supporting them, and was a stringent critic of British imperialism, especially of the Opium Wars against China: 'for refusing to buy and swallow a narcotic poison ... the blood of thousands, mingled with the dust and the mangled limbs of the ignorant and defenceless multitude, strew the battlefields'.[7]

Sacked by Braithwaite, Tweddell set up business as a printer on his own account, continuing to publish the *Stokesley News*. Braithwaite countered with a new paper of his own, the *Cleveland Repertory and Stokesley Advertiser* but there is little doubt that Tweddell's was the livelier of the two magazines. Most he wrote himself. For example under the pseudonym of Peter Flint, Tweddell penned an 'Ode to Queen Victoria': 'Unsheltered from the Winter's gloom, / With shoeless feet our streets do tread / Singing hymns for crusts of bread'. 'Arise Victoria, break the chain', the poem concluded, 'and make Britannia free again'. Tweddell was a committed Chartist, the secretary of the movement's Stokesley branch; he even announced his marriage in *Northern Star*. The latter reviewed both *Stokesley News* and Tweddell's *Yorkshire Miscellany* which replaced it in 1844, and he occasionally contributed to the national Chartist press.[8]

Tweddell espoused Chartist views from his teens. Compelling evidence of this can be found in a poem he wrote, aged 16, in January 1840. The self-styled 'Christian Republican' attacked the government for the death sentence passed on John Frost, leader of the South Wales Chartist rising the previous November.

> Think not because you are vicious,
> That we will calmly bear the wrong,
> Which you're resolv'd to heap upon us,
> Robb'd of the rights which to us belong.
> Think not because taxation robs us
> Of most of the wages that we earn,
> ...
> That we will ever cease demanding,
> The rights that are to us most dear:
> The justice of the "People's Charter"
> Does Frost e'en in his dungeon cheer.[9]

These 'Lines to Tyrants' went unpublished, but Tweddell remained committed to Frost (whose sentence was commuted to transportation to Tasmania). In the *Chartist Penny Almanack* Tweddell advertised a monthly part-work, 'now in preparation', *The Life of John Frost, the Expatriated Chartist*. He also appealed to readers for information about Frost's life, further evidence the almanac was intended to circulate nationally; for though John Frost was widely renowned as a leading Chartist, his life until 1840 had been spent in Newport, where he had been Mayor. In a long career, Tweddell was responsible for a number of projected publications that never reached fruition and his *Life of John Frost* was one of them. But, ever the literary romantic, he remained attached to the cause of radical martyrs, as an 'Address to Britons', in the *Stokesley News* indicated, with its eulogy to the Irish rebel Robert Emmet (hanged for treason in 1803) and the celebrated Chartist orator Henry Vincent:

Then let us like brave Emmet die,
Or Vincent-like in prison lie,
But ne'er succumb to tyranny,
Let come whatever may.[10]

Tweddell was not, however, the author of the five poems that appeared in the *Chartist Penny Almanack*. All were penned by the unknown William Chapel: 'The Cleveland Rose' (an anodyne love poem), 'The Martyr's Grave' (another eulogy to Emmet), 'Knowledge' (extolling self-improvement through education), 'True Fame is Liberty' (depicting the Angel of Liberty, carrying a French revolutionary *bonnet rouge*) and 'The English Slave'. The latter's sentiments echo Tweddell's 'Ode to Victoria':

Go look upon the English slave
Who labours late and hard,
His garb is ragged russet brown,
His food *"Rye bread and lard"*.

'Knowledge' and 'True Fame is Liberty' had appeared in print before, in another Chartist periodical with strong Cleveland connections, the *London Chartist Monthly Magazine*. This periodical was the work of another local Chartist, John Watkins, 'than whom a more kind-hearted, philanthropic, patriotic man breathes not', the *Almanack* commented. Watkins (1808-1858) was the eldest son of the squire of Aislaby Hall, Whitby. Insofar as Chartism made any mark upon the political backwater of Whitby, it was Watkins' doing.[11] In January 1839 he founded the Whitby Working Men's Association. Its room on Whitby Pier doubled as a Chartist Chapel, where Watkins preached each Sunday and for which he wrote a hymn collection.[12]

But in Whitby Chartism's appeal dimmed with its novelty. Instead, Watkins turned his attention to Teesside and was almost immediately arrested in September for a speech at Stockton, urging his audience to fight for the Charter 'like heroes, die for it like martyrs'. Unlike Whitby, Stockton had been profoundly shaken by the Chartist movement. That summer the government had drafted in troops, there had been numerous arrests and 235 special constables organised into a paramilitary force. 'The Stockton Magistrates … were in a panic and violently prejudiced against all chartists,' Watkins observed to his friend the marine painter George Chambers.[13] The arrest sealed Watkins' reputation and was extensively reported in the Chartist press. On his acquittal he entered into a public correspondence with Lord Normanby, the Home Secretary, demanding he intervene to restore to

Watkins copies of his pamphlet *Five Cardinal Points of the People's Charter*, confiscated by Stockton magistrates when he was arrested.

Watkins skilfully exploited the fact that Normanby's seat at Mulgrave Castle made him a near neighbour and social equal. Much of his appeal to Chartist audiences stemmed from his presenting himself as a gentleman 'friend of the people', converted by force of argument to their cause and prepared to suffer for it. There were several precedents for this, pre-eminently Feargus O'Connor, Chartism's greatest leader to whom Watkins had dedicated *Five Cardinal Points*. The *Chartist Penny Almanack* shared in Watkins' admiration. 'Who has done more for you? Who has suffered more for you in every point of view?' … He (Mr O'C.) has sacrificed pleasure, comfort, has laid out more money and has used more eloquence on your account than any man living!'

There was a strong self-promotional element to Watkins' politics but his sincerity shines through his private correspondence. 'You seem to wonder that I should be a chartist', he told Chambers, 'but if you were in the north we would soon teach you to be one too. Is it not natural that that men who do their best to deserve success, and yet find all their efforts frustrated by a cursed system that rewards the undeserving alone – is it not reasonable that such men should be discontented and desire a change? It is this that has made me a chartist'.[14] The Stockton debacle made Watkins' reputation nationally: he became one of the most prolific and regular contributors to *Northern Star*.

Watkins was also a dramatist, best known for *John Frost: A Political Play* (1841). There are passages of striking anger and bitterness in *John Frost*, articulating sentiments as close to openly espousing revolution as any Chartist in print at this time. Though written at Aislaby, by the time it was published Watkins had moved to London to further his political career. He remained there until his death, but his life was mired in controversy, following a stormy break with O'Connor in 1843. The *London Chartist Monthly Magazine* was meant to consolidate its editor's reputation in the movement. In this it was signally unsuccessful, folding after just four issues in September 1843. Or did it? It has always been assumed the four issues surviving in the library of Columbia University, New York, were all Watkins' published; but the (admittedly blatant) plug in the *Chartist Penny Almanack* – 'In my opinion his Magazine is the best periodical published' – suggests it may have endured a few months longer.

The *Chartist Penny Almanack* seems to have been the collective effort of Oliver, Tweddell and Watkins. All three were pursuing risky careers in radical publishing and – for men of their social class – espoused violent political opinions. Unsurprisingly they were bound by mutual admiration. Alongside poetry from Watkins' magazine, the almanac reprinted from the *Stokesley News* an article about teetotalism (popular among many Chartists). It assured readers that Watkins' magazine was 'the best periodical published', the *Stokesley News* 'a thorough-going Democratic periodical', and its editor an 'unflinching advocate of the entire Rights of Man ... buy it, read it, and judge for yourselves'. Tweddell reciprocated with a similar plug for the *Almanack* in the *Stokesley News*.[15] It seems likely 'William Chapel' was a pseudonym for Tweddell. Certainly, the latter's style infuses 'The Cleveland Rose' and 'The English Slave'.

William Oliver doubtless thought he had spotted a gap in the market. Although countless almanacs were published every year, those with specifically Chartist content were few in number and not apparently published beyond 1843. Alice Mann of Leeds, matriarch of a noted West Riding radical family, published a *Charter Almanack for the Year 1841*.[16] Reginald Richardson, a Salford carpenter forced into bookselling when employers victimised him for his Chartist activities, also issued *Political Almanacs*, published and distributed by Oliver's Manchester partner Heywood.[17] In 1842 and 1843 Joshua Hobson produced *The Poor Man's Companion: a Political Almanack*.[18] But none of these publishers appear to have issued further political almanacs. So it made sense for Oliver and Tweddell, in partnership with Hobson and Heywood, to fill the gap for 1844. (There may have been a *Chartist Penny Almanack* in 1843 too, for in the style of a continuing dialogue with readers that was typical of almanac compilers, the preface to the 1844 publication speaks of 'my prediction of last year'.)

What did purchasers get for their penny? The *Chartist Penny Almanack* has twenty-four pages, stitched into a yellow printed wrapper, and is in octavo format (approximately 190mm x 110mm). The pages for each month follow the convention of listing each day, with a significant anniversary or festival for each. Phases of the moon and legal dates appear in a box at the top, and household tips in a vertical column down the right-hand side. Thus in January there are 'receipts' to clean brass and knives, to treat chapped hands and to prevent foot rot in sheep. The foot of each monthly page carried six lines of seasonal gardening information. The almanac contains no astrological predictions, but abnormal weather events were predicted (e.g. 25 November: 'Downfall about this time').

In common with most popular almanacs, extensive advertisements for patent medicines were carried. The page devoted to Parr's Life Pills provided the almanac's sole illustration. 'All that is necessary to invigorate the feeble, restore the invalid to health, and do good in all cases', Parr's Pills could be obtained from Oliver's own shop, or from Davison, a Stockton tea dealer. Jenkins' Life Pills, subject of another advertisement ('no medicine acts more safely, and with equal advantage'), were also sold by Davison, and by Richard Nash, 'newsagent and innkeeper of Bishop Street or Workhouse Street, Stockton', by Guisborough chemist Daniel Duck, and at the *Stokesley News* office. Finally, Stokell's Life Pills, offered as a cure for 'scrofula, cancer, &c.,' were obtainable only from their inventor J. Stokell, pharmacist of Sedgefield. The terms in which nineteenth-century quack remedies were sold invite smiles now. However, patent medicines were often the sole medical treatment available to the poor, and retailing them was an important sideline for radical political newsagents among whose customers the working class predominated.

The specifically political content of the *Chartist Penny Almanack* appeared in two forms. First was a subtle bias towards certain political events in the calendar. These included: America's Declaration of Independence and eventual victory over Britain, the beheadings of Lady Jane Grey, Mary Queen of Scots and Charles I, the 1820 Cato Street plot to assassinate the Cabinet, the death by firing squad (guilty of neglect of duty) of Admiral Byng in 1757, Oliver Cromwell's birthday, Wat Tyler's murder, Robin Hood's death (confidently dated as Christmas Eve 1247), James II's flight at the Revolution of 1688, attempts to assassinate Queen Victoria, the passing of the 1832 Reform Act, the French and Polish Revolutions, and the deaths of the seventeenth-century radical heroes John Hampden and Algernon Sydney. Key legal dates of interest to political activists were also specified: the deadlines for elections to borough councils, Poor Law Guardians and Highway Surveyors, and the schedule for completing parliamentary electoral rolls.[19]

More obvious political content could be found in the 'fillers' and articles which populated the other 16 pages: 'Bribery is an easy step to a seat in Parliament'; a list of the six points of the People's Charter – 'Who can object to them? Not honest men I am sure! only knaves and fools!'; or the observation on the front cover that Britain boasted just 'ONE voter to about every TWENTY-NINE Persons'. Most obvious of all were the poems and several short essays on political issues. Inside the front cover was a lengthy address 'to all Classes of People, but more particularly to my Readers, the Working People':

The greatest portion of you, I know, are poor toil-worn, half-starved slaves – victims of misrule – of the odious and accursed system of

Government – though you wear not a *ring*, or any other visible mark of Slavery (excepting your emaciated forms – furnitureless houses – clotheless backs – shoeless feet – children crying for want of bread – wives bemoaning their and their children's and your fate) … you are as truly slaves as any in the universe!

This theme of 'white slavery' was a commonplace in Chartists' writing, as was the advice that followed to,

UNITE *in downright earnest, and register as one man a firm, fixed, and determined* RESOLVE *never to rest satisfied, never to cease agitating until you obtain the* PEOPLE'S CHARTER: *UNTIL YOU HAVE HURLED the Hydra-headed monster [of] Class-Legislation into a whirlpool out of which it can never again be extricated.*

Two things distinguished the political rhetoric of the *Chartist Penny Almanack*. First, as will be already apparent, was its uncompromising, and at times even violent criticism of contemporary social conditions. Second was a profound commitment to peace. As Tweddell's criticism of the Opium Wars quoted earlier indicated, Chartists were critical of what they saw as government adventurism on moral grounds. The cost of the armed forces was also attacked on the grounds that it was met from taxing the poor. Most of the national debt, the *Almanack* argued, 'was contracted by a few despotic over-bearing men, who misgoverned England without the consent of the people, and swallowed up carrying on the trade of Human Butchery'. A whole page was devoted to calculations of the cost of British wars since 1688, made by the Scottish writer on science and philosophy, Dr Thomas Dick. A further page of commentary urged that the People's Charter, 'without alteration, deduction or addition … is the only medicine that will cure the nation of the disease under which it is suffering'. Criticisms of the wars in China and Afghanistan followed.

Along with its espousal of teetotalism, the anti-war stance of the *Chartist Penny Almanack* may well have recommended it to the Quaker oligarchy of Darlington and Teesside. But it is doubtful if there was much else in its pages of which the local middle classes would have approved. Chartism was a full-frontal assault on the monopoly of political power, and the *Almanack* persisted in using the language of class antagonism at a time when nationally the movement's ferocity was abating. It was not just Chartists the *Almanack* urged to purchase Tweddell's *Stokesley News*. The middle class should do so too, for it would open their eyes from 'a social and political point of view'.

You will clearly see it to be your duty to unite with the working people in their agitation for the Charter – or as sure as you are men you will all be ruined. There will only be two Classes left in England if you do not – very rich and very poor … Unite in time with the Chartists and save not only yourselves and others from starvation, but your country from anarchy, confusion, bloodshed and murder, in fact, from the worst of Wars – a Civil War.

And Tweddell himself urged Chartists to push the *Almanack* 'into the hands of the middle classes; it may cause them to repent in time, and save, not only themselves but you from ruin, and the country from anarchy and confusion'.[20] Clearly, the *Almanack's* editor and George Tweddell thought as one: the possibility he wrote much of it cannot be ruled out. However, its language was also strongly resonant with that of local Chartists in the fevered summer of 1839, when a general strike and run on the banks was proposed and troops drafted into Stockton and Darlington. 'It is your intense and BLIND Selfishness that is rendering almost inevitable a Civil Convulsion', one County Durham *Address to the Middle Classes of the North of England* declared; and the strong language of broadsides printed by Oliver for Darlington's Chartists has already been noted.[21]

Oliver had taken risks in 1839 and although the political climate was calmer in 1843-44, there was an element of risk in inserting such sentiments in the *Chartist Penny Almanack*. Perhaps so few copies survive because it was considered 'too hot to handle' by booksellers and purchasers. But it was the nature of almanacs to be discarded. These cheap publications were designed to make a profit through a large volume of sales. The robust iconoclasm of this almanac would have had a wide appeal. In May 1842, a total of 3.3 million people had signed a mass petition for the Charter, at least 1,200 of them from the Teesside region.[22]

The *Chartist Penny Almanack* was also calculated to sell for other reasons. Unlike the fourpenny almanacs issued by the liberal middle-class Anti-Corn Law League (which also carried no adverts) it was cheap and flattered rather than patronised a working-class readership.[23] Popular almanacs circulated widely among the increasingly literate working class, finding a place in households that often contained little reading matter beyond perhaps Bunyan's *Pilgrim's Progress* and a few dog-eared old newspapers. The *Almanack* was also of relatively good quality, while the production standards and quality of some popular almanacs was execrable. For example, in 1834, the East Riding diarist Robert Sharp noted with amusement that the village publican's 'Almanack, which is a Paddy, says there will be a full moon on the 32d day of February'.[24] *Paddy* was a common Yorkshire term for an illegal almanac issued in defiance of the heavy tax imposed on almanacs by the state.[25] The abolition of this stamp duty later in 1834 opened up the almanac market, especially for provincial publishers. William Oliver and his associates were the temporary beneficiaries of this development.

The benefit was temporary because the almanac market was rapidly developing. The popular end became dominated by two distinctive types. The first was the astrological *Old Moore's Penny Almanack* (founded 1842), annual sales of which reached a million by 1900. The second, especially popular in the West Riding and Lancashire, were humorous dialect publications. Having abandoned the *Charter Almanack*, Alice Mann of Leeds published from 1844 one of the earliest: *The Bairnsla' Foaks Annual, an Pogmoor Olmenack*.[26] Dominating the middle ground, the *British Almanac of the Society for the Diffusion of Useful Knowledge* sought to drive out both astrological and radical political almanacs, and comic almanacs, notably Cruikshank's, had much the same effect. Up-market, the term almanac was claimed by specialist annuals, like *Whitaker's* and *Wisden's Cricketers'* almanacs, begun in 1850 and 1864 respectively. The term also endured in the titles of some gazetteers, such as the *Durham Directory and Almanack*, begun by the Durham city bookseller George Walker in 1846.[27] While we cannot be sure the *Chartist Penny Almanack* did not continue for a few more years, amidst this mid-Victorian explosion of popular publishing, cheap but serious-minded radical publications like it went into serious decline.

Chartism's fortunes, too, diminished the chances of the almanac continuing. It appeared at a time when Chartist activities in the region were scanty. After October 1843 there were no reports of local activity in *Northern Star* until 1845, when sporadic coverage related, significantly, solely to Stokesley. It was January 1846 before the *Star* reported any other attempt to revive the movement in the Cleveland region.[28] Nationally, after an impressive surge in 1847-48, Chartism endured only in a vestigial form.

So in the *Chartist Penny Almanack* we have a snapshot of popular publishing and politics on the cusp of significant changes, as well as an intriguing insight into the political temperature of Chartism locally during a phase when information is sparse. The *Almanack* alerts us both to the endurance of militant Chartist views in the Cleveland region, together with local activists' links with the major centres of Leeds, London and Manchester. And it illustrates the continuing commitment to improving the lot of working people of three local middle-class idealists, William Oliver, George Markham Tweddell and John Watkins.

Notes

1   B. Capp, *Astrology and the Popular Press: English Almanacs, 1500-1800* (London, 1979), p. 66. Durham County Record Office acquired, with the estate and family papers of the Salvin family of Croxdale, a box lined with pages from an eighteenth-century almanac (D/Sa/X 212).

2   See M. Chase, 'Chartism, 1838-1858: responses in two Teesside towns', *Northern History* 24 (1988), 146-171, republished with postscript in S. Roberts, ed., *The People's Charter: Democratic Agitation in Early Victorian Britain* (London, 2003), pp. 152-73; 'Chartism and the "prehistory" of politics in Middlesbrough', *Bulletin of the Cleveland and Teesside Local History Society* 55 (1988), pp. 15-29; P. Hastings, *Chartism in the North Riding of Yorkshire and South Durham, 1838-48* (York, 2004); G. Cookson (ed.), *Victoria County History: the County of Durham Volume IV: Darlington* (London, 2005), pp. 89, 94-6, 133, 242.

3   Oliver's Circulating Library: 'Library History Database', http://www.r-alston.co.uk/circ3htm accessed 5 July 2008; Cookson (ed.), *Victoria County History*, p. 244.

4   *NS* 10 Feb. 1838

5   Broadside, *To the Middle Classes of Darlington and its Neighbourhood* (Darlington, 1839), copy in TNA, HO 40/42, folio 361. See also Chase, *Chartism*, pp. 98-100.

6   Cleave and Heywood have entries in the *Oxford Dictionary of National Biography* (2004) and all three men are subjects of extensive essays in the *DLB*, Cleave and Heywood in vol. 6, and Hobson in vol. 8.

7   *Stokesley News* 2 (December 1842). See also D. Franks, *Printing and Publishing in Stokesley* (Stokesley, 1984), pp. 18-2-6.

8   *NS* 24 Dec. 1841; 4 Nov. 1843, 6 Jan. and 13 July 1843, 29 Mar. 1845, 6 Jan. 1849, 5 Jan. 1850; see also 5 Nov. 1842 and 14 Dec. 1850, *Star of Freedom* 21 Aug. 1852, *Cooper's Journal* 9 Feb., 13 and 27 Apr. 1850.

9   I am grateful to the late Paul Tweddell for permission to quote this poem, from a compendium of Tweddell's unpublished poetry in Teesside Archives, U/TW/1/1.

10   *Stokesley News* 12 (June 1844).

11   For Watkins see M. Chase, 'A forgotten Whitby author', *Annual Report of the Whitby Literary & Philosophical Society for the Year 2002*, pp. 47-51, *DLB*, vol. 12, and *Chartism: A New History*, pp. 117-25.

12   *Yorkshire Gazette* 2 Feb. 1839, *NS* 1 June and 14 Sept. 1839; *Hymns to be used at the Working Men's Chapel, Whitby* (Whitby, [1839]. See also his single sheet *Radical Hymns to be sung at the Opening of the Chartists' Chapel, Whitby, May 19, 1839* (Whitby, [1839]). Copies of both are bound into a copy of Watkins' *Lay Sermons* (Whitby, 1835) in Whitby Literary & Philosophical Society library.

13   Letter, 1 April 1840, quoted in J. Watkins, *The Life and Career of George Chambers* (London, 1841), p. 147.

14   Letter, Jan. 1840, quoted in *George Chambers*, pp. 146-47.

15 *Stokesley News* 13 (Nov. 1843).

16 *Charter Almanack for the Year 1841, containing the People's Charter ... and other matter of importance to every real Chartist* (Leeds, [1840]), copy in the International Institute of Social History, Amsterdam, call number Bro E 2340/190.

17 R. J. Richardson, *Political Almanac for 1840; and the Annual Black Book* (Manchester, 1839), and *Political Almanac for 1841; and the Annual Black Book* (Manchester, 1840).

18 *Poor Man's Companion: a Political Almanack for 1842 ... compiled from parliamentary and other documents by Joshua Hobson* (Leeds, 1841), also similarly titled 1843 issue, both in the British Library.

19 Though essentially a movement of the disenfranchised, Chartists had notable successes in local elections, including Middlesbrough's Improvement Commission: see Chase, 'Two Teesside towns', pp. 155-56 and 166. Chartists also seriously participated in the 1841 and 1847 general elections: see below, chapter 8.

20 *Stokesley News and Cleveland Reporter* 13 (Nov. 1843).

21 Broadside, *To the Middle Classes of the North of England* (Sunderland, 1839), copy in TNA, HO 40/42, folio 249, also printed in *NL* 21 July 1839.

22 Chase, 'Two Teesside towns', p. 161.

23 *Anti-Corn-Law Almanack, for the Year of Our Lord 1841* (Manchester, 1840) and *Anti-Bread Tax Almanack, for the Year of Our Lord 1842* (Manchester, 1841).

24 J.E. and P.A. Crowther (eds), *Diary of Robert Sharp of South Cave* (Oxford, 1997), entry for 9 Feb. 1834, p. 447.

25 C. C. Robinson, *Glossary of Words Pertaining to the Dialect of Mid-Yorkshire* (1876), quoted in the entry for 'paddy' in the *Oxford English Dictionary*.

26 On the nineteenth-century almanac trade see M. Perkins, *Visions of the Future: Almanacs, Time and Cultural Change, 1775-1870* (Oxford, 1996) and B. Maidment, 'Re-arranging the year: the almanac, the day book and the year book as popular literary forms, 1789-1860', in J. John and A. Jenkins (eds), *Rethinking Victorian Culture* (London, 2000), pp. 92-114.

27 S. B. Holt, 'The Durham Directory and Almanack', *Durham County Local History Society Bulletin* 26 (1981).

28 *NS* 4 Jan. and 29 Mar. 1845, 24 Jan. 1846.

8

'LABOUR'S CANDIDATES': CHARTIST CHALLENGES AT THE PARLIAMENTARY POLLS, 1839-1860[1]

Chartism was by definition a movement of the disfranchised. Feargus O'Connor's success at Nottingham in 1847 aside, it is not remembered for directly engaging in parliamentary elections. There has been a tacit assumption that only O'Connor, a barrister and Irish landowner, had the financial resources and bravura personality to mount a parliamentary challenge. Ironically he singularly lacked the financial resources. His 1835 election as MP for County Cork had been overturned because he owned insufficient property to qualify. His eligibility to be an MP in 1847 was seriously questioned and the requisite qualification manufactured by a sympathetic London financier.[2] Yet Chartist candidates had gone to the parliamentary polls on at least sixteen previous occasions (see appendix), while there were 25 other Chartist, or formally endorsed sympathetic radical, candidates at the 1847 election. In time there was even another Chartist MP, though as we shall see he never took his seat.

This essay chronicles Chartism's direct engagement with parliamentary polling and assesses its importance for our understanding of the movement and the evolution of popular politics more generally. First, however, it is necessary to clarify what early Victorian parliamentary elections actually entailed. Within Westminster, political parties were rolling coalitions of shifting interests; beyond it they did not yet exist in any formally constituted sense. A multiplicity of two-member constituencies (where voters had two votes and the highest and second placed candidates were elected) complicated electoral arithmetic. All residents of a constituency – whether enfranchised or not, men, women and children – could attend the open-air meeting where each candidate was formally nominated and seconded, and customarily gave an acceptance address. The hustings, the canopied wooden stage erected for this occasion, was frequently the focus for an elaborate ritual of processions and formal greetings. Those attending made their views clear vocally and through the use of non-verbal communication, ranging from rosettes through placards and banners, to the projection of missiles at the speakers.[3]

The climax of every nomination meeting came when the returning officer called for a show of hands for each of the candidates. '[A]ll present may hold up their hands and each lift, not one hand alone, but both, and non-electors, and even women and children, take part in the display.'[4] This could determine immediately who was elected: only if a defeated candidate demanded it, would a poll be held, one to three days later. Only at the poll was voting restricted to the legally enfranchised. Whether to demand a poll was a fine calculation. Minimal restrictions upon candidates' financial expenditure, an endemic culture of treating electors, and in many seats bribery, made electioneering prodigiously expensive. Even in 1868, after more than a decade in which bribery and treating had been steadily curtailed, an effective campaign in a metropolitan borough was authoritatively estimated to involve 'an expenditure of £5000 at the least'.[5] In addition, candidates who did go to the poll were usually required to share the returning officer's expenses for organizing the election – premises hire, the wages of poll clerks, the cost of policing and, even, claims for compensation by local traders for the loss of business.

Hence in many constituencies (fully one-third in 1841, for example) the nomination meeting completed the contest, since the chances of ousting a strong candidate were hugely outweighed by the cost involved. Even when no challenger could be found, a public nomination meeting was still legally required. The boisterous holiday atmosphere at the hustings, but also the seriousness accorded such occasions, is evident in attendance at even uncontested nominations – an estimated 20,000, for example, at Macclesfield in 1859 when the two sitting MPs were unchallenged.[6]

The contrast between nomination and polling threw into sharp relief the restricted nature of the franchise. As a movement dedicated to fighting for universal male suffrage, Chartists took hustings very seriously. It was commonplace for Chartist candidates to present themselves for election. Many returning officers would accept candidates without requiring formal proof that they possessed the requisite property qualification to be an MP (in Scotland none was required but a deposit of £180 was required on nomination). This reflected the general culture of openness and licence pervading these occasions (and doubtless a desire to maintain public order). But Chartism was never a movement solely of the dispossessed. While support from the 'middling sort' varied, there were propertied Chartists prepared to participate as candidates at election times and many who met the property qualification to vote. The latter is an important point: though candidates did not have to be constituency residents, those nominating and seconding them had to be registered local voters. In older parliamentary boroughs, those who were enfranchised before the 1832 Reform Act, and still lived within seven miles of the borough, retained the vote for life irrespective of the property qualification. Certain constituencies with significant populations of skilled craftsmen who had obtained their 'freedom' before 1832, or who enjoyed other ancient franchises, were therefore relatively inclusive.[7]

The first parliamentary hustings contested by a Chartist was at the Wigan by-election of March 1839. Edward Nightingale from Manchester was presented by two local Chartist activists. The three made pointed speeches attacking the Tory and Whig candidates; but after the show of hands, Nightingale conceded 'it would be a perfect folly for me to attempt to go to the poll'. Had he done he might have decisively affected the outcome, for a 'radical reformer' won by only two votes.[8] Nightingale's candidacy was not frivolous. It ensured Chartist views were represented in a contest attracting wide interest across Lancashire. Chartists were particularly concerned to emphasise that Whigs and even radical reformers held positions significantly short of Chartism's demands. Furthermore, with the Whig-reformers in power there were fundamental issues of government policy that Nightingale wished to attack, notably the 1834 Poor Law reforms. He also signalled that common ground existed between Chartism and Toryism, not just in their opposition to Whig-reformism, but also in their antipathy to the repeal of the Corn Laws. Nightingale, like many Manchester Chartists at this time, was a protectionist. His intervention at Wigan was therefore not just an opportunistic attack on the iniquities of the 1832 Reform Act, it was intended to make a broader policy statement. Nor was Nightingale himself a frivolous potential MP: a publican, he was a leading member of Manchester's Licensed Victuallers' Protection Society and of the town's Radical Electors' Association. He was prominent in the local anti-Poor Law movement and had been elected to the Police Commission when the Manchester constabulary was established in 1835. In short, he had a political hinterland beyond Chartism: and was not mounting the hustings to cry plague on both parties and the system that sustained them. Nightingale had a civic identity.[9]

Most subsequent Chartist challenges secured, in the phraseology of the times, 'a perfect forest of hands' at the hustings. Victors would often be designated the 'real MP' or 'people's MP' for the constituency. The political impact of a hustings' success was therefore not ephemeral. Countless Chartists participated in parliamentary elections in this way, and 'Chartist' candidates were still appearing at hustings in the late 1850s.[10] However, this article is not primarily concerned with these contests, but rather with those Chartist interventions in elections that went all the way to polling.

Little notice has been taken of the movement's direct engagement with the Westminster electoral process.[11] O'Connor's Nottingham triumph, plus two other 1847 challenges, has received passing notice but the broader picture is largely missing.[12] Here is a political movement whose very essence derived from the undemocratic character of the parliamentary process, making concerted efforts not to overturn that process but instead participate in it. The nature and extent of this activity, and the aspirations underpinning it, are essential to a more complete understanding of Chartism. They are especially pertinent to the post-Chartist period, the consequences of the movement and its interface with later Victorian politics. So the remainder of this chapter traces the early history of these challenges and then examines attempts to administer and finance electoral efforts through a central Chartist organization. Finally, it suggests how this strand within Chartism might help refine our view of the movement as a whole.

Chartism lacked central co-ordination until the National Charter Association (NCA) was established in September 1840. Unsurprisingly, its early election challenges were haphazard. They are also hard to document in detail: local newspapers showed limited interest in elections outside their region and national papers rarely recorded more than bare results, unless notable politicians were involved. Candidates did not necessarily specify a party affiliation. In the absence of centralized political parties, it was not unusual for two, three or more candidates to appear in a single constituency professing the same 'party' loyalties. Given especially the shifting political structures of the 1830s and 1840s, the retrospective designation of party affiliations in the standard reference sources can be misleading.[13] Both Dod's *Electoral Facts* and McCalmont's *Parliamentary Pollbook* list 'Chartist' challenges predating Chartism.[14] Both were apt to designate obscure candidates with radical views as 'Liberal', but did not do so consistently. For example they clearly identified Samuel Carter, unsuccessful at Tavistock in 1847 but twice returned to Westminster in 1852, as a Chartist (which makes the neglect of Carter by historians all the odder).

The difficulty of identifying unequivocal 'Chartist' candidacies reflects the broader problem of defining political loyalties in a period without clear party structures. David Nicholls, for example, analysed voting patterns to establish who were 'the friends of the people' at Westminster in the period 1832-49.[15] His conclusions were far from clear-cut. Similar lack of precision is evident even if support for the People's Charter is the key criterion. In the appendix, an attempt has been made to tabulate all parliamentary polls, 1839-60, made by known Chartists, or by radical reformers authoritatively endorsed by the movement, or which were designated 'Chartist' in contemporary pollbooks. Not all avowed Chartists belonged to the NCA or its Scottish parallel, the United Suffrage Central Committee for Scotland. But when the NCA established an official body to manage electoral matters in 1845, it failed to endorse several declared Chartists while publicly backing a number of middle-class radicals. The commitment to Chartism of these 'friends of the people' varied hugely, from the *de facto* Chartist and MP for Finsbury, Thomas Slingsby Duncombe, to William Scholefield who, as Birmingham's mayor in July 1839, notoriously directed the Metropolitan Police in the Bull Ring riots.[16]

It is hardly surprising therefore that pollbooks consistently label the first Chartist election challenger 'Liberal'. In April 1839 Hugh Craig contested a by-election for Ayrshire. Craig was a Kilmarnock draper and baillie (magistrate and councillor); he was also Ayrshire's delegate to Chartism's National Convention, chairman of the Kilmarnock Political Union and the owner of the *Ayrshire Examiner*, a Chartist newspaper. Craig was declared MP at the hustings, only to be overwhelmingly defeated when he polled 46 votes against the successful Tory's 1758, and the defeated Whig's 1296.[17] Nonetheless Craig and other Chartists welcomed the contest as an opportunity vividly to demonstrate the hugely undemocratic nature of the 1832 political settlement. Chartism now contemplated challenges in key constituencies. Henry Vincent was ready to stand at Bristol 'as a candidate on republican principles', O'Connor contested a Glasgow by-election hustings, while John Frost was linked to both Monmouthshire and Lord Russell's Stroud constituency.[18]

Events later in 1839 deflected Chartists' attention from the electoral arena. So the next test, indeed the first real test, of Chartism as a putative parliamentary force came with the General Election of July 1841. The essential context to this was the Chartists' national petition that May. This was not for the Charter, as in 1839, but an even larger assembly of signatures praying for a free pardon for the Newport Rising leaders, Frost, Williams and Jones. When Duncombe presented the petition to the Commons, a motion on its plea that the House use its influence to seek a pardon was tied and lost only on the casting vote of the Speaker – a 'Liberal'.[19]

Duncombe's central role within Chartism is insufficiently appreciated. The old-Harrovian ex-Guards officer was an unlikely champion of the Charter; but his tenacious pursuit of the government on church rates, theatre licensing, the opening of Chartists' mail, and his consistent support for all parliamentary reform resolutions, won admiration even before he took up the cause of Chartist prisoners. The best-dressed man in the Commons was no political dilettante, but a persuasive model of what a Chartist MP might be.[20] The 1841 tied vote also suggested even a small Chartist presence at Westminster could be politically potent. The proposition that Chartist candidates should stand in parliamentary elections was enshrined in the NCA constitution. The 1841 Convention sought to develop a practical policy for contesting elections. 'Prepare yourselves for the approaching elections', a special Convention sub-committee urged. 'Destroy your enemies, especially the bastile Whigs and Malthusian pack ... take up the dreaded weapon of exclusive dealing [withdrawal of custom from shopkeepers and tradesmen unsympathetic to Chartism] ... put down Whiggery first and Toryism next.' Two-member constituencies especially should be targeted: 'we have received certain and infallible evidence that in severel [sic] places either of the factions will split votes with our candidates, that is to say, a Tory and a Chartist, or a Chartist and a Whig may be returned'.[21]

The next general election would be the first since Chartism emerged. An official Chartist position had to be stated: crying plague upon both parliamentary parties was untenable. As the influential Edinburgh Chartist John Fraser had argued that February:

Public opinion may sanction the Charter; but that does not make it law. It can only be made law by a revolutionary declaration of a majority of the people in its favour, or by a decision of the majority of the members of Parliament to the same purpose. The former step is now but little contemplated by the people; we have therefore no alternative left but to promote the last ... We call on the Chartists, then, to direct their attention to elections, and make their power felt on all these occasions.[22]

Yet the decision to enter the election arena, rather than stand aloof and criticise that which every Chartist believed was patently absurd, was a bold one. Furthermore the financial outlay and organization required would be prodigious, for an election that might be delayed as late as spring 1844. Chartism would have been greatly helped had Melbourne's Whig administration clung to power longer. But the Convention was still in session when, on 4 June, a vote of no-confidence in the government triggered a general election. Whatever the timing, Chartism would never have made much impression at the polls; but faced by a sudden election its efforts could only be tokenistic. Legally qualified candidates had to be secured; enfranchised voters had to be found in each contested constituency prepared to move and second a Chartist at the hustings; and exclusive dealing needed time to bite. Realistic challenges, therefore, could be mounted in few constituencies.

So guided by O'Connor, *Northern Star* urged Chartists to support Tories where they could not field their own candidate. The movement had subsumed the campaign against the New Poor Law, while government treatment of Chartist prisoners had become a *cause célèbre*, especially since the first death in custody that January. 'A Tory minority will never oppose tyranny; a Whig minority must do so to acquire popular support, O'Connor argued, 'Therefore if you get a House of Tories, you get a good working Whig Chartist opposition'.[23] From Gammage onwards, early historians of Chartism charged O'Connor with foisting the policy of supporting Tories on the movement.[24] However, it reflected the wide consensus reached during 1839, to quote the *True Scotsman*, concerning 'how little worthy they [the Whigs] have been of that Radical support they have hitherto received'. *Northern Liberator* urged the Chartists to 'turn their strength in elections *invariably against the party that governs*'. 'It is highly desirable that things be brought to some crisis', an editorial in the LWMA's paper declared, adding 'let the Wellington party come in to-morrow'.[25]

Bronterre O'Brien, however, strenuously argued that supporting either parliamentary party should be anathema, adding that 'O'Connor is certainly mad'. Every hustings should be contested but, he argued, Chartist voters should stay away from the polls. Chartist candidates victorious at the hustings would then constitute 'a Great National Council' - effectively a standing convention.[26] Both O'Connor and O'Brien were in prison at the time. Frustration at being unable directly to influence events may partly explain the vituperative language to which both resorted. But the dispute has obscured what was achieved in 1841. Chartist candidates stood at the hustings in at least thirty constituencies. But only nine proceeded to the polls and all came bottom.[27] Only at Northampton did a Chartist make a genuine impression at both hustings and poll. Helped by Tory failure to find a second candidate to contest the two-member constituency, Peter McDouall won 176 votes, most from voters who paired him with the Tory. No voter chose both McDouall and the highest placed candidate, a Liberal, and very few paired him with the second Liberal elected, even though the latter described himself as a 'whole hog radical'. The message was clear, even in a constituency with a significant plebeian electorate (the legacy of an unusually inclusive pre-1832 franchise) the Chartist candidate would make headway only if clinging to the coat tails of a well-disposed Tory.[28]

Chartist election performance was a far cry from the guarded optimism of the 1841 Convention, and even further from McDouall's anticipation that twelve Chartist MPs would be returned who might then hold the Commons balance of power if the overall election result was close.[29] McDouall's calculation had always depended upon the additional and highly elusive return of middle-class radicals supportive of the Charter.[30] Only four MPs were returned, however, who received O'Connor's endorsement.[31] Even on the most generous definition of *Chartist*, therefore, by the conventional yardstick of seats won and lost, the 1841 general election was an abject failure for Chartism. Yet the conventional yardstick is hardly applicable.

Chartist delight that the Whigs were driven from office was almost palpable and predictably the movement claimed much credit for the Whigs' defeat. In particular, the result in the West Riding (a narrow victory for the Tories in a Whig stronghold) suggested exclusive dealing had played a contributory, even decisive, role; similarly in closely canvassed Rochdale, where the 'bold and manly' Irish radical Sharman Crawford defeated the sitting Liberal by 61 votes and was dubbed 'the Chartist member' by local Tories.[32] Complaints that Chartists were amenable to Tory blandishments, and even bribery, were not uncommon.[33] A few Chartists actively worked for the Tories.[34] Most grievously, at Glasgow the movement cleaved in two over electoral strategy, one group favouring 'Down with Whiggery at all costs', the other expressing disgust that any Chartist could ever contemplate voting Tory, even paired with Chartism's designated parliamentary candidate in the two-member constituency.[35]

However, there was never a blanket policy of opposing government supporters. The Chartist approach was pragmatic: the test of a candidate was support for the Charter, the liberation of prisoners, factory reform and repeal of the New Poor Law and rural police.[36] Chartism's concerted challenge was to the political system itself and some strikingly effective interventions were made at hustings across the country, with an especially notable victory (morally and in terms of votes cast) for the Tyneside temperance Chartist Robert Lowery over Thomas Macaulay (Secretary at War and a member of the Whig Cabinet) at Edinburgh. Every victory at the hustings was held up as another example of the iniquities of the 1832 reforms. In addition there were some blatant examples of the election process being interpreted to disadvantage Chartist candidates. Lowery contemplated a legal challenge against the Sheriff of Edinburgh's handling of the election until advised 'there was no doubt we might make out a case, but had we £2,000 to begin with?'[37] At Gateshead the mayor tried to prevent John Mason from speaking because he was not a resident of the borough, patently spurious since his opponent was also from outside the constituency. At Stockport Jonathan

Bairstow was forced to withdraw after the mayor demanded a contribution to election costs of first £50, and then £10, before even admitting him to the hustings. At Norwich the mayor demanded a surety of £200 (equivalent to three to four years' wages) from the Chartist candidate before he would organize an election. Perhaps not surprisingly Chartist supporters at the hustings then rioted. But this was one of only two instances (the other being Carlisle) where serious electoral violence was linked to support for Chartist candidates.

Although violence was almost ubiquitous at early Victorian elections, in general the crowds who supported these 'people's candidates' were impressive both for their size and self-discipline, a fact remarked upon – not without surprise – by several liberal papers and journals.[38] While violence and alleged intimidation were much in evidence at the Nottingham by-election the following year (when O'Connor himself 'fought like a dragon' in support of a radical liberal), the general point that specifically Chartist crowds usually behaved well at elections holds.[39] Recent research has even suggested that electoral violence *increased* in the post-Chartist period.[40] The explanation is complex, but frustration at the diminishing relative size of the popular electorate was probably a factor. It is likely that Chartism brought an element of discipline to popular participation in many constituency proceedings. It is difficult to sustain the argument that 'the Reform Act made little difference to the traditional tactics of electoral intimidation and violence', in the light of a detailed picture of Chartist participation in parliamentary elections.[41] Similarly, it has been argued that popular participation in the rituals of elections in this period was a form of licensed social inversion, which tended to reinforce rather than weaken local political power structures.[42] But Chartists' electoral interventions were a potent challenge to this cosy and backward-looking political world-view.

This is suggestive of a rapidly developing maturity in electoral politics, a phenomenon documented in different ways in studies of the post-1832 system by John Phillips and by Philip Salmon.[43] Electoral arithmetic, notably in reformed municipal elections from 1835, was often complex: Phillips pointed to rapidly emerging and consistent partisan voting patterns, suggesting party identities were firming up more rapidly than, even, the earlier work of John Vincent on the formation of the Liberal Party suggested.[44] Elections to local and municipal bodies, Poor Law Guardians and police commissions, each with broader franchises and greater responsiveness to the enthusiasm and application of candidates, were precisely the arena where Chartism prospered in the mid-1840s.[45] In Yorkshire alone, for example, Chartists were successful in elections for municipal councils, Poor

Law Guardians, vestries, highways boards or improvement commissions in Bradford, Halifax, Huddersfield, Leeds, Malton, Middlesbrough, Selby and Sheffield.[46] It was increasingly recognised that a key to electoral success lay in thorough registration of potential supporters and, by extension, the creation of new voters occupying properties of just sufficient value to confer the franchise.[47] As early as 1840 the Chartist Metropolitan Political Union had sought to extend the suffrage this way, and *Northern Star* editorialized on the need for Chartists to register wherever possible.[48] The economic circumstances of Chartists could never compete with those of the Liberals, who from 1847 successfully contrived wholesale accretions of support to the electoral registers through freehold land societies.[49] Nonetheless, registration of voters became a major theme in Chartist thinking, so much so that when *Northern Star* was re-launched from London in November 1844, it presented itself as 'the means of rallying the proper machinery for conducting the Registration Movement, the Land Movement, the National Trades' Movement, the Labour Movement, and the Charter Movement'.[50] As originally conceived, the Chartist Land Plan, so energetically promoted by O'Connor from 1844, would have manufactured votes just as the freehold land movement did. O'Connor, for example, predicted East Worcestershire would be wrestled from Tory 'landcrabs' by 300 Chartist forty-shilling freeholders, for the margin by which a pro-reform Liberal had lost the last contested election was only 353 votes.[51]

Only 43 colonists were ultimately settled on the Land Plan's Worcestershire estate and none was a freeholder. But such uncomfortable realities lay in the future. The optimism that led Chartists to speak in terms of a 'Registration Movement' was given additional momentum as it became increasingly apparent a general election was likely. The NCA executive began discussing the next election in early 1845, following an appeal from O'Connor to secure the return of twenty to thirty 'Duncombeites'.[52] Rapid urbanization and therefore increasing real property values could create situations in which voter registration could expand significantly. Furthermore, the system of confirming electoral rolls by a quasi-judicial process before a revising barrister meant the law was fluid and open to challenge and wide local variation. 'Revising barristers virtually recreated registration procedures from year to year.'[53] Though this could never enfranchise more than a relative handful of Chartists in any one location, with the majority of constituencies being small significant shifts in voting patterns could be effected through efficient registration. Ultra-radicals and Chartists had long understood this: the editor of the *English Chartist Circular* had published a manual on the subject within weeks of the Reform Act, and Chartist almanacs carefully flagged the revising barristers' schedule.[54] Peel's brief resignation from office in December 1845-January 1846 prompted an emergency Chartist Convention, followed by plans to levy a special subscription to meet the costs of an election campaign. In particular, the NCA executive called for the Anti-Corn Law League and the Whigs 'to be met on the hustings, and unmasked in the presence of the people'. 'Hurrah! then for DUNCOMBE', commented the *Northern Star*, 'for Labour and the Convention and D-- n the expense'.[55] When the Whigs formed a government in June 1846, after Peel's defeat in the Commons following the Corn Laws' repeal, the requirement that MPs offer themselves for re-election on appointment to the Cabinet forced several by-elections. Eye-catching Chartist challenges were mounted at Leeds, Nottingham and Plymouth and O'Connor was emboldened to predict the election of at least twelve Chartist MPs at the next general election, 'with Mr. Duncombe as our leader'.[56]

Registration, however, was time consuming and costly, as the experience of a new metropolitan registration committee established in June 1844 showed.[57] Manchester followed suit, but by the summer of 1846 the constituency's revising barrister had rejected 450 Chartist claims 'and they were not prepared with the means to carry the question into a court of law'. A large proportion of the 3,000 claims put forward by Chartists in Birmingham were similarly disallowed. So in September 1846 the NCA established a National Central Registration and Election Committee (NCREC) under Duncombe's presidency.[58] Hereon Chartism had an active body preparing for the next general election. Its weekly meetings dealt with all NCA correspondence regarding parliamentary elections; advised localities on registration issues; examined Commons division lists on key votes to identify MPs that might be supported and others a priority to oppose; approached Chartist localities to suggest particular Chartists who might stand in their constituencies; administered a fund built up from donations and subscriptions, disbursing sums to local Chartist registration committees where deemed appropriate. It was never intended candidates should explicitly declare themselves Chartists to receive support. Thus the veteran radical and anti-Corn Law campaigner, Colonel Perronet Thompson, received a £5 donation towards registration expenses at Bradford. The NCREC required, though, that candidates from outside the movement pledged to support the implementation of the Charter in any parliamentary division. With this in mind it sought personal clarification from some sitting MPs and candidates.[59] It also mounted a campaign, headed by Duncombe, to repeal the rating clauses of the 1832 Reform Act (those holding property that conferred the vote were disqualified if they were in arrears of rates). This attracted support from a handful of MPs, 38 voting for Duncombe's motion.[60]

Local registration committees harried or supported sitting MPs as appropriate and saw to the detail of registration at constituency level. How effectively this was done it is impossible to judge. The backroom work undertaken by such groups can only be guessed at. However, a letter detailing the *modus operandi* of Rochdale's [Liberal] Reform Association provides some insight:

> When the time comes to see about the payment of rates, the Secretary goes to the Overseers' Books ... and copies the names of such of our friends as have not paid – he then calls upon the defaulters, persuades them to pay up – if too poor, he lends them money, but *always is repaid by them* – he also sees that the Registration Shilling is paid, and examines the rate Book to discover if any of our friends can be placed upon the register who have heretofore been omitted.[61]

It is unlikely Chartist localities could have been so thorough, and inconceivable that they could pay a secretary £25 yearly or retain a solicitor to mount challenges before the revising barrister, both of which Rochdale's Reform Association did. The Chartist challenge at the general election of 1847 was better prepared than 1841, but was inevitably made more in hope than expectation. An early indicator – were it needed – was found in the Derby by-election on 16 June 1847. Tailor, turned Chartist lecturer, Philip McGrath made an impressive showing at the hustings; but when his Liberal opponent was declared elected and McGrath demanded a poll, the Mayor's riposte was 'let me have your money then, I am entitled in fees to your share to the amount of £23 10s. Let me have your money before we proceed'. Amidst 'great confusion' McGrath declined and the Mayor declared the Hon. Frederick Leveson-Gower, son of the first Earl Granville, elected.[62]

The following week the general election began in earnest. O'Connor called for 'a glorious month of resurrection ... our SACRED MONTH – sacred not to idleness, but sacred to Labour in Freedom's cause'.[63] Yet his own attitude to it was curiously off-hand. One cannot but question the judgment of someone who spent most of July 1847 digging and manuring a Land Plan estate, rather than election campaigning. O'Connor appeared in few constituencies and failed to attend the great annual Blackstone Edge rally on 11 July. There was, however, one conspicuous exception, Norwich. Here O'Connor made a special journey to endorse Dr Simpson, a radical liberal whom local Chartists put up in opposition to the sitting Liberal and

Tory. He, though, withdrew without explanation shortly before O'Connor arrived. Feargus was not amused: 'this picking up and hawking about of candidates, upon the modest assurance that they will condescend to represent us, is positively a disgrace to our cause'.[64] The incident demonstrated the frailty of the NCREC's authority over candidates it supported. Norwich Chartists had undertaken a full canvass of the constituency and all their efforts seemed wasted until, ten days before the hustings, William Lovett's friend, the barrister John Humffreys Parry, arrived to stand. Parry swept the hustings and the Chartists were sufficiently organised and confident to demand a poll. Although Parry lost, he polled 1572 votes, trailing the Tory by only 155. Parry trimmed his support for the Charter by advocating only triennial parliaments but that he was the Chartists' candidate was never denied.[65]

The seat Chartists felt most confident of winning was Halifax, where Ernest Jones was adopted as candidate. As in Norwich, anti-state church sentiments were an important factor. Halifax's radical-liberal dissenters formed a tactical alliance with the Chartists to contest the two member constituency against a Conservative and a Whig (the Chancellor of the Exchequer). So effective was this alliance that the other two parties were forced into running a joint campaign. However, there were tensions in the radical-Chartist camp: Chartist exclusive dealing extended beyond simply boycotting unsympathetic tradesmen to 'crowds of people congregating in front of their shops and hooting their customers'. Eventually the radical-liberal committee issued a sharp notice that the election should be 'conducted in such a manner as will least interrupt any social relationships … good neighbourhood and perfect political freedom'. Relations were particularly soured by the sudden death of a prominent Liberal employer whilst speaking at an election meeting packed by Chartist hecklers. Meanwhile, exclusive dealing by unenfranchised Chartists helped make the fortunes of several radical Halifax tradesmen and publicans. However, it was a delicate question whether Chartist tactics ultimately alienated more voters than they secured. The radical-dissenter came third by a margin of 158 votes, with Jones a further 69 behind.[66] At Blackburn, another two member constituency, W. P. Roberts mounted a similarly energetic campaign to Jones; but Roberts entered into no compacts, frankly predicting he would not be 'head of the poll, but he should have paved the way for a time that was coming, for it was his hope to "make proud power turn pale," to humble the pride of aristocracy, and defeat the treachery of Whiggism'. Roberts was bottom of the poll with 68 votes, but had the satisfaction of sharing defeat with a Liberal mill owner who had marched workers *en masse* to the hustings. At the hustings Roberts lambasted this opponent, but credited the Tories with passing the Ten Hours Act and for seeing 'humanity in the working man'.[67] Fifty-six per cent of those who voted for Roberts also voted for the Peelite who headed the poll, evidence of the *rapprochement* between Chartism and Peel which was one of the striking features of Chartism in the late 1840s.[68]

Given the effort that NCREC directed at the election, the defeat of Chartists of the calibre of Jones, McGrath and Roberts was disappointing. So too were the other contests (at least five) where Chartist candidates were unable to proceed beyond a hustings victory.[69] One Chartist was, however, elected to Parliament in 1847: Feargus O'Connor at Nottingham, a two-member constituency. This had never been predicted (O'Connor privately knew that he would struggle to meet the property qualification).[70] At its last meeting before polling began, the NCREC was informed of 'the moral certainty of Mr. Ernest Jones's return', and voted further funds accordingly. But hearing of an 'increasing prospect' at Nottingham, the committee simply wrote back with the assurance 'of its best support'. Similarly it was Halifax and not Nottingham that *Northern Star* had in its sights, devoting a whole editorial to the contest, something done for no other constituency. The *Star* did not even send a reporter to Nottingham and its initial coverage of the victory was lifted entirely from *The Times*. Unlike the remainder of the Chartist leadership who removed to their constituencies several weeks before polling, O'Connor himself barely campaigned, never addressing a meeting in Nottingham until the eve of the nomination. Since voting was public, the relative standing of candidates can be calculated for regular intervals during polling day. Even two hours before the poll closed, O'Connor had fewer votes than the other three candidates. He benefited, though, from a unique combination of factors. First his opponents were even more offhand than he in their approach: the sitting Whig MPs neither canvassed nor spoke in the constituency prior to the hustings, while the Tory never appeared at all (his father was dying). Second, the bulk of O'Connor's support came from those who supported him along with the Tory. O'Connor attracted very few disgruntled Whig voters and would clearly have lost had a second Tory contested the election, or a Whig withdrawn. O'Connor did not so much win his Nottingham seat as have it gifted to him by the other candidates, though in the ensuing euphoria few cared or even noticed.[71]

The 1847 general election was important in giving Chartism a platform for the reassertion of core principles and to distance these from the Land Plan. This participation in the election provided, even when there was no Chartist candidate to support. For example, in return for their support, Bury St Edmunds Chartists extracted from the Whig candidate a promise to vote for a free pardon for John Frost.[72] Strikingly, O'Connor alone spoke of the Land Plan in his election address. Other candidates adhered closely to a common programme, drawn up by the NCREC, which confined discussion of land issues to the repeal of primogeniture and entail and a simple call for 'an extension of the small proprietary system'. Demands to separate church and state and for a voluntary system of education (as opposed to state subsidies paid mainly to Anglican schools) were intended to appeal to radical nonconformist electors. Other measures included the restoration of church property to the purpose of poor relief; the abolition of the New Poor Law; the repeal of the game laws; abolition of capital punishment; an extension of direct taxation and of free trade; and opposition to participation in 'all foreign wars, not rendered necessary for self defence, or the purposes of humanity'. Some, like Irishman John West at Stockport, also advocated self-government for Ireland. At the programme's heart was what the Greenock candidate John McRae referred to as 'the great Charter of your liberties', involving a pledge by all candidates that, if returned, they would submit to re-election each year.[73]

O'Connor's success obscured the fact that the outcome of the 1847 election fell well below expectations. Nine radical-liberal candidates endorsed by the NCREC were elected,[74] compared to the five claimed as effectively 'Chartists' in 1841; but O'Connor's call had been for twenty to thirty 'Duncombeite' MPs, of whom twelve would be active Chartists. In the event, the movement brought to the polls only three more candidates (nine) than it had done in 1841; more critically still, it had candidates at far fewer hustings. Depleted Chartist strength was particularly apparent in Scotland but by no means exclusively so, for there were fewer English hustings challenges. The election also exposed tensions in the movement. Even the *Northern Star* was equivocal about exclusive dealing:

> The Electors themselves are harassed by the exclusive privilege they possess. All long for the BALLOT, many for the CHARTER. They look for this to screen them from the arrows of party hate – and so wretched is the system that numbers run away at an election time, others intentionally disqualify themselves, and many boldly refuse to vote at all, since they cannot do so with safety'.[75]

The total funds raised by the NCREC paled by comparison with the Land Plan. The committee's balance sheet for the campaign revealed that its total income was only £470, compared to over £1420 for the Land Plan in the week of publication alone; also that it made direct contributions to only seven constituencies, averaging under £32 each. Expenditure at Nottingham was £95, mostly incurred retrospectively by gifts to O'Connor's committeemen.[76] From a number of quarters there were criticisms that Land Plan members were apathetic about the election.[77] There was also an understandable reluctance on the part of many Chartists to be seen to take the electoral process too seriously. Something of this was evident in O'Connor's conduct; it was certainly visible at Worcester where the Chartists' candidate, complete suffragist Robert Hardy, lost the election by 214 votes. In the admiring yet appalled words of a *Star* reporter, Hardy 'did not canvass a single elector, employ a single lawyer, or spend one shilling; he is not an eloquent speaker'.[78] At the two-member seat of Ipswich, Vincent came close to being elected in an unofficial compact with the Liberal. Whether he desired election is debateable. Vincent was the least successful parliamentary candidate, in numbers of contests mounted and lost, between 1832 and the mid-twentieth century. It was a point of pride on his part not to conform to the customary glad-handed assault on a constituency prior to an election. As a close friend observed of Vincent's previous challenge at Ipswich, 'He had no committee rooms, carriages, banners, or band … neither had he made any canvass.' Vincent only entered the borough on a Thursday evening – the nomination was on the following Monday, and the polling on Tuesday.[79] It is questionable whether Vincent ever sought victory: without payment for MPs, the financial consequences of winning could have been disastrous – as indeed they were for George Thompson, the NCREC-endorsed radical reformer at Tower Hamlets in 1847.[80] A decade later, veteran Chartist Abel Heywood adopted the same approach when he contested Manchester as the nominee of the town's Manhood Suffrage Association, winning the hustings but losing the poll.[81]

O'Connor was not a particularly adept parliamentarian.[82] This was of some significance for Duncombe, a chronic asthmatic, was seriously ill and played little part in Westminster affairs during the next two years. O'Connor's presence in the Commons therefore had an even greater totemic value; but totemic rather than substantial is what it largely was. He was often immersed in Land Plan business; he lacked Duncombe's skill as a parliamentary operator, and was too-suspicious of radical liberalism to attempt to form the 'Duncombeite' circle he once had argued was needed. His ostentatious practice of sitting on 'the foremost seat of opposition' with Peel, Disraeli, and other leading Tories, both symbolized his negative relationship with radical liberals and ran counter to the growing disposition of Chartists across the country to make common cause with them.[83] This, as much as the tragic and unheralded collapse of his mental faculties from

1850, gave Chartists reason to ponder how far participating in parliamentary elections was either desirable or feasible. 'The very name Chartist has become a by-word and a reproach', one old Chartist believed:

> Yet we are not without hope, I believe, Sir, that a real People's Party is now forming, which will secure the confidence of the great mass ... But you will say, what are we doing? I answer, we are forming ourselves into Local Societies, we are getting ourselves on the Register for Municipal Electors. We think this is a step in the right direction. It is true that we are not bawling and making a great noise, but we have begun to work.[84]

It was within the realm of municipal, not parliamentary, politics that Chartism would have a significant impact.[85]

Chartism's challenges at the parliamentary polls reflected the fortunes of the movement generally: an early flourish, followed by buoyant optimism in the early 1840s, the incomplete recovery of lost ground in 1847, and finally protracted decline during the 1850s. The NCREC, debt-ridden, collapsed under the weight of supporting a successful radical reformer at the 1850 Lambeth by-election.[86] Only seven constituencies were contested by designated Chartists at the next general election in July 1852: a contest overshadowed by deepening sectarian disputes within what remained of the movement. Six of these candidates came bottom of the poll, including Ernest Jones at Halifax with just 37 votes (in 1847 he had polled 249). The engineers' leader William Newton made the best showing at Tower Hamlets, polling 1095 votes (less, however, than 4.6 per cent of the total cast in what was Britain's largest constituency). The sitting MP John Williams, the closest to a true supporter of Chartism among the liberals the NCREC approved in 1847, lost at Macclesfield.[87] George Harney failed to win even the hustings at Bradford. O'Connor, committed to an asylum the month before, could not contest Nottingham. In his place Chartism ran Charles Sturgeon, a lacklustre candidate with limited credentials.[88] By the time the next opportunity arose to contest Nottingham (1857) the situation was irretrievable, even with the energetic Jones as candidate. In 1859 the votes in Jones' favour collapsed. Chartist candidates contested polls on only two further occasions. Charles Wordsworth, a lawyer, stood at Paisley in 1857. And Frederic Lees, noted temperance campaigner and formerly a Chartist member of Leeds Town Council, contested Ripon in 1860. Lees won the hustings and then declined to poll, but the returning officer insisted one was held to satisfy doubt about the legality of returning an MP who had lost the hustings. Thus did Chartism's challenges at the parliamentary polls conclude in a fusion of farce and bathos – even Lees' proposer and seconder failed to vote for him.[89]

However, in the 1852 general election there was a seventh contested constituency, Tavistock in Devon, where Samuel Carter was elected, a candidate both Dod and McCalmont designated a Chartist. He also won a by-election in April that year, too late to take his seat and had also contested Tavistock unsuccessfully in 1847.[90] However, his was a pyrrhic victory: Carter was unseated weeks later when it was shown he did not meet the property qualification.[91] At one level Carter's election was no more than a quirk, as its subsequent neglect at the hands of historians of Chartism suggests. Though he favoured women's suffrage, he was a very moderate Chartist, declaring 'if so instructed by his constituents, [he] would give the Charter his cordial support; but, in the absence of that authority, would vote for an extension of the suffrage, the ballot, and triennial Parliaments'.[92] But his misfortune also underlines how the odds were stacked against Chartist parliamentary election success. Not only did the property qualification to vote or become an MP exclude almost all Chartists, those who administered the electoral system as revising barristers or returning officers were, as we have seen, often ill-disposed to Chartism. Tavistock's returning officer permitted an opposing candidate's agent to stop electors as they were about to poll and tell them Carter's qualification was disputed and if they gave him their vote 'it would be liable to be thrown away'.[93]

Equally significant, Chartism was numerically strongest in constituencies where the popular electorate was weakest: expanding industrial boroughs whose large working-class populations lived in low-quality housing, ineligible for the householder franchise of occupying property with a rateable value of £10. Those constituencies most amenable to popular influence at the polls were small country town boroughs like Banbury, Bury St Edmunds, Tavistock or Tiverton, where Chartism was organizationally weak but whose housing stock was of better quality and often over-valued for rating purposes.[94] Tavistock Chartists had a premonition of this in 1839 when they canvassed for signatures for the National Petition, 'without scarcely missing a door': of the 1,366 signatures obtained, the best response came from surrounding villages, beyond the borough boundary.[95] When Carter stood for the constituency in 1847, the NCREC was ignorant of his challenge until after it had happened. These were also constituencies where the popular electorate was shrinking, as the number of working men who retained the vote as of 'ancient right', having been members of the pre-1832 electorate, inevitably dwindled. Furthermore, the relative size of 'the popular electorate' within urban constituencies generally was shrinking.[96]

This drew such teeth as Chartism might have had in expanding non-industrial boroughs such as Bath, where by 1853 only four 'ancient right' electors remained and even £10 householders had declined by nearly 20 per cent since 1832, or Cheltenham or Brighton, where increased numbers of £10 householders were not matched by a commensurate growth in the electorates.[97]

Not only the physical but also the cultural landscape of 'the popular electorate' was changing. Recent research into popular Conservatism suggests that 'the intense correspondence between national and local politics' evident after the Reform Act diminished sharply in the late 1840s.[98] Conservatism's vicissitudes after Peel's defeat in 1846 were a major factor in the decline of popular Tory organization. Given Chartism's much smaller purchase on the national parliamentary arena, slippage in grassroots' appetite for participation in Westminster elections was inevitable and proved terminal.

Clearly, there were systemic factors within both the electoral system and Chartism itself which made the election of Chartist MPs almost impossible. Has Chartism's involvement in parliamentary polling therefore real significance? It has, for several reasons. Firstly, without an informed understanding of Chartism's repeated and concerted attempts to secure its own MPs our comprehension of the movement as a whole is incomplete and fractured. The NCREC was a serious initiative. It did not comprise aspiring dilettante politicians; nor were those involved activated by self-interest. Duncombe aside, the Committee comprised active Chartists who had not, and never would, enjoy the vote – men like its treasurer the Black London tailor William Cuffay, transported for his role in the 1848 Chartist insurgency. Cuffay's Soho garret home would not have qualified its occupier to vote under any definition of the suffrage extant before 1918. Irish-born handloom weaver Thomas Clark was another stalwart member. Having made a living as a Chartist lecturer, he ended his life selling insurance, dying 'in the utmost distress' in 1857.[99] Cuffay, Clark and others like them worked for Chartist and radical-liberal candidates because they believed success might bring direct tactical advantages at Westminster. That they did so underlines that Chartism, even under O'Connor's dominance after 1841, was never monolithic. There was far greater scope for creative co-operation with radical liberals than historians of the movement have supposed. One ventures to suggest, however, that the wrong Chartist was elected to Parliament in 1847 for their aspirations to have a realistic chance.

Second, this strand within Chartism alerts us to how Chartism's status as the quintessential industrial protest movement can mislead. In the late-nineteenth and early twentieth centuries considerable political energy was invested in creating a particular version of Chartism's history, one that emphasised how its 'moral force' was blunted by physical force tendencies of a backward-looking and reactionary nature, and by the movement's thraldom to political adventurers from outside the ranks of the working class. Perhaps the most significant of the late Chartist challenges occurred in 1852 when William Newton, a formative influence on the Amalgamated Society of Engineers, contested Tower Hamlets. 'A Chartist in principle', Newton described himself as 'willing to accept, but not to agitate, for a lesser measure of reform'.[100] But by 1938, when the Trades Union Congress issued a history commemorating its seventieth anniversary, TUC General Secretary Sir Walter Citrine could write that 'Newton's candidature challenged three other candidatures – one of them a Chartist and a Radical'.[101] Historically well-informed (he had been largely responsible for the TUC's tribute to the Tolpuddle Martyrs in 1934), Citrine's confusion nonetheless indicated the Fabian historiographical orthodoxy of the inter-war years, with its emphasis on how Chartism was superseded by 'modern' trade unionism. [102] Ernest Jones' vituperative criticisms of trade unionism, and of the Engineers especially, compounded this interpretation; and at Tower Hamlets specifically, the presence of George Thompson (the popular anti-slavery campaigner, endorsed by NCREC in 1847) among those whom Newton opposed may have abetted Citrine's confusion. However, Thompson had no links with Jones, while Newton's election address shows him fully committed to the Charter. Harney, writing in the *Star of Freedom* (as *Northern Star* had become) believed the return of 'Labour's candidate', William Newton, 'would be a victory worth any labour, any sacrifice'.[103] Historical developments rarely come neatly packaged or pigeonholed. Attempting to divide off Chartism from a 'modern' political world, as Citrine subconsciously did, reflected the Fabian historiographical orthodoxy of the inter-war years.

This is not to argue for a rigidly teleological interpretation of parliamentary labour history with Chartism enshrined at its inception. This brings us to a third aspect in which Chartist participation in parliamentary polling is significant: the interface between Chartism and Liberalism. The career of Leeds Chartist Robert Meek Carter illustrates this. Chartism recorded some of its earliest municipal victories at Leeds.[104] A mill hand and then, from 1844, a coal merchant's weighman, Meek Carter acquired his education through Chartism and night schools. His entry into electoral politics was achieved through the lowest rung of the municipal ladder, a highways board. In 1852 he was elected to Leeds Town Council, one of the two last candidates explicitly standing as Chartists. Carter's habit of regular saving had allowed him to start a coal merchant's business on his own account; subsequently he expanded into cloth finishing. Guardedly at first, he began to work with leading Leeds liberals on a manhood suffrage agenda.[105] Carter's track record as a local councillor and as a radical recommended him to office in a range of progressive causes and in 1866 he became a vice-president of the National Reform League. Then in 1868 he became one of the Liberal MPs for Leeds. In parliament Meek Carter pursued, according to *The Times*, 'thoroughly Radical opinions', including legal protection for trade unions and the disestablishment of the Anglican church. Re-elected in 1874, his parliamentary career was cut short by the failure of his business and he resigned in 1876. Like so many Chartists he made a restless radical even late in life: despite the humiliation of bankruptcy he returned to serve two more years on Leeds Town Council, proudly recording his occupation in the 1881 Census as 'Town Councillor & Cloth Finisher'.[106]

Carter's career was exceptional only for culminating at Westminster and, to a lesser extent, for its longevity. In Glasgow James Moir provides a very similar exemplar. From the early 1850s there were ex-Chartist councillors without number. Naturally a minority of those who had called themselves Chartists sought and attained elected office. More typical would have been the conscientious former Chartist who simply 'exerted himself strenuously at election times in the Liberal interest'.[107] Such lives were seldom well-documented, but it was this kind of municipal activity, rather than Ernest Jones' isolated and unsuccessful forays as a parliamentary candidate, which was the truest expression of Chartism's democratic aspirations.

Inevitably this involved an accommodation with Liberalism (an accommodation Ernest Jones also made before he died). Yet this was not the betrayal of Chartist principle that it might seem. Liberalism's version of popular constitutional reform was sufficiently close to that of Chartism, in language and content, for it to seem a natural conjunction. Both shared a common genealogy of Protestant dissent, the revolutions of the seventeenth century and the radical patriotism of the eighteenth. Factors that had kept Chartism and Liberalism apart were the New Poor Law, Corn Law repeal and radical liberalism's exaggerated deference to free market economics. However, in mid-Victorian England the routine operation of the Poor Law mitigated its most draconian intentions while Corn Law repeal was removed as an object of contention. Moreover, former Leaguers, in seeking to instate land reform in its place, chose a cause with which every Chartist concurred. Free market economics endured longer, but even here diminishing dogmatism in the third quarter of the century laid the grounds for a broadening progressive coalition, though a certain 'practical sacrifice and ideological cost' was required of middle-class liberals to achieve rapprochement with ex-Chartists.[108] In many localities, vigorous Chartist activity in the 1830s and 1840s contributed to the emergence of popular liberalism in the 1850s and 1860s.[109] Conversely, localities where Chartism had been weak tended to be those where subsequent Liberalism inclined to orthodoxy. Soon, radical liberals would embrace Chartism and work it into their own pedigree. When George Thompson, William Newton's opponent in 1852, returned to Tower Hamlets for a reform demonstration in 1859, he declared to general applause: 'The Charter can stand by the Declaration of Independence in America, by Magna Charta, or the Bill of Rights'.[110]

Notes

1   This study was prompted by a conversation at the University of Exeter in 1983, when Dr Bruce Coleman asked me why *McCalmont's Parliamentary Pollbook* listed a Chartist MP for Tavistock. I apologize to Bruce for taking a quarter of a century to provide an answer.

2   P. A. Pickering, *Feargus O'Connor: A Political Biography* (Monmouth, 2007), pp. 59-61; G. Airey, 'Feargus O'Connor, 1842-55: A Study in Chartist Leadership', (unpublished DPhil thesis, Staffordshire University, 2003), pp. 29-30, 49-50; S. Roberts, 'Feargus O'Connor in the House of Commons, 1847-52', in *Chartist Legacy*, ed. by O. Ashton, R. Fyson and S. Roberts (Rendlesham, 1999), pp. 105-6.

3   F. O'Gorman, 'Campaign rituals and ceremonies: the social meaning of elections in England, 1780-1860', *Past & Present* 135 (1992), 79-115; J. Vernon, *Politics and the People* (Cambridge, 1993), pp. 80-104; P. Salmon, *Electoral Reform at Work: Local Politics and National Parties, 1832-41* (Woodbridge, 2002).

4   E. W. Cox and S. G. Grady, *The New Law and Practice of Registration and Elections* (10th edn, 1868), cited by H. J. Hanham, 'Introduction' in C. R. Dod, *Electoral Facts from 1832 to 1853* (Brighton, 1972), p. lxi.

5   *Idem*, p. xliv.

6   J. Vincent, *Formation of the Liberal Party* (London, 1966), p. 15

7   M. Taylor, 'Interests, parties and the state: the urban electorate in England, c. 1820-72', in *Party. State and Society: Electoral Behaviour in Britain since 1820*, ed. by J. Lawrence and M. Taylor (Aldershot, 1997), 50-78.

8   *Preston Chronicle* 9 Mar. 1839; *Charter* 10 Mar. 1839; *Liverpool Chronicle* 15 Mar. 1839. The political affiliations of non-Chartists used here follow M. Stenton, *Who's Who of British Members of Parliament, Volume 1: 1832-1885* (Hassocks, 1976), itself based on contemporary editions of C. R. Dod, *Dod's Parliamentary Companion* (first published 1833 as C. R. Dodd, *Parliamentary Pocket Companion*). Dod based his data on information supplied by MPs themselves: see Hanham, 'Introduction', pp. x-xi.

9   P. A. Pickering, *Chartism and the Chartists in Manchester and Salford* (London,

1995), pp. 201-2.

10   For example: 1840 John Fraser at Edinburgh; 1841 Jonathan Bairstow and
Thomas Cooper for South Leicestershire and Cooper again at Leicester,
George Binns at Sunderland, William Dixon and Edward Nightingale at
Wigan, Abram Duncan for Kinross & Clackmannanshire, John Duncan
for Fifeshire, William Eagle at Norwich, John Fraser for Roxburghshire,
J. B. Hanson at Carlisle, G. J. Harney and Lawrence Pitkethly for the West
Riding, James Jack for the Ayrshire burghs, James Leach and James Williams
at Leeds, Robert Lowery at Edinburgh, John McCrae at Greenock, Richard
Marsden at Preston and Sheffield, William Martin at Bradford, John Mason at
Gateshead, Bronterre O'Brien at Newcastle upon Tyne, Reginald Richardson
at Perth, John Skevington and Dean Taylor for North Leicestershire, Andrew
Wardrop for the Dumfries burghs, Morgan Williams at Merthyr Tydfil; 1842
O'Connor and Vincent at Nottingham; 1847 Thomas Dickenson at South
Shields, William Dixon at Wigan, Harney at Tiverton (erroneously reported
as polling nil votes by McCalmont), Samuel Kydd at Greenwich and John
McCrae at Greenock; 1848 Joseph Barker at Bolton, William Dixon at Kings
Lynn, Samuel Kydd for the West Riding; 1852 Harney at Bradford and Knight
[forename unknown] at Greenwich; 1856 Richard Hart at Newcastle upon
Tyne.

11   D. A. Hamer, *Politics of Electoral Pressure: a Study of Victorian Reform Agitations*
(Hassocks, 1977), pp. 305-8, is especially disappointing. But see M. Taylor,
'The Six Points: Chartism and the reform of parliament', in *Chartist Legacy*,
ed. Ashton *et al*, pp. 16-7.

12   R. Challinor, *A Radical Lawyer in Victorian England: W. P. Roberts and the
Struggle for Workers' Rights* (London, 1990), pp. 155-9; M. Taylor, *Ernest Jones,
Chartism, and the Romance of Politics, 1819-1869* (Oxford, 2003), pp.102-4.
See also M. Chase *Chartism: A New History* (Manchester, 2007), pp, 253-4 and
279-86.

13   Dod, *Electoral Facts from 1832 to 1853*; F. H. McCalmont, *Parliamentary
Pollbook of All Elections* (London, 1879), 8th edn, enlarged and edited by
J.Vincent and M.Stenton as *McCalmont's Parliamentary Pollbook* (Brighton,
1971). On problems arising from imposing 'a modern set of party labels on
the early and mid-Victorian system' see Taylor, 'Interests', pp. 67-9.

14   O'Connor at Oldham and John Moore at Reigate in 1835 by-elections.
McCalmont also designated as Chartist J. R. Stephens at Ashton-under-Lyne
in the 1837 general election. On this basis John Taylor's candidacy for the Ayr
burghs in 1832 and 1834 could also be designated 'Chartist': see W. H. Fraser,
Dr John Taylor, Chartist: Ayrshire Revolutionary (Ayr, 2006), pp. 19-20 and 24.

15   D. Nicholls, 'Friends of the people: parliamentary supporters of popular
radicalism, 1832-49', *Labour History Review* 62:2 (Summer 1996), 127-46.

16   C. Behagg, *Politics and Production in the Early Nineteenth Century* (London,
1990), pp. 189, 203, 205, 208-11, 213.

17   *Caledonian Mercury*, 29 Apr. 1839; *Morning Chronicle*, 2 May 1839; N[orthern]
S[tar], 29 June 1839; A. Wilson, *Chartist Movement in Scotland* (Manchester,
1970), p. 74.

18 *Blackburn Standard* 6 Feb. and 19 June 1839; *NS*, 6 July 1839; *Western Vindicator* 12 Oct. 1839; D. J. V. Jones, *The Last Rising* (Oxford, 1985), p. 63.

19 *Hansard* vol. 58, 25 May 1841, cols 742ff; Chase, *Chartism*, p. 178.

20 For Duncombe see the cumulative portrait in Chase, *Chartism*.

21 *NS*, 5 June and *McDouall's Chartist & Republican Journal*, 12 June 1841.

22 *True Scotsman*, 13 Feb. 1841.

23 'To the independent non-electors of the Empire', *NS*, 19 June 1841.

24 'Had it not been for the pro-Tory policy recommended by O'Connor, the election of 1841 might have conferred immense benefit on the cause', R. G. Gammage, *History of the Chartist Movement* [first published 1854] (Newcastle, 1894), p. 194.

25 *True Scotsman*, 15 June 1839; *NL*, 22 June 1839; *Charter*, 30 June 1839.

26 Letters to Newcastle and Carlisle Chartists, *NS*, 12 and 19 June 1841.

27 See Note 10 above and appendix.

28 J. A. Phillips, *The Great Reform Bill in the Boroughs: English Electoral Behaviour, 1818-41* (Oxford, 1992), pp. 169-70.

29 *McDouall's Chartist & Republican Journal*, 12-26 June and 10-24 July 1841.

30 For such radicals seeking Chartist support, see M. J. Turner, 'Thomas Perronet Thompson, "'sensible Chartism" and the chimera of radical unity', *Albion* 33:1 (2001), 51-74.

31 See appendix; to the four should be added Duncombe, unaccountably excluded from O'Connor's election commentary, *NS* 26 June 1841.

32 *NS*, 26 June 1841; undated contemporary newscutting, cited by D. S. Gadian, 'Class-consciousness in Oldham, 1830-50', *Historical Journal* 21 (1978), p. 171.

33 *P[arliamentary] P[apers]* 1842 (457), Southampton Town Election Inquiry, minutes of evidence 129, 153. For similar subsequent complaints see *PP* 1852-3 (1685), Corrupt Practices in the Borough of Cambridge, pp. 381-82; *Leader* 8 Jan. 1853; *PP* 1867 (3776), Corrupt practices at Totnes, p. 610.

34 The best documented example is Nightingale at a by-election that February: *PP* 1841 (219), Walsall Election Petition, minutes of evidence 151-2, 200 and 215.

35 Wilson, *Chartist Movement in Scotland*, pp. 163-65.

36 Chartist endorsement of Liberal candidates included Salford, *Manchester Times*, 19 June 1841 (see also Pickering, *Chartism and the Chartists*, p. 246), Preston, *Preston Chronicle*, 19 June 1841 and Bath, *Manchester Times*, 26 June 1841.

37 B. Harrison and P. Hollis (eds), *Robert Lowery, Radical and Chartist* (London, 1979), p. 186.

38 *Nonconformist*, 6 Oct. 1841; J. Epstein, *Lion of Freedom: Feargus O'Connor and the Chartist Movement* (London, 1982), p. 285.

39 T. Cooper to S. Cooper, [Aug. 1842], TNA, TS 11/601; *PP* 1843 (130), Nottingham town election petition; Chase, *Chartism*, pp. 208-9. F. Mather, *Public Order in the Age of the Chartists* (Manchester, 1959), pp. 86, 116 and 137, links just three serious incidents of electoral disorder to Chartism – at Newtown, Congleton and Ashton-under-Lyne (all 1841).

40   J. Wasserman and E. Jaggard, 'Electoral violence in mid-nineteenth century England', *Historical Research* 80 (2007), 124-55.

41   J. Stevenson, *Popular Disturbances in England, 1700-1870* (London, 1979), p. 287; see also N. Gash, *Politics in the Age of Peel* (London, 1953), pp. 137-53.

42   O'Gorman, 'Campaign rituals and ceremonies', pp. 108-9.

43   J. Phillips, 'The unnoticed political revolution of 1835', in *Partisan Politics, Principle and Reform in Parliament and the Constituencies, 1689-1880*, ed. by C. Jones, P. Salmon and R. W. Davis (Edinburgh, 2005); Phillips, *Great Reform Bill*; Salmon, *Electoral Reform*.

44   Vincent, *Formation of the Liberal Party*.

45   Taylor, 'Six Points', pp. 17-18; Pickering, *Chartism and the Chartists in Manchester and Salford*, pp. 73-85; Chase, *Chartism*, pp. 343-4. The Glasgow Chartist leader James Moir was elected to the city's police commission in 1844, see 'Moir, James (1806-1880)', *Oxford Dictionary of National Biography*, on-line edn, Oxford University Press, May 2006.

46   *NS*, 8 Oct. 1842, 1 and 8 Nov. 1851; A. Elliott, 'Municipal government in Bradford', in *Municipal Reform and the Industrial City*, ed. by D. Fraser (Leicester, 1982); B. Wilson, *Struggles of an Old Chartist* (1857), reprinted in *Testaments of Radicalism*, ed by D. Vincent (London, 1977), pp. 203-4, 208; M. Chase, 'Chartism, 1838-58', *Northern History* 24 (1988), 156, 166; *NS*, 9 Apr. 1842; S. Pollard, *History of Labour in Sheffield* (Liverpool, 1959), pp. 48-9.

47   On the importance of registration to the constituency organization of the two main parties see J. Prest, *Politics in the Age of Cobden* (London, 1977) and M. Cragoe, 'The Great Reform Act and the modernization of British politics: the impact of Conservative Associations, 1835-41', *Journal of British Studies* 47 (July 2008), 581-603.

48   *NS*, 25 Apr. 1840, 17 July 1841, 25 May 1844. See also F. C. Mather (ed.), *Chartism and Society* (London, 1980), pp. 77-80.

49   See below, chapter 12.

50   *NS*, 30 Nov. 1844.

51   *Labourer* vol. 2 (1847), 181; *NS*, 19 Dec. 1846, 20 Feb. 1847.

52   *NS*, 28 Dec. 1844.

53   K. T. Hoppen, 'The franchise and electoral politics in England and Ireland, 1832-1885', *History* 70 (1985), p. 203.

54   W. Carpenter, *The Elector's Manual; comprising ... information ... connected with the exercise of the franchise ... with the necessary instructions to the new constituency* (London, 1832); *Chartist Penny Almanack for 1844* (Darlington, [1843]), p. 5. For a later example, James Watson's *Handbook of Registration* ('Chartist committees should see to its circulation'), see *NS* 4 May 1850.

55   *NS*, 27 Dec. 1845, 7 Mar. 1846.

56   *NS*, 4-18 July, 8 and 15 Aug. 1846.

57   *NS*, 22 June, 10 and 17 Aug. and 12 Oct. 1844.

58   *NS*, 8 Aug., 12-26 Sept. 1846.

59   *NS*, 13 and 20 Feb., 6 Mar., 24 Apr. 1847.

60   *Hansard*, vol 90, 23 Feb. 1847, col. 406; *NS*, 6 Mar. 1847.

61   J. Bright to G. Crosfield, quoted by H. J. Hanham, *The Nineteenth-Century*

Constitution (Cambridge, 1969), p. 242.

62   *Derby Mercury*, 23 June 1847, c.f. *The Times*, 17 June and *NS*, 19 June 1847.

63   *NS*, 26 July 1847.

64   *NS*, 10 July 1847. The putative candidate, Simpson, was probably the same who reneged on an agreement to stand for Bradford in 1841, see *NS*, 19 June 1841.

65   *NS*, 10, 17 July 1847; *Norfolk Chronicle*, 24 July 1847; *Ipswich Journal*, 31 July 1847; J. K. Edwards, 'Chartism in Norwich', *Yorkshire Bulletin of Economic and Social Research* 19:2 (Nov. 1967), 85-100. Parry was later defence counsel for some Chartists tried after the attempted 1848 rising (*NS*, 30 Sept. 1848).

66   Wilson, *Struggles*, p. 205; T. Iwama, 'The middle class in Halifax, 1780-1850', (unpublished DPhil thesis, University of Leeds, 1983), pp. 196-204. A reported 2,000 people packed the Halifax Oddfellows' Hall to organize the Chartist exclusive dealing campaign, see *NS*, 31 July 1847.

67   *Blackburn Standard*, 29 July 1847.

68   Pollbook printed in *Blackburn Standard*, 4 Aug. 1847; Chase, *Chartism*, pp. 125, 271-4, 284, 286, 297

69   See Note 10 above.

70   See Note 2 above.

71   *NS*, 31 July and 7 Aug. 1847; C. Binder, 'The Nottingham electorate and the election of the Chartist, Feargus O'Connor, in 1847', *Transactions of the Thoroton Society* 107 (2003), 145-62; R. Church, *Economic and Social Change in a Midland Town: Victorian Nottingham, 1815-1900* (London, 1966), pp. 144-5.

72   A. F. J. Brown, *Chartism in Essex and Suffolk* (Chelmsford, 1982), p. 78.

73   O'Connor, see *NS*, 5 June 1847; McCrae, see *NS*, 31 July 1847; West, see *DLB*, vol 7; other quotations from Ernest Jones' address, *NS*, 3 July 1847.

74   Muntz and Scholefield (Birmingham), Bowring (Bolton), Perronet Thompson (Bradford), Duncombe and Wakley (Finsbury), John Williams (Macclesfield), George Thompson (Tower Hamlets), Crawford (Rochdale).

75   *NS*, 7 Aug. 1847.

76   *NS*, 1 Jan. 1848.

77   Except at Leicester where the local branch claimed its canvass and handbill 'gained the election' for the Liberals, see *PP* 1847-8 (381), Leicester election petition, p. 112 and *NS*, 7 Aug. 1847.

78   *NS*, 7 Aug. 1847.

79   *Ipswich Journal*, 24 July 1847; W. Dorling, *Henry Vincent: A Biographical Sketch* (London, 1879), pp. 34-5.

80   R. M. Griffin, 'George Thompson and Trans-Atlantic Antislavery, 1831-1865', unpublished PhD thesis, Indiana University, 1999), pp. 267, 270-1.

81   *Manchester Times*, 30 Apr. 1859; R. L. Greenall, *The Making of Victorian Salford* (Lancaster, 2000), pp. 130-31.

82   Chase, *Chartism*, pp. 286, 321-3. Roberts, 'O'Connor in the House of Commons', and Pickering, *Feargus O'Connor*, pp. 129-37, offer more-positive assessments.

83   O'Connor's preferred seating was well-attested: see I. and P. Kuczynski (eds),

A Young Revolutionary in Nineteenth-century England: Selected Writings of Georg Weerth, (Berlin, 1971), p. 169; *Daily News*, 9 Dec. 1847; Lord Stanley, diary entry for 23 Mar. 1849, reprinted in J. Vincent (ed.), *Disraeli, Derby and the Conservative Party* (Hassocks, 1978), p. 2; Pickering, *Feargus O'Connor*, p. 130.

84   *Star of Freedom and National Trade Journal*, 25 Sept. and 27 Nov. 1852.

85   For England see above, Notes 45 and 46; for Scotland see *NS*, 22 Jan. 1848 (Glasgow Chartist Electoral Association) and 'James Moir', *Oxford Dictionary of National Biography*; for Wales, R. Wallace, *Organise! Organise! Organise! A Study of Reform Agitations in Wales, 1840-86* (Cardiff, 1991), pp. 97-8 and A. V. John, 'Chartist endurance', *Morgannwg* 15 (1971), 36-44.

86   See appendix.

87   Williams 'declared himself in favour of universal suffrage, and other "points of the People's Charter"' - quoted in Stenton, *Who's Who of British MPs*, p. 410. The *Macclesfield Courier* claimed he boasted supporting the National Holiday and Chartist Land Plan (quoted in *North Wales Chronicle*, 2 July 1852).

88   As a Liberal Sturgeon came bottom at Knaresborough (1841); he went on to challenge Peel's former Home Secretary, Sir James Graham, at the Carlisle by-election in January 1853, lost at the hustings and declined to poll, see *Reynolds Newspaper*, 9 Jan. 1853 and *Leader*, 8 Jan. 1853.

89   *The Times*, 22 and 25 Dec. 1860. See also B. Harrison, *Dictionary of British Temperance Biography* (Coventry, 1973), pp. 77-8. Standing as a Liberal, Lees subsequently came bottom of polls at Northampton (1868) and Leeds (1874).

90   C. R. Dod, *Electoral Facts, from 1832 to 1852, Impartially Stated* (London, 1852), p. 300 designated Carter 'Conservative' for the 1847 contest. In the following year's edition this was amended to 'Liberal' (*Electoral Facts from 1832 to 1853*, p. 310). Dod labelled the 1852 by-election challenge 'Liberal', but the second 'Chartist'. His *Parliamentary Companion* unequivocally used the label Chartist: see Stenton, *Who's Who of British MPs*, p. 68. McCalmont consistently described Carter as 'Chartist'.

91   Having successfully petitioned against Carter's election, the liberal-conservative he defeated was declared elected by Parliament: *PP* 1852-53 (227), Select Committee on Tavistock Election Petition, p. 57. Carter stood unsuccessfully as a Liberal for Tavistock (1865), but was finally elected at the Coventry by-election (March 1868) only to be defeated at the general election that November. He was again defeated at Coventry in 1874.

92   Stenton, *Who's Who of British MPs*, p. 68. For Carter's support of female suffrage see *Plymouth and Devonport Weekly Journal*, 5 Aug. 1847.

93   S. C. Tavistock Election Petition, pp. 25 and 29.

94   For disparities in rateable value see Hanham, 'Introduction', pp. xiii-xiv.

95   E. Williams to the National Convention, 28 Apr. 1839, British Library (Department of Manuscripts), Place Papers, Add. MSS 34245A fo 323.

96   M. Taylor, 'Interests', pp. 56-60.

97   Conclusions based on data given by Dod, *Electoral Facts from 1832 to 1853*, pp. 17, 35-6 and 59.

98   Cragoe, 'The Great Reform Act and the modernization of British politics', pp.

602-3.

99   *Reasoner*, 26 Apr. 1857. There are entries for both in *DLB*, vol. 6; see also S. Roberts, *Radical Politicians and Poets in Early Victorian Britain* (Lampeter, 1993), pp. 89-106 on Clark, and Chase, *Chartism*, passim.

100 *Star of Freedom and National Trade Journal*, 3 Apr. 1852.

101 W. Citrine in *70 Years of Trade Unionism*, ed. by H. Tracey (London, 1938), p. 13.

102 On the Fabian historiography see D. Thompson, 'Chartism and the historians', in her *Outsiders: Class, Gender and Nation* (London, 1993), esp. pp. 27-30. *The Book of the Martyrs of Tolpuddle, 1834-1934*, [ed. by W. Citrine] (London, 1934) – Citrine personally wrote the historical section, 'The Martyrs of Tolpuddle', pp. 1-101.

103 *Operative*, 12 Apr. 1852; *Star of Freedom and National Trade Journal*, 8 May and 5 June 1852; 'William Newton', in *DLB*, vol. 2. J. Saville, *Ernest Jones: Chartist* (London, 1952), pp. 47-8, 190-95 remains the fullest analysis of Jones' relations with trade unionism.

104 *Leeds Mercury*, 9 Jan. 1841; *NS*, 8 Jan., 19 Mar., 2, 9 and 30 Apr., 6 Aug. 1842; D. Fraser, 'Politics and society in the mid-nineteenth century', in *History of Modern Leeds* ed. by D. Fraser (Manchester, 1980), pp. 286f; see also D. Fraser, *Urban Politics in Victorian England* (Leicester, 1976).

105 G. J. Holyoake, *Jubilee History of the Leeds Industrial Co-operative Society* (Leeds, 1897), p. 249; C. Godfrey, *Chartist Lives* (New York, 1987), pp. 475-6.

106 *The Times*, 11 Aug. 1882; 1881 Census RG12/4539 fol. 133.

107 *Ashton Reporter*, 5 Dec. 1874, commenting on William Aitken.

108 T. Koditschek, *Class Formation and Industrial Society: Bradford, 1750-1850* (Cambridge, 1990), p. 569; M. Finn, *After Chartism: Class and Nation in English Radical Politics, 1848-74* (Cambridge, 1993).

109 For example Halifax, see K. Tiller, 'Working-class Attitudes and Organisation in Three Industrial Towns, 1850-75', (unpublished DPhil. thesis, University of Birmingham, 1975) and her 'Late Chartism: Halifax, 1847-58', in *The Chartist Experience: Studies in Working-class Radicalism and Culture, 1830-60*, ed. by J. Epstein & D. Thompson (London, 1982); Leicester, see B. Lancaster, *Radicalism, Co-operation and Socialism: Leicester Working-class Politics* (Leicester, 1987), pp. 76-84; Rochdale, see Vincent, *Formation of the Liberal Party*, p. 111; Bradford, see Koditschek, *Class Formation*, pp. 517-65; Banbury, see B. S. Trinder, 'The radical Baptists', *Cake and Cockhorse: the Magazine of the Banbury Historical Society* 2:11 (Jan. 1965), 179-92 and B. S. Trinder, *A Victorian MP and his Constituents* (Banbury, 1969), pp. 38-39.

110 *East London Observer*, 12 Mar. 1859, quoted by Vernon, *Politics and the People*, p. 321.

Parliamentary polls contested by Chartist and Chartist-endorsed candidates

Date and Constituency	Name	Votes	Placed	Comments
1839 Ayrshire County	Hugh Craig [L]	46	3/3	USCCS
1841 General Election				
Aberdeen	Robert Lowery [Ch]	30	3/3	NCA
Banbury	Henry Vincent [Ch]	51	3/3	NCA
Bath	J.A. Roebuck [L]	1157	2/2 *elected*	OC
Brighton	Charles Brooker [Ch]	19	4/4	1
Cheltenham	Col. T.P. Thompson [L]	4	3/4	2
Glasgow	George Mills [Ch]	353	4/4	USCCS
Hull	Col. T.P. Thompson [L]	1645	4/4	OC
Marylebone	W.V. Sankey [L]	61	5/5	3
Monmouth District	William Edwards [Ch]	0	2/2	4
Northampton	Peter M'Douall [Ch]	176	4/4	NCA
Oldham	John Fielden [L]	unopposed	*elected*	OC
ditto	Wm Augustus Johnson [L] unopposed	unopposed	*elected*	OC
Paisley	J. Thomason [Ch]	0	2/2	USCCS
Reigate	Dr James Bedford [Ch]	9	2/2	5
Rochdale	Sharman Crawford [L]	339	1/2 *elected*	OC
Tower Hamlets	T.E.P.Thompson [L]	831	5/5	OC

1842				
Brighton	Charles Brooker [Ch]	16	3/3	1
Ipswich	Henry Vincent [Ch]	473	4/5	NCA
1843				
Tavistock	Henry Vincent [Ch]	69	2/2	NCA
1844				
Kilmarnock	Henry Vincent [Ch]	98	3/3	NCA
1845				
Southwark	Edward Miall [L]	352	3/3	6
1846				
Plymouth	Henry Vincent [Ch]	188	2/2	NCA
1847 General Election				
Birmingham	G. F. Muntz [L]	2830	1/4 *elected*	NCREC
ditto	W. Scholefield [L]	2821	2/4 *elected*	NCREC
Blackburn	W.P. Roberts [Ch]	68	4/4	NCA/ NCREC
Bolton	Dr J. Bowring [L]	652	2/3 *elected*	NCREC
Bradford	Col. T.P. Thompson [L]	926	2/4 *elected*	NCREC
Coventry	William Williams [L]	1663	3/3	NCREC
Derby	Philip McGrath [Ch]	216	4/4	NCA/ NCREC
Finsbury	T.S. Duncombe [L]	unopposed	*elected*	NCREC; 7
ditto	Thomas Wakley [L]	unopposed	*elected*	NCREC
Halifax	Ernest Jones [Ch]	280	4/4	NCA/ NCREC
ditto	Edward Miall [L]	349	3/4	NCREC

Ipswich	Henry Vincent [Ch]	546	4/4	NCA/NCREC
Leeds	Joseph Sturge [L]	1980	3/3	NCREC
Macclesfield	John Williams [Ch]	500	2/3 *elected*	NCREC
Marylebone	Robert Owen [Ch]	1	5/5	8
Northampton	Dr John Epps [Ch]	140	5/5	9
Norwich	J. Humffreys Parry [L]	1572	3/3	10
Nottingham	Feargus O'Connor [Ch]	1257	2/4 *elected*	NCA/NCREC
Oldham	John Fielden [L]	612	4/4	NCREC
Rochdale	Sharman Crawford [L]	unopposed	*elected*	NCREC
Sheffield	Thomas Clark [Ch]	326	3/3	NCA/NCREC
Stockport	John West [Ch]	14	4/4	11
Tavistock	Samuel Carter [Ch]	56	4/4	12
Tower Hamlets	George Thompson [L]	6268	1/3 *elected*	NCREC
Worcester	Robert Hardy [L]	927	3/3	NCREC
1848				
Carlisle	Peter M'Douall [Ch]	55	4/4	NCA
York	Henry Vincent [Ch]	860	2/3	NCA
1850				
Lambeth	William Williams [L]	3834	1/3 *elected*	13
1852 (April)				
Tavistock	Samuel Carter [Ch]	115	1/3 *elected*	12
1852 General Election				
Finsbury	T.S. Duncombe [L]	6678	2/3 *elected*	SF

Halifax	Ernest Jones [Ch]	37	4/4	NCA
Hull	Viscount Goderich [L]	2242	2/4 elected	SF
Macclesfield	John Williams [Ch]	468	3/3	14
Northampton	John I. Lockhart [Ch]	106	4/4	15
Nottingham	Charles Sturgeon [Ch]	512	3/3	SF
Southwark	Apsley Pellatt [L]	3887	2/3 elected	SF
Tavistock	Samuel Carter [Ch]	169	2/3 elected	12
Tower Hamlets	William Newton [Ch]	1095	5/5	SF
Westminster	William Conningham [L]	1716	3/3	SF
York	Henry Vincent [Ch]	886	3/3	NCA
1857 General Election				
Nottingham	Ernest Jones [Ch]	614	3/3	NCA
Paisley	C.F.F. Wordsworth [Ch]	4	3/3	16
1859				
Nottingham	Ernest Jones [Ch]	151	4/4	NCA
1860				
Ripon	F.R. Lees [Ch]	0	2/2	17

Key

Ch: Chartist

L: Liberal (McCalmont's designation)

NCA: member of the National Charter Association (not necessarily at time of election).

NCREC: endorsed by NCA National Registration and Elections Committee, NS (24 July 1847).

OC: endorsed by O'Connor and the NS (26 June, 24 July 1841).

SF: endorsed by the *Star of Freedom* (26 June 1852), the successor to *Northern Star*.

USCCS: member of the United Suffrage Central Committee for Scotland.

Notes

1   Unclear if Brooker was NCA member, but he was officially sponsored by Brighton NCA locality and endorsed by *Northern Star*.

2   'The Chartist candidate' (*NS* 3 July 1841). Thompson was nominated by the proprietor of the Chartist *Cheltenham Free Press* and seconded by another local Chartist activist. He was able to contest both this and the Hull because consitutency contests were staggered over several weeks during general elections at this time.

3   Elected to the 1839 National Convention; unclear if he belonged to the NCA.

4   Veteran Newport Chartist, but not regional Chartists' first choice of candidate. Declined to stand down when latter arrived late for nomination. Edwards won the hustings but his insistence on going to poll was deeply unpopular with Newport Chartists. See D. Osmond, 'After the Rising: Chartism in Newport, 1840-48', *Gwent Local History* 98 (Spring 2005), 8-52.

5   A Brixton merchant, not recognised as Chartist by *Northern Star* but elsewhere described as standing 'in the reform interest' (*Examiner*, 26 June 1841). McCalmont and Dod also described as Chartist John Moore, a candidate at Reigate's 1835 by-election.

6   By-election fought by Miall on a radical dissent and anti-Maynooth platform, supported by metropolitan Chartists and endorsed by O'Connor as 'a Chartist and nothing else' (*NS*, 23 Aug. 1845).

7   As an MP, Duncombe supported Chartism from its inception, but oddly was not endorsed by O'Connor or *Northern Star* in 1841. Nor is it clear if he was a NCA member at this time. The Chartist R. J. Richardson (*Dundee Chronicle*, 9 July 1841) stated T. S. Duncombe was the Chartist candidate at Finsbury.

8   The NCA locality had tried and failed to secure a qualified candidate. Owen, nominally Chartist, used the occasion to issue an address extolling his highly individualistic vision, without mention of Chartism or the Charter. See R. Owen, *To the Electors of the Borough of Marylebone* (n.p, 1847).

9   Supported Lovett's National Association and People's League. 'His success is to be wished and worked for' (*NS* 24 July 1847) and candidature received NCREC's retrospective praise ('vindicated the cause of the people at the hustings') *NS*, 11 Sept. 1847.

10   See *NS* 10 and 17 July 1847; *Norfolk Chronicle*, 24 July 1847; *Ipswich Journal*, 31 July 1847.

11   Chartist missionary, land plan lecturer, gaoled for his part in 1848 rising. Editorial in his support and received NCREC's retrospective endorsement, *NS*, 24 July, 11 Sept. 1847.

12   See main text above for details.

13   Endorsed and supported financially by NCREC. A Liberal candidate but was described in a *NS* editorial (10 Aug. 1850), and by metropolitan Chartists, as the Chartist candidate. See also Coventry, 1847.

14   'Declared himself in favour of universal suffrage, and other "points of the People's Charter"', *Dod's Parliamentary Companion* (1852) quoted in Stenton, *Who's Who of British Members of Parliament*, p. 410.

15 Unclear what authority Dod or McCalmont had for designating Lockhart a Chartist.
16 Charles Favell Forth Wordsworth QC, author of legal textbooks.
17 See main text above for details.

9

THE CHARTIST MOVEMENT AND 1848

John Saville's contribution to the historiography of Chartism would be recognized as significant, even without his *1848: The British State and the Chartist Movement*, whose publication in 1987 in many ways represented the pinnacle of his career as a historian. Saville's authorial contribution to the *Dictionary of Labour Biography* includes an impressive array of biographical essays on Chartists. To volume six alone he contributed an outstanding entry for the black Londoner, trade unionist and Chartist William Cuffay, plus further fine-grained accounts of Robert Gammage and Thomas Martin Wheeler and, as co-author, of Catherine and John Barmby, Thomas Clark and Arthur O'Neill.[1] Similarly invaluable are the editorial introductions he wrote in the 1960s for four reprints of key Chartist texts: G. J. Harney's journal *Red Republican*, Gammage's *History of the Chartist Movement*, and the autobiographies of W. E. Adams and Thomas Cooper.[2] The cumulative importance of these works is considerable. But the publication of *1848* marked Saville out as a historian of real distinction: it is a book of fundamental importance to understanding not Chartism alone, but the nineteenth century as a whole. Chartism really mattered to John Saville, just as it had mattered to early Victorian government and society.

The weight of biographical studies in any simple numerical tally of Saville's output as a Chartist historian might suggest to the uninitiated that he was concerned primarily with empirical retrieval. However, the power of *1848* as a work of historical scholarship derives not from its author's command of historical detail (great though that was) but his rootedness in the Marxist tradition. It is worth examining the book's gestation in some detail for, despite the late date of its publication, there are good grounds for claiming a place for it as a product of the Historians' Group of the Communist Party of Great Britain (CPGB) alongside stellar earlier works by, for example, Christopher Hill, Eric Hobsbawm and E. P. Thompson.[3] In fundamental respects, *1848* expands and explicates attitudes towards its subject that emerged within British communism in the immediate post-war years.

Europe's year of revolutions was not, however, where John Saville's career as historian of Chartism began. He never particularly explained why he chose as the subject of his first substantial publication in 1952 the Chartist leader Ernest Jones. Presumably he assumed that Jones' importance as the labour leader who did most to bridge the Chartist period and the 1850s would speak for itself.[4] Saville began researching Jones' career soon after he was demobilized in April 1946, during his brief career as an economist in the Chief Scientific Division of the Ministry of Works. It was only in September 1947 that he took up the post at Hull which initiated his academic career.[5] The pressure of the early months of his appointment probably explains his otherwise puzzling non-appearance in the 1948 'Chartist Centenary Issue' of the CPGB's cultural journal *Our Time*. To that issue, Dorothy Towers – Dorothy Thompson after her marriage later that year – contributed the first ever scholarly examination of the work of the Chartist poets; while the lead feature on 1848, by the veteran CPGB organizer and orator Tommy Jackson, in some ways anticipates arguments in Saville's subsequent work.[6] Jackson was not only alert to the inspirational impact of continental events on British Chartists but was mindful of the critical dimension that developments in Ireland added to the government's handling of events in Britain. He also emphasized that the well-known Chartist rally on Kennington Common on 10 April had been 'systematically and persistently made the theme of a whole embroidery of falsification … Actually, Chartism began to grow more formidable after April 10th than it had been before.' Jackson concluded that the Chartist conspiracy the followed in August had entirely 'been worked up by police agents'.[7]

Almost certainly Jackson was drawing from Theodore Rothstein's *From Chartism to Labourism: Historical Sketches of the English Working Class Movement*. This had been published in 1929 as the second item in Martin Lawrence's 'Marxist Library' imprint, following Plekhanov's *Fundamental Problems of Marxism*. In his introduction to the 1983 reprint, Saville commented that *From Chartism to Labourism* had been neither widely reviewed nor especially well-received in 1929; and he speculated that, long out of print, it was effectively unknown to scholars before the late 1950s.[8] Saville himself, however, had first come across the volume in the 1930s, gaining, he said, a deal from it; and his *Ernest Jones: Chartist* gives some prominence to Rothstein and its bibliography of recommended modern works on Chartism is confined to him and just two other authors.[9] The recognition of Rothstein's work by both Jackson and Saville contrasts with the neglect of later Chartism in other pre-1950 Marxist scholarship.[10]

None of this early scholarship, even Rothstein's, offered a full evaluation of Chartism after 1848. Non-Marxist historiography offered nothing better.[11] In choosing to study Jones, Saville, by contrast, was able to explore the later phases of Chartism. His book has remained an important source of information on the movement in the 1850s, even as the interpretation of its subject has been superseded. This is partly because its bulk consists of selections from Jones' speeches and writing, with brief editorial introductions. The introduction proper makes a concerted case for taking seriously Jones, and likewise Chartism, during the years it operated as a pressure group rather than a mass movement. The young Saville saw these years as pivotal in the evolution of the labour movement due to its synergies with Marx's influence. That Jones should have accepted, towards the end of his life, a place in the Liberal sun somewhat discomfits this interpretation. Saville did not ignore it, citing Jones' acceptance of 'household suffrage, untrammelled and unfettered' alongside a eulogy to Gladstone and Bright. But to remember Jones in this way, Saville briskly claimed, is to present 'a distorted picture', over-emphasizing the 'end product' of a career during 'the greater part of which Jones rejected in uncompromising fashion, middle-class ideals and policies'.[12]

Saville was similarly brisk in addressing the abruptness of Jones' conversion to Chartism. The context, Saville recognized, was the collapse of Jones' finances and his failure to persuade the Anti-Corn Law League to support him in launching a newspaper. But ultimately, Saville thought '[i]t was not despair born of financial catastrophe that drove him into the Chartist ranks ... the world into which he was jolted by the necessity of having to earn a living was one in which a sensitive nature could not fail to be moved at the suffering and misery of so many of his fellow countrymen'. Even so, the sudden intensity of Jones' acceptance of the politics of class conflict could only 'without exaggeration, be called his conversion'.[13] Perhaps the unselfconscious religiosity of British communism at this time led the avowed atheist historian to believe he could understand Ernest Jones' behaviour. Jones' modern biographer is more cynical.[14]

If *Ernest Jones: Chartist* showed the limitations of Saville's historical method in explaining the intimate and personal, two other works from 1952 reveal the acuity of his approach to broad, structural issues. The first, a review of Cole and Filson's *British Working Class Movements: Select Documents, 1789-1875*, took issue with what Saville perceived as its stale assumptions about the inner life of Chartism and its consequences. Echoing Jones' tribute to O'Connor as the man above all others who had created and organized 'the democratic mind', Saville argued for O'Connor's decisive role in 'buttressing the confidence of the working men in their own power', and for the energizing contribution to this of his 'striking, polemical English' oratory and prose. 'The historian must not underestimate the effect of such things upon the morale of a political movement.'[15] Among historians of Chartism at the time Saville was unique, and remained so into the late 1970s, in his emphatic belief that 'it is time that O'Connor, with all his faults and with a proper recognition of his strength, was given careful analysis'.[16]

The review also noted in passing 'a most extraordinary bias and prejudice' on the part of the judiciary against the Chartist prisoners in 1848. Saville had not made this point anything like as forcibly in *Ernest Jones*. However, once he had completed the latter in December 1951, he turned to a major re-evaluation of 1848, the fruit of which was the second of his articles from 1952, appearing in Lawrence & Wishart's *Modern Quarterly*.[17] In this Saville attacked 'a theme which has become a commonplace in historical writing in this country, where the story of Chartism in 1848 is almost always the same account of fiasco and inglorious decline'. Saville's nuanced interpretation was to remain influential for three decades. He emphasized how first the media and then public opinion became fixated with the French Revolution of 1848, so that 'the identification between Chartist, rioter and foreign revolutionary was complete … Parallel with these developments went the consolidation and deployment of the coercive power of the State.' The leitmotiv of government policy was the avoidance of any precipitate clash which might inflame working-class opinion. In contrast to continental Europe, 'and here was the secret of its stability', the British government cultivated and retained the support of both the propertied classes and many others further down the social scale. In decline since 1842, and with its energies diverted into the Land Plan, Chartism according to Saville was 'half paralysed'. O'Connor's increasingly deficient leadership was especially significant here: for the first time since 1838 he unequivocally threw his weight 'upon the side of the right-wing moral force advocates', a development compounded in November by what Saville termed 'a violent swing to the right' which O'Connor warmly welcomed. The reference here was to a policy of concentrating on social rather than political issues, endorsed by an emergency congress in Birmingham as those leading Chartists not in prison wrestled to get the movement back on course.[18]

Subsequent historians have viewed 'the social turn' adopted at Birmingham more positively.[19] The central thrust of Saville's account of 1848, however, has proved far more enduring. The conclusion 'that Chartism collapsed into insignificance after the defeat of April 10th', he pointed out, 'has no basis in fact'. The late spring and summer of 1848 in Britain was marked by growing unrest, culminating in the exposure of a conspiracy in mid-August. What brought Chartism to a standstill, Saville argued, was extensive government use of spies and *agents provocateurs*, confident in the knowledge that judges and middle-class juries could be relied upon to convict Chartists once in court. Critical here was the Crown and Government Security Act pushed through Parliament after a first reading on the very evening of 10 April. The act created new offences of 'treason felony', for which the penalty was imprisonment or transportation for life, in place of the capital offences set out in the Treason Act of 1795. The latter made martyrs of the convicted, as the Whig government had discovered after the 1839 Newport Rising. Furthermore, the rights of prisoners accused of capital offences were more extensive than those charged only with felonies, and juries were more likely to convict where the death penalty did not apply. No less significantly, speech alone had not been deemed treasonable before the 1848 Act, but treated as a misdemeanour with relatively modest penalties. However, under the new act it became a 'treason felony' to 'compass, imagine, invent, devise, or intend' to levy war against the Crown, either by word or 'by open and advised Speaking'.[20]

Saville's realization that the gestation of this act and its application is pivotal to understanding 1848 in Britain was a major development. It is all the more significant when one realizes that the standard work on the legal history of the period confidently asserts that 'no one was charged in England' under the legislation.[21] Saville had now arrived, with a degree of rigour and detail unmatched in the earlier interpretations of Jackson and even Rothstein, at the conclusion all his subsequent work on Chartism would reiterate and expand: that 'the working class movement was opposed by a political strategy which combined apparent reasonableness and tact with a ruthlessness whose vigour was matched by an insistence upon victory to be achieved by any and all means possible'.[22]

A problem followed, however, from Saville's choice of a relatively obscure Marxist journal for the publication of this interpretation. Read and Glasgow's biography of O'Connor (1961) was oblivious to it; so too was F. C. Mather's *Public Order in the Age of the Chartists* (1959), a work Saville nonetheless declared 'invaluable' for its detailed research into authority's handling of Chartism.[23] The contributors to the seminal *Chartist Studies* collection of 1959, which in any case was stronger on earlier than on later Chartism, never cited it. A decade later, at a conference devoted to Chartism, Saville reiterated his interpretation of the movement's decline. He was particularly attacked for claiming 'Chartism was not only physically destroyed' but 'intellectually and spiritually annihilated'. He was reported to have characteristically 'made a spirited and unrepentant reply'. Significantly, however, the essence of his interpretation of 1848 went unchallenged. Indeed he reinforced it by also emphasizing the relevance to his argument of economic recovery from late 1848, both as a short-term explanation for the decline of the movement and as the motor for structural social shifts (principally, expansion in the number of skilled workers and the growth of consumer of cooperation) that were unconducive to Chartism's recovery.[24]

By the time of that conference Saville had consolidated his reputation as a historian of Chartism with an introductory essay to a new edition of the *History* that the second tier leader Robert Gammage had published in 1854. The essay was a *tour de force* which lay bare the shortcomings of Chartist historiography at the end of the 1960s.[25] On the specific issue of the movement in decline, Saville entered a more measured comment that 'it would not be wrong to speak of the submergence, in the national consciousness, of the Chartist movement' in the second half of the nineteenth century. This perception possibly stemmed from, and was certainly reinforced by, a remark of Engels in 1890 about the 'forty years winter sleep' of the English proletariat.[26]

To a significant extent, the force of Saville's thesis about 1848 at this stage depended upon his assertion concerning this 'submergence'. Yet it is in this very introduction, full of meticulously crafted, detailed footnotes, that the shortcomings of this assertion were perhaps most apparent. Almost every page contains references no serious student of Chartism, even now, can afford to ignore, many of them garnered from the years 1850-90. Footnote 73 alone encompasses references to 28 articles in *Newcastle Weekly Chronicle*, and thirteen other publications issued between 1857 and 1887. It is clear that Saville was beginning to rethink aspects of his interpretation of Chartism. He now freely admitted that *Ernest Jones, Chartist* was 'too narrow' in interpreting the decline of Chartism in largely economic terms. He now believed '[t]he explanation of Chartist decline must be sought in the total context of social and economic life'. Three years earlier, introducing the reprinted *Red Republican*, he had commented that '[e]xplanations of political defeat and decline which omit the role of human agency, or ignore the many factors which shape and mould social consciousness, are never likely to offer satisfactory conclusions'.[27]

The introduction to the Gammage reprint is also notable for a remarkably rounded account of the Chartist Land Plan, anticipating the turn in that organization's historiographical fortunes from the late 1980s.[28] Saville himself had not been exempt from the once customary dismissal of the Land Plan, deeming it 'Utopian' and 'unquestionably reactionary' in 1952.[29] However, 'I have come ... to be more sympathetic to the Land Plan than I was ten years ago,' he wrote in a 1961 contribution to the *Bulletin* of the Society for the Study of Labour History. This was a well-informed survey of the 'constant ferment of ideas and discussion about land questions and problems' that had both preceded the plan and survived it, and which helped explain the considerable interest with which the Chartist scheme was received. 'The Land Plan was certainly not bizarre', Saville concluded, 'it was a good deal less utopian than most of the millenial [sic] schemes of these years,' and it helped to hold Chartism together in the doldrums years of the mid-1840s: a point he acknowledged had earlier been made by Morton and Tate.[30]

Saville's earlier works had only touched on the land question.[31] However, his considerable command of the subject was again evident twelve months later in a critical bibliography, 'Henry George and the British Labour movement'.[32] These pieces emerged from a larger scale project which he never brought to fruition. David Martin has explained how while a postgraduate at Hull in the late 1960s, Saville 'passed to me some of his unpublished work on the land question and left the way open to me to follow an avenue of research that he might have taken himself'. From this there emerged both Martin's doctoral thesis and one of the 'Hull Occasional Papers' on Mill and the Land Question.[33] However these treated only a facet (albeit an important one) of a question that preoccupied radicals of all persuasions across the long nineteenth century. Enigmatically, *Strict Settlement: A Guide for Historians*, which Saville co-authored in 1983, remains his most substantial work on the land question. However, on its authors' own admission, it is 'not in any way concerned with its economic, social and political consequences'.[34] One senses that John Saville on the English Land Question was one of the great unwritten volumes of the second half of the twentieth century.[35] Only in 2010 was the subject brought at last into the compass of a single volume (and it took a team of fifteen authors to do it).[36]

In the context of his uncompleted projects it is also worth noting the cumulative significance of Saville's work on Owenism. In addition to providing an introduction to Robert Owen's *New View of Society*, he contributed to an important collection of essays published for Owen's bicentenary what remains the best account of the radical journalist and proto-syndicalist James Elishma Smith. And Saville's 1978 essay on Owenite thought concerning the family and marriage appeared 'ahead of the curve' of feminist historiography, published five years before Barbara Taylor's now standard treatment, *Eve and the New Jerusalem*.[37]

Clearly, by the 1970s John Saville was in a position to publish a major work on Chartism, equipped as he was with both a clear understanding of the trajectory of the movement as a whole, and a deep understanding of important contextual elements such as agrarianism and Owenite socialism. Indeed, in his autobiography he noted the book was 'ready to put together but this had to wait until my retirement [1982]'. Even then it would be another five years before *1848* was published. What deflected him in between were *Strict Settlement* and his new edition of Rothstein (both 1983); volumes 7 (1984) and 8 (1988) of the *Dictionary of Labour Biography*, plus the second volume of its French abridgement (1986); and substantial pieces for the *Socialist Register* on Bevin and the Cold War and on the British miners' strike of 1984-5. Having been, as he later recollected, 'much involved in the grassroots politics of this major confrontation', the strike itself cannot but have had a disruptive effect on Saville's academic work.[38] But it arguably also sharpened his perception of the operational realities of how the state handled unrest. As we have seen, he had long been impressed by the combination of apparent reasonableness and ruthlessness in the handling of Chartism in 1848. Reasonableness and tact were hardly the defining features of the response to the miners' strike. The experience of it appears to have sharpened Saville's rueful admiration of the effectiveness of Whig policy in 1848.

One ventures to suggest, therefore, that had it been published in the 1970s, *1848* would have been a very different book and a less powerful intervention in the historiography of either the British labour movement or of nineteenth-century Britain generally. But the events of 1984-5 are not the sole explanation for this. By 1987 the historiography of Chartism had reached something of an impasse. Since 1959, with the publication of the seminal collection *Chartist Studies* edited by Asa Briggs, the movement had been subjected to intense but often locally specific, highly empirical and under-theorized scrutiny. Saville himself summarized the situation thus:

Too much, I thought, was becoming antiquarian and insufficiently probing of the political structures within which the various social groups were located. In particular, it was the nature and ideology of the different ruling groups that was absent from too many accounts of historical change.[39]

However, three books forced John Saville to re-evaluate his interpretation of 1848. Each was a major addition to the historiography of Chartism and needs individual consideration. Saville declared he was 'especially grateful' for David Goodway's *London Chartism* (1982) which constituted the death-knell for the hoary old interpretation of 10 April and left the way clear for

Saville to concentrate upon his broader vision of the significance of 1848.[40] Goodway's meticulous reconstruction of metropolitan Chartism, which reached its considerable zenith in 1848, also flagged that the threat to the capital provided an ingredient that had been absent in the earlier crisis years of 1838-9 and 1842. Implicit, too, in Goodway's narrative was the importance of political espionage and *agents provocateurs* to the government.

The second key work influencing Saville's outlook was likewise published in 1982. Saville had not participated in the seminars in 1977 and 1978 that led to James Epstein and Dorothy Thompson's edited collection *The Chartist Experience*. One way of reading his *1848* is as a critique of the deficiencies of this volume, intended to set a new paradigm for Chartist studies. An extensive and fully integrated coverage of Ireland in 1848 is one of the great strengths of Saville's book. It is noticeable that the interconnectedness of Ireland with the fortunes of British radicalism in 1848 was not addressed by Thompson in her own contribution to the volume, despite its title 'Ireland and the Irish in English radicalism before 1850'. Indeed, she candidly observed, 'the full story of 1848 in England remains to be told'.[41]

Issues relating to 1848, however, were addressed in two of the volume's essays. Kate Tiller's case study of Halifax, 1847-58, confirmed the demoralizing impact of 'depleted leadership, threatened reprisals and waning support' by late 1848; but it also illustrated the frequently vital character of Chartism into the late 1850s at a local level, albeit within an overall context wherein 'the working-class movement [had] lost direction and is characterized by increasingly localized responses to different conditions and a breakdown of wider links'.[42] John Belchem's essay on 1848 itself leaned heavily on Saville's *Modern Quarterly* article to establish the over-arching context of press hostility to Chartism. However, it attacked Saville's argument that O'Connor's behaviour in 1848 constituted any kind of 'abnegation of leadership. Rather, it was the forceful assertion of a redirection of radical endeavour'. Belchem also took issue with Saville's claim there had been 'a violent swing to the right' that November. Rather, the emergency conference in Birmingham anticipated the inclusion of social democratic policies alongside parliamentary reform by the NCA in 1851, and was an important stage in the evolution of 'mid-Victorian "consensus and cohesion"'. Belchem also emphasized the continuing importance of O'Connor who 'remained the cynosure of the movement'. Although Belchem conceded 'the total failure of 1848' and never denied state policy was critical in determining its course, he somewhat diluted this emphasis by referring to 'the percipience' of the Whigs in 'overpowering a somewhat decrepit protest movement'. For Belchem, Chartism collapsed in

1848 because its defining strategy of the mass platform was unsuited to the circumstances of the time.[43]

The impact of Gareth Stedman Jones' contribution to the collection, 'Rethinking Chartism', was primarily felt through the extended version that appeared the next year in Stedman Jones' book *Languages of Class*.[44] This was the last of the trio that helped shape Saville's final appraisal of 1848. There was much about Stedman Jones' seminal study with which Saville doubtless identified. It made a powerful case that the plethora of local studies had atomized understanding of Chartism, obscuring both the movement's strengths and weaknesses; and it convincingly argued that, in the final analysis, Chartism was a political movement that cannot fully be understood or defined in terms of the disaffection of particular social groups. Jones also placed great emphasis upon the state's agency in containing and defeating Chartism. In the same year as Stedman Jones' book appeared, Saville in his edition of Rothstein's *From Chartism to Labourism* emphasized the emergence of the state's apparatus to contain proletarian dissent. This was the primary reason, Rothstein had argued, why Chartism took the form of a movement for parliamentary reform. In this Saville saw a strong resonance with Stedman Jones, specifically setting an extended quotation from him in parallel with one from Rothstein.[45]

Saville found in Rothstein an acute appreciation of the importance of state formation and its coercive capabilities and therefore an informed understanding of the critical importance of 1848. He found historians' failure to develop and extend Rothstein's analysis 'inexplicable'.[46] Despite the acuteness of Stedman Jones' arguments, one looks in vain for any such development or extension there. Saville's *1848* constituted an extended critique of 'Rethinking Chartism'. The most profound feature of 'Rethinking Chartism' was its seemingly authoritative dismissal of class consciousness as having any explanatory traction for the history of early Victorian Britain in general and Chartism in particular.[47] This was achieved by a detailed examination of the language of Chartism, through which Jones confronted the apparent exceptionalism of the movement. Chartism certainly appears exceptional, as the one epic and truly national mass agitation for electoral reform in modern Britain. It is questionable if even the early twentieth-century movement for women's suffrage approached Chartism in extent or potency. As Jones himself pointed out, though he was widely misinterpreted as arguing the opposite: 'Chartism could not have been a movement except of the working class, for the discontents which the movement addressed were overwhelmingly, if not exclusively, those of wage earners, and the solidarities upon which the movement counted were those between wage earners'.[48]

However, in analysing Chartism in relation to class and the languages by which class is understood, 'Rethinking Chartism' focused almost exclusively upon one linguistic trope, 'Old Corruption'. It therefore underplayed the potency that class analyses brought to the ideology of the movement, especially from 1842 onwards. This flaw was compounded by the relatively narrow range of contemporary references cited in the essay. Significantly more than half of Jones' citations of historical material *pre-date* 1838, while fewer than 15 per cent relate to the 1840s. The pivot of Stedman Jones' argument overall, however, was that reforms passed by Peel's government from 1841 fatally undermined the Chartist case for parliamentary reform. They demonstrated that Parliament was capable of passing legislation that was not in the selfish interests of MPs. Once Parliament ceased to behave corruptly, his argument runs, 'Old Corruption' lost its ideological force as a medium for critically analysing parliamentary politics and seeking reform of the legislature.

Saville emphasized there was little that was novel in the pivotal point of Stedman Jones' overall argument. Not only had Rothstein anticipated Stedman Jones' explanation for why Chartism took the form of a parliamentary reform movement; another British Marxist historian, Paul Richards, had recently argued that government policy in the 1840s marked a fundamental departure from the 'aggressive liberalism' of the previous decade.[49] However, Saville also questioned the efficacy of Richards' and Stedman Jones' explanation for the decline of Chartism by demonstrating that far from having become (as Stedman Jones believed) stale and anachronistic, Chartist rhetoric and the wider movement had recovered sufficiently from the doldrums of the mid-1840s to constitute a serious threat to the authority of the state. Furthermore in reaffirming the strength of the Chartists' continuing attachment to parliamentary reform, both as a principled objective and as the political means to socio-economic ends, Saville powerfully argued the movement was at heart class-conscious. More than that, he also argued that the actions of the state in 1848 exploded Stedman Jones' claims about 'the high moral tone of the proceedings of the government and the effective raising of the state above the dictates of the particular interests – whether landlords, financiers or manufacturers'.[50] In addition, he argued Jones had over-estimated the dominance of the ideological trope of 'Old Corruption' from the start, a failing Saville ascribed to Jones not consulting Noel Thompson's doctoral research on popular political economy.[51]

Saville predictably had little time for claims about 'the high moral tone' of the state in 1848:

What is missing from Stedman Jones' general thesis is the recognition that coercion is the other side of the government coin marked conciliation. If consent can be obtained without violence, so much the better; and the history of British domestic politics after 1850 is eloquent testimony to the success of hegemony in the sense used by Gramsci. But the 1840s came at the end of half a century of popular discontent and radical agitation … [I]t was not until 1848 itself that there was demonstrated, beyond question and doubt, the complete and solid support of the middling strata to the defence of existing institutions.[52]

Saville's *1848* both consolidated and built on the author's earlier work on Chartism. However, it also emphasized new lines of argument, for example about the potent intersection, in London especially, of British Chartists and Irish Confederates. For Saville, unrest in Ireland in 1848 was far wider and potentially more destabilizing than the fracas even he referred to as 'the abortive cabbage-patch rising'.[53] Critical to his interpretation was a perception that British domestic politics in 1848 could be comprehended only within the 'triangle of revolutionary Paris, insurgent Ireland, and a revitalised native Chartist movement in London and the industrial North'.[54] Thanks to Goodway's research, *1848* was stronger on London than it was on the industrial North; and of the Midlands, where the Chartist revival that year was manifestly weaker, the book was largely silent. At least one reviewer took Saville to task for his uneven narrative of Chartism's history in his chosen year. Yet the careful wording of his subtitle indicates the book is not a history of Chartism per se but rather an analysis of the British State in and through its treatment of the movement in 1848. Saville was emphatic that the political temperaments of localities and regions moved to their own rhythms, and these he did not pretend to describe, still less explain. He was no less emphatic, though, that Chartism's unique claim on the attention of the historian was that far more than any preceding political movement, 'it had a national leadership, with a national journal, to bind the parts of the movement together'.[55] It was as a threat to national security, not as a chain of localized disturbances, that the state dealt with Chartism in 1848.

It is in this context, especially given his 'visible and powerful' influence upon the movement's great newspaper *Northern Star*, that Feargus O'Connor is central to Saville's interpretation of Chartism. Given the absence in the 1980s of any sustained account of his life beyond 1842, the cumulative argument of *1848* was also important to understanding the strengths and failings of O'Connor. The rehabilitation of his reputation was a defining feature of Epstein's and Dorothy Thompson's work around this time. But

O'Connor's influence (for good or ill) upon Chartism in 1848 was an issue evaded by Epstein, whose biography of O'Connor terminated in the early 1840s. And it was only treatable in broad terms by Thompson in her general history of the movement.[56]

Without denying the importance of police agents in securing Chartist prosecutions in 1848, Saville's earlier stress on *agents provocateurs* now diminished, but his emphasis on the malevolent partiality of the legal system was if anything greater, not least because of his careful dissection of treason trials in Ireland. But the final way in which Saville's *1848* differs from the synoptic accounts he offered earlier in his career is in the contextualization of the state's impact upon working-class culture and politics in a longer perspective. In the book's 'commentary by way of a conclusion', Saville reiterated the longer term significance of economic growth during the 1850s in shaping the political attitudes of working people. He also stressed that '[i]t is not uncommon for radical historians to confuse party, or movement, with class'. Like E. P. Thompson, on whose 'Peculiarities of the English' his argument lent heavily at this point, Saville stressed the creation of mutual support movements by members of the working class, 'to counter the insecurities, the harshness and the exploitation of the capital order they inhabited'.[57] Saville believed this process was more deeply rooted by 1848 than Thompson (who saw it essentially as a phenomenon of the second half of the century). While it no way explained Chartism's defeat in 1848, in Saville's view it did help explain 'the apparent smoothness of the transition from the turbulent 1840s to the less disturbed fifties'.[58]

The smoothness of the transition was also assisted negatively, Saville suggested, by the failure of British radicalism to build on the achievements of the 'Smithian socialists' of the 1820s – primarily Thomas Hodgskin and William Thompson – and extend their intellectual challenge to the orthodoxies of industrial capitalism. Saville argued the steadily narrowing Owenite movement offered little to Chartism and his interest in James Elishma Smith, already noted, was as a potential heir to Hodgskin and Thompson's mantle. In *1848* he explicitly lamented how Smith 'shrug[ged] off his militant socialism without any apparent emotional or intellectual difficulty'. Later Saville (like Rothstein before him) would point to the need to understand James Bronterre O'Brien as the pivotal figure between the alternative political economy of the 1820s and late Chartism. However, *1848* barely mentions him.[59] Arguably this accurately reflects O'Brien's stature in both the year of revolutions and after. Saville concluded his digression on the cultural and intellectual factors reinforcing the state's victory over Chartism in 1848 with the observation that working-class radicalism after the 1850s lacked 'anything approaching a theory of capitalist exploitation – even something equivalent to the fuzzy analysis that that has served the greater part of the labour movement in the twentieth century'.[60]

That remark is no polemical aside. It underlines that for Saville the defeat of Chartism in 1848 mattered. It mattered not as a simple historical conundrum in need of explication but as a fundamental fracture, a point where history *did* actually turn – to reverse A. J. P. Taylor's dictum about the course of German history in 1848.[61] 'The great Chartist movement', Saville would recapitulate a few years later, 'was the greatest challenge the British State faced throughout the whole of the last two centuries'.[62] He saw its defeat as eclipsing in importance even the accommodation reached between the traditional landed political elite and the industrial and commercial bourgeoisie. Indeed the spectre of Chartism arguably sealed that accommodation. In Saville as a historian of Chartism we have a remarkable example of a muscular thinker, hammering out the essential framework of his interpretation at an early stage but then refining it over the course of nearly four decades. 'Spirited and unrepentant' in the face of new thinking when he thought it justified to be so, he nonetheless showed a refreshing preparedness to acknowledge where previously he had been mistaken. His approach to Chartism was rooted in his own lived experience as a political actor, and the account he has left is a powerful blend of structural economic and social analysis, with an unusual attentiveness to legal history and a deft deployment of cultural and intellectual insight.

Notes

1   *DLB*, vol. 6. His co-authors were A. L. Morton (Catherine and John Barmby); Naomi Reid (Thomas Clark); John Rowley and Eric Taylor (Arthur O'Neill).

2   *Red Republican & The Friend of the People*, (London, 1966), introduction, vol. 1, pp. i-xv; R. G. Gammage, *History of the Chartist movement, 1837-1854 ... Second edition, 1894*, (New York, 1969), 'Introduction: R. G. Gammage and the Chartist movement', pp. 5-65; W. E. Adams, *Memoirs of a Social Atom*, (New York, 1968), introduction pp. 5-26; T. Cooper, *The Life of Thomas Cooper*, (Leicester, 1971), introduction pp. 7-33.

3   E. Hobsbawm, 'The Historians Group of the Communist Party' in M. Cornforth, ed., *Rebels and their Causes: Essays in honour of A L Morton*, (London, 1978), pp. 21-48.

4   J. Saville, *Ernest Jones: Chartist; selections from the writings and speeches of Ernest Jones*, (London, 1952).

5   J. Saville, *Memoirs from the Left*, (London, 2003), pp. 77-8, 86.

6   D. Towers, 'The Chartist poets', and T. A. Jackson, 'Eighteen forty-eight', *Our Time*, April 1948, pp. 168-9 and 163-6.

7   Curiously the *Our Time* article is missing from the bibliography of Jackson's

writings appended to the *DLB* entry Saville co-authored with Jackson's daughter Vivien Morton in vol. 4.

8   J. Saville, 'Introduction' to T. Rothstein, *From Chartism to Labourism: Historical Sketches of the English Working Class Movement*, (London, 1983), p. xviii.

9   Saville, *Ernest Jones*, p. 280. The other two were G. D. H. Cole, *Chartist Portraits*, (London, 1941) and P. W. Slosson, *The Decline of the Chartist Movement*, (New York, 1916). For Saville's initial encounter with Rothstein, see his 'The Communist experience: a personal appraisal' in R. Miliband and L. Panitch, eds, *Communist Regimes: the Aftermath, Socialist Register 1991*, (London, 1991), p. 13.

10   R. Groves, *But We Shall Rise Again: A Narrative History of Chartism*, (London, 1938), pp. 171*ff*; A. L. Morton, *A People's History of England*, (London, 1938), pp. 425-6; S. A. Dutt, *When England Arose*, London, 1939 and *The Chartist Movement*, (London, [1944]), pp. 44-5; M. Morris, 'Chartism and the British working-class movement', *Science & Society*, 12:4 (1948), 415.

11   E. Dolléans, *Le Chartisme, 1831-1848*, (Paris, 1912) stops abruptly at April 1848; M. Hovell, *The Chartist Movement* (Manchester, 1918), and see above, chapter 2 ; J. West, *A History of the Chartist Movement* (London, 1920), pp. 258-93 is descriptive rather than analytical. Even Slosson, *Decline of the Chartist Movement*, by seeing Chartism as essentially doomed from its inception, offers little by way of analysis for the years from 1848.

12   Saville, *Ernest Jones*, pp. 81-2.

13   *Idem*, p. 17.

14   E.g. Jones 'did not so much cross the Rubicon as wander over the road', M. Taylor, *Ernest Jones, Chartism, and the Romance of Politics, 1819-1869* (Cambridge, 2003), p. 77. On the religious overtones of much of the internal life of the CPGB see R. Samuel, *The Lost World of British Communism* (London, 2006), esp. pp. 45-68.

15   'A note on the present position of working-class history', *Yorkshire Bulletin of Economic and Social Research* 4 (1952), 130.

16   Quotation from J. Saville, 'Labour movement historiography', *Universities and Left Review* 3 (winter 1958), 76. A rounded understanding of O'Connor is the hallmark of Dorothy Thompson's work and of those younger historians she influenced, but had to wait until her *The Early Chartists* (London, 1971) for its first iteration. Meanwhile, oblivious to Saville's work, D. Read and E. Glasgow produced their truly lamentable *Feargus O'Connor: Irishman and Chartist* (London, 1961).

17   'Chartism in the year of revolution, 1848', *Modern Quarterly* (winter 1952), pp. 23-33; also Saville, 'Labour movement historiography', p. 129; Saville, *Ernest Jones*, p. 10.

18   'Chartism in the year of revolution', pp. 23, 25-6, 32; Saville made the same point in his introduction to *Red Republican*, vol. 1, p. ix.

19   E.g. J. Belchem, '1848: Feargus O'Connor and the collapse of the mass platform', in J. Epstein and D. Thompson, eds, *The Chartist Experience: Studies in Working-Class Radicalism and Culture, 1830-1860* (London, 1982), pp. 301-

2; M. Chase, *Chartism: A New History* (Manchester, 2007), pp. 331-2.

20   'Chartism in the year of revolution, 1848', pp. 28, 30-31. Treason Felony Act (its modern name) as cited in L. Radzinowicz, *A History of English Criminal Law and its Administration from 1750: Volume 4, Grappling for Control* (London, 1968), p. 325.

21   L. Radzinowicz and R. Hood, *The Emergence of Penal Policy in Victorian and Edwardian England* (Oxford, 1990), p. 419, n52. For prosecutions in English courts under the Act see J. E. P. Wallis, *Reports of State Trials. New Series, Volume VII, 1848-50* (London, HMSO, 1896), cols 381-484, 1110-16 and 1127-30.

22   Saville, 'Chartism in the year of revolution, 1848', p. 33.

23   J. Saville, 'Introduction', to *Red Republican*, vol. 1, London, 1966, p. ix.

24   J. Saville, 'Some aspects of Chartism in decline', *Bulletin of the Society for the Study of Labour History* (henceforth *BSSLH*) 20 (1970), 16-18.

25   Saville, 'Introduction' to Gammage, pp. 5-65.

26   Saville, 'Introduction' to Gammage, p. 30, also pp. 45 and 47, citing Engels, 'The fourth of May in London' in Donna Torr, ed., *Karl Marx and Friedrich Engels: Correspondence 1846-1895* (London, 1934).

27   Saville, 'Introduction' to Gammage, pp. 44-5; *Red Republican*, introduction p. xiv.

28   Saville, 'Introduction' to Gammage, pp. 48-62. For the later historiography of the Land Plan see above chapters 4 and 5; J. Bronstein. *Land Reform and Working-class Experience in Britain and the United States, 1800-1862* (Stanford, CA, 1999).

29   Saville, 'Chartism in the year of revolution', p. 23; *Ernest Jones*, p. 24.

30   J. Saville, 'The Chartist Land Plan', *BSSLH* 3 (1961), 10-12. A. L. Morton and G. Tate, *The British Labour Movement, 1750-1920* (London, 1956), p. 95.

31   Saville, *Ernest Jones*, pp. 45, 152; 'Labour movement historiography', p. 73.

32   J. Saville, 'Henry George and the British labour movement: a select bibliography with commentary' *BSSLH* 5 (1962), 18-26.

33   D. Martin, *John Stuart Mill and the Land Question*, University of Hull Occasional Papers in Economic and Social History, 9 (1981), p. i.

34   J. Saville and B. English, *Strict Settlement: A Guide for Historians*, University of Hull Occasional Papers in Economic and Social History, 10 (1983), 5.

35   For an indication of what might have been, in addition to the *BSSLH* contributions cited above, see Saville's entries on Robert Outhwaite, William Saunders and Frederick Verinder in *DLB*, vol. 8. With characteristic disregard for his own writing commitments, John set work to one side on *1848* to write these, to complement the entries by the present author on earlier land reformers that appear in the same volume.

36   M. Cragoe and P. Readman, eds, *The Land Question in Britain, 1750-1950* (Basingstoke, 2010).

37   R. Owen, *A New View of Society ... with an introduction by John Saville* (London, 1972); J. Saville, 'J. E. Smith and the Owenite movement, 1833-34' in S. Pollard and J. Salt, eds, *Robert Owen: Prophet of the Poor* (London, 1971), pp. 115-44; Saville, 'Robert Owen on the family and the marriage system of the

old unmoral world', in Cornforth, *Rebels and their causes*, pp. 107-21.

38   Saville, *Memoirs from the Left*, pp. 161 and 175.

39   Saville, *Memoirs from the Left*, p. 180.

40   D. Goodway, *London Chartism: 1838–1848* (Cambridge, 1982).

41   Epstein and Thompson, *Chartist Experience*; quotation from Thompson, 'Ireland and the Irish in English radicalism before 1850', p. 142.

42   K. Tiller, 'Late Chartism: Halifax, 1847-58', *Chartist Experience*, pp. 317 and 341.

43   Belchem, '1848: Feargus O'Connor and the collapse of the mass platform', *Chartist Experience*, pp. 275-6, 301, 303 and 280-1.

44   G. Stedman Jones, 'The language of Chartism', *Chartist Experience*, pp1-58; G. Stedman Jones, 'Rethinking Chartism', in his *Languages of Class: Studies in English Working-Class History, 1832–1982* (Cambridge, 1982), pp. 90–178.

45   Saville, 'Introduction' to Rothstein, pp. xx-xxi.

46   Saville, 'Introduction' to Rothstein, p. xxiii. Rothstein had devoted a forty-page appendix to analysing 1848 in England, in addition to the treatment in his main text.

47   The analysis in this and the following paragraph draws on M. Chase and J. Allen, 'Great Britain, 1750-1900' in J. Allen, A. Campbell and J. McIlroy, eds, *Histories of Labour: National and Transnational Perspectives* (Pontypool, 2010), pp. 72-5.

48   Jones, 'Rethinking Chartism', p. 95.

49   Saville, *1848*, pp. 217-18, citing P. Richards, 'State formation and class struggle, 1832-48', in P. Corrigan, ed., *Capitalism, State Formation and Marxist Theory* (London, 1980).

50   Saville, *1848*, p. 219; and see Stedman Jones, 'Rethinking Chartism', p. 177.

51   Saville, *1848*, pp. 214-15 and 280n7, citing N. Thompson, *The People's Science: The Popular Political Economy of Exploitation and Crisis, 1816-34* (Cambridge, 1984).

52   Saville, *1848*, p. 220.

53   Saville, *1848*, p. 39.

54   Saville, *1848*, p. 1.

55   D. Thompson, review in *History Workshop Journal* 28 (1989), 160-6; Saville, *1848*, p. 212, cf. 207.

56   J. Epstein, *The Lion of Freedom: Feargus O'Connor and the Chartist Movement, 1837-42* (London, 1982) and D. Thompson, *The Chartists: Popular Politics in the Industrial Revolution* (London, 1984). P. A. Pickering, *Feargus O'Connor: A Political Life* (Monmouth, 2008) has since gone some way to address the limitations of Epstein's focus on the early years of Chartism.

57   E. P. Thompson, 'The peculiarities of the English' (1965), revised edition in his *The Poverty of Theory and other Essays* (Woodbridge, 1978).

58   Saville, *1848*, p. 211.

59   See his call for 'a modern analysis of Bronterre O'Brien' in 'The crisis in labour history: a further comment', *Labour History Review* 61:3 (1996), 327; and compare 'Introduction' to Rothstein, p. xxii, where Saville comments O'Brien was 'Rothstein's especial hero'.

60   Saville, *1848*, p. 216.
61   A. J. P. Taylor, *The Course of German History* (London, 2001), p. 67.
62   J. Saville, *The Consolidation of the Capitalist State, 1800-1850* (London, 1994),
     p. 69.

10

'RESOLVED IN DEFIANCE OF FOOL AND OF KNAVE'?: CHARTISM, CHILDREN AND CONFLICT

One Sunday morning in 1848, when I was barely nine years old, on coming home from chapel I saw two men washing the blood off their heads and faces at the pump opposite our house in Haggerston. I asked my father who had done this, and he replied that the police had beaten them at a meeting in the 'the Ruins' (now known as Columbia Gardens), because they had held a meeting to demand the vote. He explained as simply as he could what a vote meant. Then I asked him if he had a vote, and he replied 'No', he being then a compound householder, whose rates were directly paid by the landlord of the house. My father was to me then the perfection of wisdom and goodness; so I said, 'What do you call these men?' He replied, 'Chartists'. I at once said, 'Then I am a Chartist.' That was my first object lesson in politics.[1]

Howard Evans, author of the above account, grew up in a terraced house, in the shadow of a gasworks in Haggerston Lane, East London. His recollections almost certainly relate to Sunday 4 June 1848, the morning of which saw a series of running battles across Bethnal Green between, on the one hand the Metropolitan Police, and on the other Chartists and Irish Confederates. Later that evening, violence broke out again on a wider scale, 'an indiscriminate, wanton, unhuman, and brutal attack was made upon Men, Women, and Children by the Police not only in the Field where the Meeting was held but in all the various Localities for near a Mile around', according to one of many letters of protest lodged by residents of the area.[2]

Uniquely among Victorian political movements, Chartism placed children and youth at the forefront of its conflict against forces opposed to reform. Within a broader defence of its particular vision of the working-class family, Chartists both mobilized to defend childhood and frequently located it at the centre of a conflict with the economic and political establishment. Neither historians of Chartism nor childhood have, however, given much thought to this phenomenon.[3] Only the practice of dedicated Chartists naming their children after prominent figures in the movement is routinely noted in studies of Chartism. All too often, historians have allowed the humorous aspects of this practice to deflect attention from the substance of what it meant to grow up in a Chartist household: for who can resist smiling at the thought of Fanny Amelia Lucy Ann Rebecca Frost O'Connor McDouall Leach Holberry Duffy Oastler Hill Boden, whose birth was registered at Birmingham in 1842?[4] The naming of children after radical heroes was no novelty – Henry Hunt was a popular choice earlier in the century – but it required nerve on the part of parents and the act of naming potentially thrust the newborn infant into a situation of conflict: 'I suppose they want the child hanged', the vicar of Selby told the congregation at the baptism of little Feargus O'Connor Mabbot. The vicar of Sowerby, near Halifax, disputed the choice of Feargus O'Connor Vincent Bronterre for one child. When the parents held firm, he retained the baby after baptism to say additional prayers over it.[5] Even Civil Registrars were not above arguing with parents who sought to register 'a young patriot'.[6] Nor was life necessarily plain sailing for the child afterwards. Feargus O'Connor Holmes, born in 1842 the son of two Keighley woolcombers, went through school referred to only as 'F' by a master who refused to let such names pollute his lips. He toughed it out, however, and still gave his full name to the enumerator of the 1901 Census, by which time he was a worsted machine maker, and still living in Keighley.[7]

However, the overwhelming majority of Chartist parents resisted such adulatory gestures as the Mabbots or Holmes. Around 3¼ million people signed the Chartist petition of 1842 but judging by the 1851 Census, fewer than 500 English or Welsh couples named their child after Feargus O'Connor.[8] Furthermore, the concentration of historiographical attention on this phenomenon has perpetuated a view of children within Chartism as essentially passive objects, serving only to signify the political convictions of their parents. For some children, as we shall see, this was certainly the case. However this chapter explores the broader implications of the central position children assumed within Chartist rhetoric and associational activity, tracing its implications both for the role of women within the movement, and for the stress Chartism placed on the integrity of the family in the face of the destructive forces of industrialization. This was a recurrent theme in Chartist rhetoric and it connected closely to the ideal of the male breadwinner, the defence of which was central to Chartism's broader social objectives, increasingly so in the mid-1840s.

Critics of Chartism tended to see the presence of youths and children at

Chartist demonstrations as compelling evidence that the movement lacked seriousness of purpose or solid support.[9] In 1839 the patriotic Sheffield dialect poet 'Dame Flatback' attacked so-called physical force Chartists for recruiting 'prentis lads into yer regiment' – a generalization that proved spectacularly wide of the mark when, just weeks later, plans for a Sheffield rising were exposed. For the Sheffield conspirators – like the overwhelming majority of Chartists receiving custodial sentences nationally in 1839-41 – were not the ill-disciplined youths of popular imagination but older men, usually married, with a median age of 31 and of whom 62 per cent had dependent children.[10] Few hostile press reports of Chartist meetings, however, could resist diminishing their importance by stressing that youths were present in large numbers. The frequency with which such comments embraced young people of both genders may well have derived from a particular wish to denigrate the movement; but it also reflected the wide communal basis for Chartism. Thus at Whitsuntide 1848, the *Manchester Guardian* commented that '[i]n Stockport, the numbers who attended were insignificant, and the great majority were boys and girls, actuated by a thoughtless love of mischief [rather] than by political feelings'.[11]

To what extent might children's participation in Chartism have been actuated by political feelings; and was their attendance at meetings in large numbers (where it occurred, as opposed to being claimed by hostile critics to belittle the movement) ever a conscious decision? Whether their motivation derived primarily from themselves or was learnt, or even imposed, by their parents is difficult to discern, though it will be argued shortly that a rare surviving Chartist sampler is suggestive of at least one child expressing political opinions largely independently of direct adult intervention. More conventional evidence than needlework, however, does yield a number of examples of children who reacted sympathetically to Chartism independently of parental influence. For example Charles Bradlaugh, the great radical and freethinking controversialist of the second half of the nineteenth century, dated his political conversion to 1843-44. Aged ten and living in Hackney, he was inspired by the conversation of an elderly Chartist to buy a copy of *The People's Charter* for a halfpenny.[12] In Nottingham, the thirteen-year old William Booth (later founder of the Salvation Army) experienced the first stirrings that led to his religious conversion, a process that began – he freely admitted to W. T. Stead – from listening not to hellfire sermons but to the impassioned oratory of Feargus O'Connor: '"The Chartists were for the poor," so the boy reasoned, "therefore I am for the Chartists"'.[13] In 1838 in Bingley, West Yorkshire, 'a man lent me his paper when it was a week old for a penny', recalled Thomas

Wood, a sixteen-year old apprentice mechanic at the time, 'I giving him the paper back when I had had it a week'.[14] In 1846, when O'Connor opened the Ancoats' People's Institute, seventeen-year old William Chadwick had to be called to order by the chairman for a speech from the floor in which he declared 'the blow should be struck and the tyrants upset that very night'. Thus too did William upstage his younger brother Richard, who merely recited a poem he had written honouring O'Connor: '... the bright flag of Liberty shall shed, / Its heavenly signal over the patriot's head'.[15]

More typically, children were led to Chartism as part of the natural process of growing up in a politicized household. 'My father frequently took me to Radical meetings', Howard Evans remembered, 'where I listened to Ernest Jones, George Thompson, Edward Miall, Henry Richard and Henry Vincent.'[16] Evans' participation in politics was primarily as a spectator, and the mention of Miall, Thompson and Vincent signals that his father's Chartism was very much in the constitutional tradition of agitation. However, there are several recorded examples of lads in their late teens serving as officers in local National Charter Association (NCA) branches: for example William Chadwick, the seventeen-year old Ancoats hothead, had matured into the corresponding secretary of the Manchester Chartists less than two years later. At a similar age Henry Clubb of Colchester combined the secretaryship of both the town's NCA and Land Plan branches.[17] Other households, especially in the early years of the movement, propelled children into more combative roles. For example at Lye Waste (a squatters' settlement comprised mainly of nail makers and their families) near Stourbridge, children were widely employed in the summer of 1839 making 'craws' feet' or caltrops (a spiked iron ball that, when thrown to the ground, disabled cavalry horses).[18]

More prosaically, there are numerous accounts in later Victorian working-class autobiographies of children who had some schooling being enlisted to read Chartist newspapers to adults. 'Before I entered my teens I was a sympathetic Chartist, and early in my life read with avidity the pages of the "Northern Star"', wrote Joseph Kavanagh of Barnsley, the son of immigrant Irish linen weavers. He recalled how, in March 1848:

One Sunday night I read, for a houseful of listeners, ten columns of the proceedings on the banks of the Seine which culminated in the deposition and flight of Louis Philippe, king of the French. Of course the Chartists in England and the Young Irish Repealers in the sister isle were jubilant, for they nursed the delusion that the revolutionary waves would soon beat up against the White Cliffs of Dover.[19]

Another youngster, Ben Grime of Oldham, purchased the paper every Saturday to read aloud to his father and neighbours over 'a tot of whoam-brewed'.[20] A teenage handloom velvet weaver from Failsworth, Lancashire, recollected that the *Star* was 'subscribed for by my father and five others. Every Sunday morning these subscribers met at our house to hear what prospect there was of the expected "smash-up" taking place. It was my task to read aloud so that all could hear at the same time'.[21]

The political education of some Chartists' children was more dramatic. Referring to Thomas Paine's *Rights of Man* (1789-92), a Birmingham journeyman silversmith told an open air meeting in November 1839 that 'he intended for his children to learn the whole of it and if they did not he would give them a jolly good thrashing'.[22] This statement was probably alehouse rhetoric. But it underlines that children were far from being autonomous subjects in the eyes of many working people, especially perhaps their fathers. Working-class males made a significant emotional investment in their children, one that was increasingly evident through their commitment to the ideal of the male breadwinner. Indeed, the ideal of the male breadwinner increased during the early nineteenth century, as the status of many male wage earners *outside* their families diminished through the erosion of their command in the labour market, their independence as producers, and their capacity to exercise discretion and control over the work process.

Within that context, attachment to the notion that a husband's primary role was that of provider for their whole family had considerable appeal. (It also helped rationalize male workers' hostility to female intrusion into masculine workspace.) The timing of the main three surges of support for Chartism paralleled downturns in the economy, when unemployment and wage cuts hit the family economy of the working class. The significance of this was vividly apparent in powerloom weaver Richard Pilling's explanation for his leading role in the 'general strike' of 1842. For three weeks, at rally after rally across Lancashire, Pilling urged workers to strike 'for a fair day's wage for a fair day's work, and until the Charter becomes the law of the land'. Defending himself at his subsequent trial, Pilling spoke of fathers carrying babies to the cotton mills to be suckled by their wives at meal times, of the sexual harassment of women on the factory floor, and of his own feelings of injured masculinity:

> I have ... a good wife – a dear wife – a wife that I love and cherish, and I have done everything that I could in the way of resisting reductions in wages, that I might keep her and my children from the workhouse, for

I detest parish relief. It is wages that I want. I want to be independent of every man, and that is the principle of every honest Englishman; and I hope it is the principle of every man in this court.[23]

Child rearing then, was not just a biological or personal and emotional process, it was a political act. Chartist parents took pride in raising their children to share in their principles. Salford carpenter Reginald Richardson wrote from gaol in 1840 that 'detestable faction ... never can destroy, except with my life, the firm and deep-rooted hatred that animates my bosom. My children, like young Hannibals, shall be trained to hate my persecutors, so that for one martyr the Whigs make of me, I will leave FOUR SONS trained to my principles.'[24] The leading Baptist divine of Edwardian England, John Clifford (born 1836) recollected, 'I was brought up to admire Will Lovett ... and to detest Feargus O'Connor as a wild demagogue'.[25] There was nothing novel about Chartist parents radicalizing their children: interviewed by a prison inspector in 1841, Chartist Isaac Johnson blamed his lack of formal education on the fact that he was expelled from school 'at Peterloo time', for wearing at his father's insistence a white hat – the badge of the Regency ultra-radical.[26]

Children were naturally at the heart of the educational initiatives many branches developed. Almost two-fifths of Lovett and Collins' seminal 1840 book *Chartism: A New Organisation of the People*, is actually about children's education; and the *Gazette of the Working Men's Association*, with which Lovett was closely associated, even went so far as to have a children's column.[27] Chartist culture in this respect contrasted sharply with the middle-class anti-Corn Law agitation, but it had much in common with Owenite socialism.[28] Owen's views on the formation of character naturally led to an emphasis upon children's education and their participation within the cultural life of the community. Lovett, who had originally entered radical politics through Owenism, remained convinced that nurture, not nature, shaped children's character and intellect. A clumsy generalization within early Chartist historiography was that education was mainly the preoccupation of Lovett and his circle, and not O'Connor's.[29] However, education for all age groups was emphatically at the heart of the O'Connorite Chartist project. The influence of religious nonconformity infused Chartism's educational initiatives and Chartist Sunday schools were commonplace, in many localities along with day schools. These might be situated in a Chartist Hall or institute (as at Stalybridge for example) or more typically in the home of a Chartist activist, as at Bethnal Green, where Elizabeth Neesom ran a school in the room behind the radical newsagency run by her husband Charles, one of the leading teetotal Chartists.[30] Neesom was the author of one of the most trenchant arguments for a distinctively Chartist education, embedded within the *Address* of the female Chartist total abstinence group, of which she was the prime mover. In it she urged her fellow female Chartists to 'secure a sound and proper education for our children, in accordance with our views and feelings', adding:

> Depend upon this fact, the charity and policy badge of national schools, is the remnant of the ancient Saxon serf's collar. Why should our feelings be wounded by seeing the finger of scorn pointed at our children, and the sad appellation of 'charity brat' applied to them? A well-regulated mind disdains servility and cringing. Let us reject their Church and State offers of education for our children, which is only calculated to debase the mind, and render it subservient to class interest; let us teach our offspring to do unto others as they would others should do unto them.[31]

Opportunities for self-directed education were seen as an important factor in the struggle to reform society. Such was the social and political gulf between Chartists and their social 'betters', there was widespread suspicion of initiatives designed by others to 'improve' workers and their children. Reports of Chartist schools uniformly stressed that they were autonomous: for example the 'Democratic Sunday School' in Thwaites, west Yorkshire, proclaimed it was 'the people's own', 'their little commonwealth' and 'entirely of the labouring class'.[32] These were powerful attractions even in Scotland, where provision of publicly funded education was more generous and carried little stigma. 'Let us, therefore, send all our juveniles to their [i.e. Chartist] schools', the *True Scotsman* argued, 'and not to any of the rotten old regime.'[33] Choosing a Chartist schooling was therefore an overtly political act on the part of the parents. It placed the child in a potentially conflictual situation both because the political content of Chartist curricula met with establishment hostility, and because young Chartists were expected to understand and assert their rights. 'The minds of all children naturally incline to *good*', Sophia, a Birmingham Chartist, argued. 'Children *should* ask questions, they have a *right* to do so', she continued, adding 'Children are much more acute observers than they are generally supposed … Let us, as Chartist women and mothers, instruct and encourage each other, that our children shall be better informed of their rights as citizens.'[34] The corollary of this stance was that the Chartist educational project was held to reside as much in the home as in formally organized schools. Henry Vincent, a charismatic orator with an extensive following in western England and South Wales, addressed the women of this region thus:

So long as our rulers could persuade women they had nothing to do with politics, the present unjust system was bound to continue. The tyrants knew that all the children would grow up slaves; but now that women think for themselves, the tyrants feel their end approaching! Talk of putting down the Chartists, forssoth, why every kitchen is now a *political meeting house*; the little children are members of the unions, and the good mother is the political teacher … [C]hildren will suck in Radicalism with their mothers'-milk.[35]

Some Chartist localities went so far as to establish separate branch organizations specifically for young people. The constitution of the National Charter Association tacitly encouraged the recruitment of all ages.[36] Young people's associations were particularly evident in 1842, the peak popular community-based mobilization for the Charter. Examples include the Bristol Young Men's Charter Association, Dundee Youths' Democratic Charter Association, Sheffield Chartist Youth Association, the Salford Juvenile Chartists and the Stockport Youth Association, described as 'in connection' with the local branch of the NCA. 'The Stockport Youths are resolved to extend the association of young men into every town of the County of Chester', the *Northern Star's* local correspondent reported.[37] These juvenile associations imitated the organizational and cultural forms of NCA localities, in order both to strengthen the sense of solidarity among their members as young Chartists and to make visible Chartism's assault upon conventional definitions of political personhood. Thus in June 1843 the Manchester Youths' Charter Association organized the funeral of one of its number at the Ancoats Bible Christian Chapel. A band played the dead march as the cortege wound its way round the monument to Henry Hunt in the Chapel grounds and after several orations proceedings concluded with the singing of the Marseillaise and a wake, fuelled by tea, in the Ancoats' Chartist rooms.[38]

The participation of children in Chartist demonstrations was everywhere apparent and, occasionally, even demanded by the movement's leaders. For example the Nottingham NCA, in organizing O'Connor's visit to the town in February 1842, circulated extensive details of his processional route and instructed the 'Men & Women of Nottingham!! DO YOUR DUTY, Prepare Flags for your Children, and let us have a glorious demonstration'.[39] Prepare they did and the *Nottingham Review* duly reported that a large number of children processed with these flags en masse, behind a brass band and in front of portraits of O'Connor, the factory reformer Richard Oastler and the United Irish hero Robert Emmet.[40] The general strike later that year affords further examples of children's concerted participation in public demonstrations: 'the first day the mills were stopped, a body of five-hundred girls, belonging to the dissenting Sunday-schools at Oldham, marched at the head of the rioters, singing their school-hymns'.[41]

Chartism was at heart a constitutional agitation, exemplified in the three great petitions presented by the movement to Parliament in 1839, 1842 and 1848. At its heart was *The People's Charter*, and each petition was presented not from the movement, nor its constituent members, but from 'the People', 'the industrious classes'. The addition of children's names to Chartist petitions was encouraged and this was done not clandestinely but openly. It is debatable whether the Chartists ever truly believed that petitioning would succeed. Rather, it had a totemic significance as the righteous expression of a people's will and the people in this context was frequently construed to include children of all ages. 'Silence them, give it to them: let every man, woman and child sign the Petition; disarm all your enemies at once', declared Feargus O'Connor in 1839. 'Go on, good men! Go on, virtuous women! Go on little children! We are engaged in the cause of justice, which is the cause of God. *Sign the Petition. It is the last, the very last.*'[42] During the 1848 controversy over the integrity of the third Chartist petition, the Rector of Alfreton, Derbyshire wrote to the Home Secretary that one of his parishioners, whose name was recorded on the petition, was an infant just three weeks old.[43] The admission of children to the ranks of a people seeking redress was simply another facet of the Chartist redefinition of what constituted the political nation. Some Chartists, for example the Scot John La Mont, argued for the further 'extension of the Suffrage to sane minded males of 18 years of age, instead of 21, already provided by our Charter; and the enfranchisement of females – notwithstanding the amount of blackguardism, folly and coercion which will be arrayed against this extension by the aristocratic *debauchés*'.[44] To seek to legitimate youths' and women's political voices was thus to intensify Chartism's challenge to unrepresentative old corruption.

What did children's participation in Chartism mean, especially given that the movement's greatest leader, Feargus O'Connor, was apt to characterize his adult followers as 'my children'? Did Chartism privilege childhood or, perhaps, efface much of its distinctiveness from adulthood? Can we tell if children were themselves 'resolved in defiance of fool and of knave'? This is the verse worked into a needlework sampler around 1847 by Ann Dawson, born 1842:

Britannia's the land where fell slavery's chain
Had bound fast its victims in hunger and pain
Where no eye would pity, when no hand would save
Then came forth to break it o connor the brave
A band of brave fellows, whose hearts caught
The sound arose from their slumbers and
Rallied around resolved in defiance of fool
And of Knave for freedom to fight with
O Connor the brave for
The Charter and No Sorender [45]

Ann was the daughter of Isaac Dawson, a journeyman baker and NCA activist from Droylsden, east Lancashire, and his wife Hannah.[46] Hannah, Ann's brother and her older sister Betty were all card room operatives, employed in the mills in the tedious, dust-ridden drudgery of preparing cotton fibres for spinning. Their family of seven had to supplement its income by taking in three factory weavers as lodgers. Despite their precarious economic situation, Ann Dawson, her sister and two of her three brothers were all enrolled by their parents in the Chartist Land Plan. The enrolment of children in the plan was not uncommon, though few families' incomes stretched to enrolling four. This was a sizeable financial investment. Momentarily, we are afforded a very human glimpse of the aspirations of a grassroots Chartist family. Ann's sampler is one of the most affecting, and certainly most colourful, material remnants of Chartism. Naivety of execution combines with vibrancy of colour to create an impression at once youthful and sunny, elegiac and optimistic. Ann's needlework, depicting the O'Connorville schoolhouse, is a vivid reminder that Chartism embraced men, women and all ages, and at its heart was a profound commitment to education and self-improvement. But this commitment does not translate into political quietism: far from it, for an allegiance to O'Connor's uncompromising commitment to the politics of the mass platform is the sampler's central poetic statement.

One of the great attractions of O'Connor's Land Plan was that it appeared to offer both a practical means to end children's employment in factories and reinstate the mother at the heart of domestic life. Both the rhetoric of the plan and the geography of its settlements contrasted sharply with those of early Victorian socialism. Communal living was at the heart of the Owenite vision; but the Chartist colonies comprised isolated cottages (wherein the kitchen was the largest room), each situated within an individual landholding.[47] O'Connor's vision, however, resonated powerfully with the factory reform movement, which consistently argued that the employment of women outside the home inverted the 'natural' order. If the Dawsons were among the Lancashire pilgrims to the opening of the Land Plan's first colony on May Day 1847, they would have heard O'Connor warm to this theme in a speech delivered in the schoolhouse itself. 'I have brought you out of the land of Egypt, and out of the house of bondage', he declared, 'this is a portion of the great feature of my plan to give the fond wife back to her husband, and the innocent babe back to its fond mother ... Let the father nourish, and the fond mother nurture, their own offspring (cheers) and then we shall have a generation of FREE CHRISTIANS.'[48] O'Connor's sentiments on this occasion, as so often, show how powerful the idea of independence was among Chartists, independence from the caprice of undemocratic government and a state church, and from industrialism's 'house of bondage'. The key to his popularity as a Chartist leader, especially in the Pennine textile districts, was his capacity to reflect back to his audience and readers their own perceptions of their place in society and their aspirations to improve it. Casting his audience in the role of Israel was a shrewd rhetorical device. Though religion meant little to O'Connor, he well knew how close it lay to the heart of popular radical feeling: In the sampler this is vividly conveyed by the bible and anchor, recalling the words of St Paul: 'hope we have as an anchor of the soul, both sure and steadfast'. For Ann Dawson and her family the concept probably also resonated with the words of Benjamin Stott, a Chartist poet from nearby Middleton:

Lift up your faces from the dust,
Your cause is holy, pure and just;
In Freedom's God put all your trust,
Be he your hope and anchor.[49]

Ann Dawson's is the only known Chartist sampler. Thousands of other nineteenth-century samplers survive, typically worked with exacting precision and often expressing sententious or religious sentiments that lead almost inevitably to the conclusion that they were accomplished only under close adult supervision. Ann Dawson's work, however, has a subversive quality, for several reasons. Firstly, the expression of overt political sentiment in samplers is extremely rare; the inclusion even of secular verse is atypical.[50] The increasing prominence during the later eighteenth and nineteenth centuries of improving verse, in a genre that had formerly been confined to the depiction of stylized icons and abstract decoration, has been seen by feminist textile scholars as inculcating profoundly patriarchal ideals of femininity.[51] The verse Ann Dawson chose, however, is certainly not 'improving' in any conventional sense. Although its dedication to O'Connor clearly reflects the patriarchal nature of authority within the Chartist movement, the overall effect is equally indicative of the key role played by mothers and other older women in working-class households in the politicization of children.

Ann's Dawson's handiwork, however, is also subversive in terms of technique as well as content. By the 1840s samplers worked by working-class children tended to be highly stylized. Teaching embroidery to the poor gathered momentum in the late eighteenth and nineteenth centuries. Books were published setting out how this should be done and needlework became a major component of the curriculum of both secular and religiously organized schools. One consequence was a marked move away from spontaneity, ornament and variety of colour as samplers typically came to be dominated by cross-stitched alphabetical and numerical sequences and tended to the monochromatic. By contrast, the work of Ann Dawson decidedly does not exhibit the order and precision of the overwhelming majority of Victorian samplers. For example, from the fifth line she loses sight of the structure of her verse and submerges its rhymes.[52] This is suggestive of something natural and unforced rather than the regimented presentation of school work based on a copybook or teacher's worked example. It is also riotously colourful and situates its political verse amidst stylized elements typical of earlier centuries which had become uncommon in the Victorian period.

No other Victorian social movement posed so extensive or searching questions to the social or political establishment of its day as did Chartism. We may conceptualize its activities as constituting a multiplicity of sites of conflict; and this generalization extends even to the ostensibly more innocuous activities of education and self-improvement in which children were quite naturally involved. The active participation of children is evident across the whole spectrum of Chartist opinion, 'physical' and 'moral' force, those who idolized Feargus O'Connor and those who felt most comfortable with the artisan intelligentsia typified by William Lovett. Children's involvement in Chartism extended far beyond its educational initiatives. They were consistently participants in virtually all Chartist political and cultural activities short of conspiracy and insurrection. Even here some Chartists suggested children should potentially be mobilized if peaceful resistance to tyranny failed: 'let the women take the scissors, the child the pin or needle',[53] Joseph Rayner Stephens declaimed; and there were examples – as at Lye Waste in 1839, quoted earlier – of children actively preparing weaponry.

A more rounded appreciation of the role of children within Chartism may help us to understand more fully the political work that issues of gender and patriarchy undertook within the movement. Female Chartists emphasized their role as educators in order to reinforce their own claims to participate in the political arena: 'Mothers, claim the Rights of your children' a banner unfurled at an early Chartist rally declared.[54] The involvement of children often stemmed from the initiative of their parents, but it could be autonomous and even spontaneous. Children's participation reflected Chartist notions of active citizenship, a concept that, although with increasingly emphatic gender distinction, embraced both males and females. Chartism also privileged childhood through its emphasis upon a particular version of the domestic ideal and the integrity of the working-class family in the face of the corrosive effects of industrialism. However, while it fought to preserve the distinctiveness of childhood that the employment of children outside the family unit eroded, Chartism's politicization of children arguably diminished distinctions between children and adults. For Anglican reformers, such as the contributors to John Sinclair's study of the causation of the 1842 strike wave, the politicization of the family provided compelling evidence of the need to expand provision of education by the establishment.[55] The family and childhood were not merely among those things male Chartists mobilized to defend: they were themselves primary locations of Chartist conflict against the economic, social and political establishment of the period. As a social institution, families lay at the heart of Chartist rhetoric.

Notes

1   H. Evans, *Radical Fights of Forty Years* (Manchester, [1913]), pp. 19-20.
2   TNA, MEPO 2/66 (Complaints against police conduct, May-August 1848). For a detailed account see D. Goodway, *London Chartism, 1838-1848* (Cambridge, 1982), pp. 83-84 and 119-22.
3   P. A. Pickering, *Chartism and the Chartists in Manchester and Salford* (Basingstoke, 1995), pp. 40-45 is the only serious consideration of Chartist youth.
4   General Register Office (London), *England & Wales Civil Registration Index, Births*: June-September 1842; cf. D. J. V. Jones, *Chartism and the Chartists* (Harmondsworth, 1975), p. 24.
5   *NS* 31 July 1841, 12 Dec. 1840.
6   See for example reports of disputes in *NS* 3 Oct. 1840 and 13 Mar. 1841.
7   A. Briggs, 'Industry and politics in early nineteenth-century Keighley', *Bradford Antiquary* ns 9 (1952), p. 314; 1901 Census for Keighley, RG 13/4077/90/12.

8   An electronic search of the 1851 English & Welsh Census reveals 316 children given 'Feargus' as a first name, 46 of whom had 'O'Connor' as their middle name. A critical contextual point here is that the 1851 Census lists only seven English-born males named Feargus who had born before 1837.

9   Similar claims were subsequently made by critics of women's suffrage: see, for example John Tenniel's cartoon, 'An ugly rush', *Punch* 28 May 1870.

10   *Dame Flatback's Advice to t' Queen … a Supplement to the Shevvild Chap's Annual for 1840* (Sheffield, 1839), p. 1; C Godfrey, 'The Chartist prisoners, 1839-41', *International Review of Social History* 24 (1979), 199.

11   *Manchester Guardian* 7 June 1848.

12   H. B. Bonner, *Charles Bradlaugh: A Record of His Life and Work* (London, 1895), p. 6.

13   W. T. Stead quoted in H. Begbie, *Life of William Booth, the Founder of the Salvation Army* (London, 1920), vol. 2, p. 50.

14   Wood quoted in J. Burnett, *Useful Toil* (London, 1974), p. 308.

15   *DLB*, vol. 7, p. 53.

16   Evans, *Radical Fights*, p. 8.

17   For Clubb see A. F. J. Brown, *Chartism in Essex and Suffolk* (Chelmsford, 1982) and Anon., *History of the Philadelphian Bible-Christian Church* (Philadelphia, 1922), pp. 67-89.

18   *Charter* 28 July 1839.

19   J. Kavanagh, 'A Barnsley Man's autobiography', *Barnsley Chronicle* 9 June 1900.

20   B. Grime, *Memory Sketches* (Oldham, 1887), p. 26.

21   B. Brierley, *Home Memories and Recollections of a Life* (Manchester, 1886) p. 23.

22   Prosecution notes, R. v Brown, 1840 in TNA, TS 11/813 fos 4-8.

23   *The Trial of Feargus O'Connor, Barrister at Law, and Fifty-eight Others* (Manchester, 1843) p. 254. See also M. Chase, *Chartism: A New History* (Manchester, 2007), pp. 229-35.

24   *NS* 25 Apr. 1840.

25   Quoted in P. d'A. Jones, *The Christian Socialist Revival, 1877-1914* (Princeton NJ, 1968), p. 343.

26   TNA, HO 20/10, quoted in D. Thompson, 'Women and nineteenth-century radical politics', p. 120.

27   *Gazette of the Working Men's Association* 2 (1 June 1839), copy in British Library, Add MSS 27,835 fos 161 *et seq.*

28   The cultural dimensions of the Anti-Corn Law League are explored by P. A. Pickering and A. Tyrell, *The People's Bread: A History of the Anti-Corn Law League* (London, 2000), esp. pp. 116-216. For Owenism see E. Yeo, 'Robert Owen and radical culture', in S. Pollard and J. Salt (eds), *Robert Owen, Prophet of the Poor* (Basingstoke, 1971).

29   For example, M. Hovell, *The Chartist Movement* (Manchester, 3rd edn, 1966), pp. 203-9; R. H. Tawney, introduction to W. Lovett, *Life and Struggles* (London, 1920), vol. 1, p. xxviii; D. Read and E. Glasgow, *Feargus O'Connor: Irishman and Chartist* (London, 1961), p. 92; J. T. Ward, *Chartism* (London,

1973), p. 144.

30 M. Tylecote, *Mechanics' Institutes of Lancashire and Yorkshire before 1851* (Manchester, 1957), p. 241. For Elizabeth Neesom see especially *DLB*, vol. 8 and 'Chartist Lives: Elizabeth Neesom', in Chase, *Chartism: A New History*, pp. 184-91.

31 East London Female Total Abstinence Association, 'Address', *Northern Star* 30 Jan. 1841.

32 *NS* 8 Aug. 1840.

33 *True Scotsman* 29 Feb. 1840.

34 'The true principles of education', *English Chartist Circular* vol. 1, no. 19 [June 1841].

35 *Western Vindicator* 28 Sept. 1839.

36 'Aims and rules of the National Charter Association', *NS* 1 Aug. 1840.

37 *NS* 8 and 29 Jan., 12 Feb. 1842; 16 Dec. 1843; Wilson p. 273.

38 *NS* 24 June 1843.

39 Nottingham NCA poster, 21 Feb. 1842, TNA, HO 45/254 fo. 2.

40 *Nottingham Review* 4 Feb. 1842, quoted in R. Church, *Economic and Social change in a Midland Town* (London, 1966), p. 139.

41 J. Sinclair, *National Education and Church Extension* (London: Rivington, 1849) p.67.

42 *NS* 23 Feb. 1839 (original emphasis).

43 TNA, HO 45/2410 pt 1, fo. 350 [Apr. 1848].

44 John La Mont, 'The Movement', *English Chartist Circular* vol. 2, no. 33 [Sept. 1842]. See also Dorothy Thompson, 'Who were 'The People' in 1842?', in M.Chase and I.Dyck (eds), *Living and Learning* (Aldershot, 1996), p. 130.

45 Anon., text of needlework sampler embroidered by Ann Dawson, 1847, private collection. Photographs of this remarkable artifact can be found on the covers of S. Roberts and D. Thompson, *Images of Chartism* (Woodbridge: Merlin, 1998) and Chase, *Chartism*. The latter also contains a more detailed study of Dawson and her significance for our understanding of Chartism, on which the following paragraphs are based.

46 *NS* 10 Apr. 1841; 1851 Census for Droylsden, HO 107/2234/37/15.

47 E. Royle, *Robert Owen and the Commencement of the Millennium: A Study of the Harmony Community* (Manchester, 1998), pp. 118-21, 145-48. See also chapter 4 above.

48 *NS* 8 May 1847. For fuller extracts from this speech and further analysis see chapter 4 above.

49 Hebrews 6: 19; B. Stott, 'Song for the million', *NS* 24 Sept. 1842, reprinted as 'Friends of Freedom', in his *Songs for the Millions* (Middleton, 1843), p. 28. For Stott see *DLB*, vol. 4.

50 National Society for Promoting the Education of the Poor in the Principles of the Established Church, *Instructions on Needlework and Knitting* (London: the Society, 1847); J. Toller, *British Samplers* (Chichester, 1980); S. Mayor and D. Fowle, *Samplers* (London, 1990), plate 6; L. Synge, *Antique Needlework* (London, 1982), pp. 71-2.

51 See especially R. Parker, *The Subversive Stitch* (London, 1984).

52   See quotation above. A rhyming and metrically 'correct' rendering of the poem would be as follows:

> Britannia's the land where fell slavery's chain
> Had bound fast its victims in hunger and pain,
> Where no eye would pity, when no hand would save.
> Then came forth to break it O'Connor the brave.
> A band of brave fellows, whose hearts caught the sound,
> Arose from their slumbers and rallied around,
> Resolved in defiance of fool and of knave
> For freedom to fight with O'Connor the brave
> For the Charter and No Surrender.

Although unlikely to be the work of Ann Dawson herself, the poem does not appear to have been published (I am grateful to Mike Sanders for his help in searching for it).

53   *NS* 6 Jan. 1838.

54   Quoted in J. Schwarzkopf, *Women in the Chartist Movement* (Basingstoke, 1991), p. 302.

55   See Sinclair, *National Education and Church Extension*, pp. 49-83.

11

CHARTISM AND THE LAND:
'THE MIGHTY PEOPLE'S QUESTION'

Patronage, which is a consequence of, and springs from, the Large Farm System, *withholds the land from you*; while the law of primogeniture, and the barbarous law of settlement and entail, prevents such as are able from buying small allotments of land. To break through these barriers is easy and simple, and should be the great national object. By its accomplishment alone can you now set up the principle of individualism against that of centralisation … [T]he land of a country belongs to society; and … society, according to its wants has the same right to impose fresh conditions on the lessees, that the landlord has to impose fresh conditions upon a tenant at the expiration of his tenure. Society is the landlord: and as society never dies, the existing government are the trustees … Society looks on the performance of all requisite duties as the only condition on which its lessees can make good that title. (Feargus O'Connor, 'The Land! Its Value: And How to Get It', *Northern Star* 9 November 1844)

Between 1838 and 1848 Chartism held a place at the centre of British domestic politics. Then, for a further decade, it exercised an intermittent influence on the trajectory of radical politics. As a political movement its concerns extended far beyond the six points for parliamentary reform, embodied in the People's Charter from which it took its name.[1] Studies of the movement in relation to landed property, however, have overwhelmingly focused upon the Chartist Land Plan. This scheme to settle its supporters on four-acre cottage holdings, located in a network of national colonies, attracted over 70,000 subscribers at its peak in 1847-8. Its inelegant and protracted demise, after only 234 subscribers had been located on the land, tarnished the subsequent reputation of Chartism. The movement's greatest leader, Feargus O'Connor (whose personal investment in the scheme – financially, politically and emotionally – was considerable) was similarly blighted. It is tempting to explain both the appeal and failure of the Land Plan by reference to naïve nostalgia for a pre-industrial society. Yet the sentiments underpinning its appeal were far from simple 'back to the land' platitudes, as O'Connor's attack – quoted above – on the way private property and political patronage were mutually sustaining, reveals.

Until recently, the tendency among historians of the movement has been to view this sprawling and, organizationally, deeply flawed edifice as a scheme of O'Connor's invention alone.[2] Early studies largely analysed it is as a *sui generis* phenomenon, linked to the Chartist movement for practical and promotional purposes, whilst being intellectually and politically somewhat detached from it. Yet paradoxically, this near-exclusive historiographical focus on the Plan has prevented a fully rounded understanding of it. This chapter will argue first, that the Land Plan cannot be understood in isolation from the broader issue of how Chartists regarded landed property; and second, that despite widespread differences of opinion among Chartists throughout the movement's history, a consistently critical stance on private property in land was maintained.

The Land Plan, launched in April 1845, was the object of unalloyed negativity from early historians of the movement. The only favourable response to the Land Plan among them came from continental European authors, unencumbered with the baggage of Fabian socialism, which viewed the leadership of O'Connor with distaste and land reform generally as a distraction from the central purposes of working-class politics in an industrializing society.[3] Since the 1970s, however, the interpretive pendulum within the historiography of Chartism has swung decisively in O'Connor's favour and in parallel to this there has occurred a surge of interest in the Land Plan, extending even to the acquisition of a Chartist cottage by the National Trust.[4] However, the historiographical renaissance enjoyed by the Land Plan has obscured the extent to which agrarian ideas were central to all currents within Chartism. A powerful intertwining of the long-established ideologies of the Norman Yoke and of Old Corruption provided the basis from which Chartists advanced arguments for, variously, forcible re-appropriation, land and building societies, a free market in landed property, deeply radical taxation regimes, the moral imperative of agricultural reform to maximize food production and, from 1851 'the Charter and something more', a social democratic programme with land nationalization at its heart. Three elements underpinned them all. First was an outright hostility to large accumulations of landed property, irrespective of the legal form in which they might be held. Thus, secondly, Chartism was suspicious of central government as the putative owner or manager of the national estate. Thirdly, all Chartist conceptions of the reform of landed property shared a 'way of seeing' land that was shaped by ideas of shared access, usage and control rather than by possessive individualism.

At their heart, most if not all Chartist ideas about landed property derived from the concept of the Norman Yoke. Chartism was rooted in the tradition of earlier radicalism, especially the conviction that 'Old Corruption' determined both the tone and fiscal character of government.[5] Thus Chartists were naturally inclined to endorse the view that, as the Tyneside Chartist weekly *Northern Liberator* put it, 'the illegitimate William had legitimated usurpation.'[6] However, Chartist usage of the concept was as much connotative as denotative. The extent to which Chartists actually believed in the Norman Yoke's historical veracity is debateable; but it was a powerful tool to think with, and the concept was freighted with critical judgments about the institution of landed property. It was in this manner, rather than as part of a factual account of the evolution of private property in land, that Chartist speakers and authors deployed the language of the Norman Yoke. For example, according to a Derby police informer Jonathan Bairstow, a NCA missionary, depicted England 'in the days of Alfred the Great' thus:

> There was no Factorys, no mill owners, the manufacture and farming was about Equal and the price and food and Labour was Regulated by the King and parliament and all lived happy and Comfortable; things went on this way for several Centurys until Wm the Conqueror came over with his hired tools to make you subservient to is will ... the Land was the property of all and was only now held by the few from the share of power they held in the Government of the country.[7]

This trope in Chartist thought was equally appealing to the movement's Irish and Scottish supporters. Indeed, Alfred the Great was potentially a figure in admiration of whom both English and Irish, and Catholic and Protestant, could combine. Blessed with a clean pair of hands as far as Ireland was concerned, he stood for a different concept of English authority, untainted by landlordism. 'England became *feudalised*', explained the leader of Irish Chartism, as a result of the 'Norman banditti – the great progenitors of England's boasted barons, with William the Illegitimate – founder of the present illustrious dynasty! – at their head'.[8] Following the death of Daniel O'Connell, a growing rapprochement with Irish nationalists saw Liverpool Chartists seek to overcome the sectarian divisions that undermined the movement on Merseyside through the formation of 'the Alfred League'. Described by its promoters as 'a National Co-operative Cheap Justice

Association', the League was dedicated to the 'recovery of property *Stolen from the People*, including the plunderings of the Norman Robbers'.[9] Behind this rhetorical smokescreen, the League actually operated as a friendly society. (More familiarly known by its later title, the Loyal Order of Alfred, it was one of many fraternal initiatives that emerged from Chartism.)

The Norman Yoke endured as a trope in English radical thought far longer and pervasively than Christopher Hill, in his prescient and pioneering essay on the subject suggested.[10] As late as 1856, Ernest Jones, O'Connor's former lieutenant who had assumed the latter's mantle from 1850, opined that 'the seizure of the Saxon land by the Norman robber' was 'the parent wound, from which we bleed to-day':

> Join with me for the re-conquest of the land. It is the task of the age – the mission of the century. You talk of unchaining yourselves: unchain the land, and your own chains will fall. The franchise is the bond that binds your hands; but land monopoly is the dungeon that surrounds your bodies.[11]

The Norman Yoke reinforced the radical assault upon the landed aristocracy. Successive imitations of John Wade's *Black Book*, the Ur-text of the fight against 'Old Corruption', argued that the reformed House of Commons was still dominated by Britain's landed elite.[12] Monopoly of political power and monopoly of land were decidedly not coincidental. It was political monopoly that had made possible the consolidation of the land monopoly through parliamentary enclosure, 'Robbery', according to the *Northern Liberator*, 'by means of Enclosure Bills, of the COMMON LANDS, consisting of MILLIONS OF ACRES, from the industrious and poorer part of the population … under colour of legislation, *filched*, in the most barefaced manner.'[13] Bronterre O'Brien, one of the most articulate and thoughtful of the Chartist leadership put it bluntly: 'Knaves will tell you that it is because you have no property that you are unrepresented. I tell you, on the contrary, it is because you are unrepresented that you have no property.'[14] Thus the Norman Yoke also licensed the notion that social reformation might not be entirely peaceable. Land which had been forcibly appropriated might, morally and necessarily, be the legitimate object of draconian measures for its re-appropriation. William Hill, a former handloom weaver, Swedenborgian minister and the founding editor of the greatest of the Chartist newspapers, *Northern Star*, argued in a leader on the law of primogeniture:

The thousand modes of plunder by which the nation's bones are being constantly picked, arise, in the first instance, out of the determination of those whose ancestors first obtained a monopoly of the soil, by what is called 'right of conquest'; that is to say, by robbery and murder, not only to retain all the ill-gotten spoil of their fathers; but, under colour of the letter, though in defiance of the spirit, of this law of primogeniture, to make the people from whom the land was originally stolen, support, at least, five-sixths of the whole number of thieves and thieves' descendents by extraordinary labour, independent of the land.[15]

Yet this coruscating attack went on to propose simply that 'by Universal Suffrage, the people [will] get the power to annihilate the law of primogeniture, along with every other relic of the barbarous ages'.[16] As so often in Chartism, the language of Hill's editorial projected not just truculence but violence, even though the underlying objective for which it argued is a legal reform of relatively limited extent (and we might note, had it ever been implemented, of limited effectiveness).[17]

However, the supposedly forcible nature of the Norman land grab did justify draconian remedies in the minds of many Chartists, including those typically associated with its 'moral force' (as opposed to 'physical force') tendency. For example in 1849, the poet and engraver, William J. Linton called for the confiscation of that year's harvest. This, he argued, should then be re-allocated to paupers, the unemployed and to the labourers who had produced it, as the first instalment of what Linton termed a 'national rent'. Linton's national rent would have been almost identical to the single tax of later Georgeite land reformers: levied at the rate of 20 shillings per acre it would encourage the maximization of agricultural production, render unnecessary all other forms of taxation, and along the way assist the formation of a national estate since the property of defaulting landowners would be surrendered to the state.[18]

Linton's argument crystallizes a further dimension of Chartist views of land reform, namely that it was a practical and moral imperative, necessary to maximize agricultural production and alleviate poverty as well as a means to right a political injustice. The argument that thoroughgoing land reform alone could maximize the productive capacities of the soil was well established long before Chartism. It can be traced to radical opposition to Malthusianism and, beyond that, to the view that parks and landscaped gardens were a facet of effeminizing luxury, a physical manifestation of corruption that constituted the ultimate affront to the poor. 'Why are huge forests still allowed to stretch with idle pomp and all the opulence of eastern grandeur?' Mary Wollstonecraft had demanded in 1792. 'Why does the brown waste meet the travellers view when men want work?'[19] This theme had particularly been developed during the Regency years by the Spencean Philanthropists.[20] Three Spenceans – Allen Davenport, Charles Neesom and Thomas Preston – lived long enough to exercise a significant influence on metropolitan Chartism.[21] 'If there were no parks, and no pleasure grounds', Davenport claimed in 1822, 'the whole face of the country would present to the eye cornfields, meadows, gardens, plantations of all kinds of fruit trees, etc., all in the highest state of cultivation.' The Spencean tradition was a vital part of London Chartism. Through George Julian Harney, the principal guiding hand on *Northern Star* from 1843 to 1850, it came to shape Chartist ideology more widely. 'His creed was – and Thomas Spence had taught it him – that "the Land is the people's farm", Harney declared in 1845, 'and that it belongs to the entire nation, not to individuals or classes.'[22]

The view that landed estates had been siphoned off from the nation at large paralleled the notion that 'Old Corruption' continually annexed the income government derived from taxation. Similarly, an unproductive landscape mirrored 'The Thing' – idle, parasitic and bloated in luxury. These ideas were given wide voice by Chartists, including those without any connection to the Spencean tradition. In a speech from the pulpit of a Methodist meeting room at Charlestown, Ashton-under-Lyne, in 1848, Scottish-born surgeon Peter McDouall

> said that Population has now so fast increased that every part of the land that has hitherto remained unproductive must be broken into tillage; that gentlemen's parks, as well as commons, must be divided into pastures, to feed the people – that is a proposition in which a great many of you must agree ... everything tells us that no portion of this land can any longer lie idle; and ere long, the aristocracy will find themselves obliged to cut up their parks, and enclose the forests, and render them productive for the rest of the community.[23]

This argument was mutually reinforcing with the abiding radical belief that – of all the possible methods of organizing the cultivation of the land – smallholding maximized productivity returns relative to the input of labour. It could thus alleviate poverty both by widening employment opportunities and facilitating the production of plentiful food, countering the Malthusian spectre. 'When I see a man with his foot upon his spade', declared O'Connor in his seminal *Practical Work on the Management of Small Farms*, 'I think I recognise the image of his God, and him in that character which even the Malthusian deigns to assign him – A MAN STANDING ON HIS OWN RESOURCES.'[24] This notion was itself powerfully reinforced by contemporary idealization of spade husbandry, perhaps the only principle held consistently and unanimously by the three commanding personalities of early nineteenth-century radicalism, William Cobbett, Robert Owen and Feargus O'Connor. Even Bronterre O'Brien, one of the fiercest critics of O'Connor from within the Chartist movement, eulogized smallholding. 'The hope of individual reward', he explained, 'is the most natural incentive to labour.' Though he strongly favoured free trade, O'Brien rejected the notion that the leaders of the Anti-Corn Law League 'mean to give you as cheap bread as O'Connor's four acres would give you. Mind, I am no admirer of Feargus O'Connor – it's quite otherwise I assure you. But truth is truth, come from whom it may.'[25]

The long-established radical call for small farms was widely configured as the means through which both to reform agricultural production and alleviate poverty. In the words of Christopher Doyle, a Manchester powerloom weaver and NCA activist who became a full-time official for the Land Plan:

> It was the duty of the government of the country to cause the waste lands to be cultivated so as to give employment and food to those who were willing to labour, but were too often, as that the present time, in consequence of the artificial state of the labour market, thrown out of employment in large masses, to the great injury of society at large.[26]

To argue for collectivized agriculture was an ideological Rubicon no Chartist ever crossed. Land nationalizers and land planners alike favoured small-scale cultivation. Ernest Jones consistently espoused small holdings, even as he abandoned the tenets of the Land Plan in favour of land nationalization, Hostility against centralization, a consistent trope in O'Connor's argument for the Land Plan, featured prominently in Jones's case for nationalization of the land. 'By the state retaining for ever as national property the land once purchased, the centralisation of the land in the hands of a few rich individuals becomes impossible ... the occupiers of the land are to be *tenants*.'[27] This concept meshed well with post-Chartist radical Liberalism, of which Jones was an exemplary exponent after the demise of the NCA in 1858. 'England's wealthiest Ballarat is England. Our goldfields are golden fields of wheat ... Give us a million peasant farmers.'[28]

For Chartists, therefore, the first duties of a reformed parliament would necessarily include legislation to reform landed property, as a critical part of righting injustice, fighting poverty, producing cheap foodstuffs and eliminating unemployment. 'Behold *cause* and *effect* at once presented to view! Behold evil and remedy. Down with … landed monopolists! Restore the wages-slaves to those lands of which their forefathers were plundered. And behold the means in political power, and in that alone.'[29] Chartism consistently argued that land reform would be an imperative once the Charter was law. For example in September 1839, in virtually its last act before it dissolved, the Chartist National Convention adopted a *Declaration of the Rights of the People* that committed the movement to an elected magistracy, to the abolition of the standing army, and to taking into public ownership any land that had once been 'appropriated to public and general use'.[30] Historians, distracted by the heat and fury of 1839, have usually overlooked this detailed exposition of the policies that a parliament, elected on the basis of the People's Charter, would have sought to enact. The immediate colonization of Crown lands even found its way into some strike resolutions during the 1842 strike wave, alongside a call for the Charter to be made law of the land.[31] Subsequently, the NCA briefly adopted (1843-44) a constitution in which all mention of the Charter was expunged from NCA objectives, but provision 'for the unemployed, and means of support for those who are desirous to locate upon the land' was explicitly avowed.[32] The emergence of the Chartist Land Plan in 1844-5 is only explicable within the context of the commitment to agrarian reform that had been central to Chartism almost from its inception.

Private landed property's place at the heart, as Chartists saw it, of a chain of political and social oppression, justified calls for its reform as a matter of both pressing urgency and irrefutable moral rectitude. However, Chartism faced a dilemma in that the arguments it advanced often appeared to favour the spoliation and destruction of private property. There were moments in 1839 when the equation appeared absolute, for example when *The Times* reported the Dukinfield Chartist Abraham Lee producing bullets from his pocket as he declared, 'it was every man's right to have a piece of land, and every man should never rest 'till everyone had his own right'.[33] Generally, however, Chartists drew clear distinctions between various categories of land and the reforms that should be applied to each. Calls for the immediate confiscation of private property were usually confined to common land enclosed by parliamentary act, for 'upwards of six millions of acres of commons lands have been taken from the working classes'.[34] In addition, economic necessity was often advanced as justifying the cultivation of so-called waste over the heads, if necessary, of whoever held it. Crown and Church of England lands were to be released for intensive cultivation as soon as feasible. For the rest, Chartists projected a gradualist reformation in land holding, to be achieved by the introduction of free trade in land, usually reinforced by state acquisition of freeholds at the death of owners 'by surrender, or by any means concordant with justice and a generous treatment of all classes'.[35]

Perhaps no more vile falsehood was ever invented than that laid to the charge of the Chartists, asserting that they require a spoliation and division of property ... They merely ask for the old mode of dividing and leasing land, in small portions, so that the same measure which now supports one, may support hundreds ... For most assuredly, when the laws are made by UNIVERSAL SUFFRAGE, as ere long they must be, though no one will be robbed of the property which he has now acquired, means will be taken to prevent the future acquisition and accumulation, in individual hands, of large heaps of wealth and property by the oppression and starvation of the people. The 'classes' know this, and hence the bitterness of their animosity against the people, whom they perceive to be rising to their due station in society; hence their anxiety to put down the charter agitation; and hence the lying absurdities about equalizing property which they have so industriously propagated.[36]

After 1848 Chartism matured as a political movement and its leading figures began to think in more sophisticated terms than the surge of reactive reforms that, it had hitherto been anticipated, the enactment of the People's Charter would initiate. Critical awareness grew that even the simultaneous repeal of the laws of primogeniture, strict settlement and entail would not immediately force large quantities of land onto the market; and such land as did become available might not be in the form of small parcels. Such small acreages as were flushed onto the market might not be readily affordable, even through the mechanism of lotteries or mutualist strategies such as loan or land clubs. Furthermore, the increasing interest taken by former Anti-Corn Law Leaguers after 1846 in land redistribution (via the rapidly expanding Freehold Land Society Movement) and land law reform (on a gradualist basis) suggested that as a specifically Chartist tactic, the repeal of primogeniture, strict settlement and entail was deficient.[37] Harney neatly encapsulated this problem in February 1850:

The people are promised wonderful felicity by the repeal of the laws of primogeniture and entail, bringing the land to the public market. Mr. Bright and others desire to have the land as free to traffic in as labour is now. What would be the effect of such a 'reform'? Those who had the money to buy land would become landlords, and every landlord, whether lord of five or of fifty-thousand acres, would be a conservative – the sworn enemy to further change. Moreover, monopolizing the soil, and commanding the sources of toil in the manufacturing districts, the new aristocracy would possess a power over the lives of both agricultural and manufacturing workers unexampled in the world's history.

The proletarians need another sort of reform. The feudal aristocracy being doomed to expire, care should be taken that no new aristocracy be allowed to take their place. With that view THE LAND MUST BE MADE NATIONAL PROPERTY.

Harney was the pivotal figure in re-orientating Chartism explicitly to embrace a social programme that was incapable of confusion with liberalism: 'push forward a propaganda of social democracy. Let them struggle for *the Charter and something more* – THE CHARTER, THE LAND, AND THE ORGANISATION OF LABOUR!'[38]

'The Charter and something more', an adaptation of the traditional Chartist slogan 'the charter and nothing less', was the basis on which the NCA adopted a social democratic programme in March 1851. Features of this programme included proposals to settle the unemployed on the land via 'the restoration of poor, common, church and crown lands to the people. Such lands to be divided among the poor in suitable proportions. Those located to be tenants of the State, paying a proportionate rent-charge for their holdings'. Nationalization of other land was to be achieved gradually through purchase. Taxation would be levied on land and accumulated wealth only.[39]

It should be noted, however, that arguments for nationalized ownership had circulated within Chartism prior to 1851. The 1848 programme of the National Association for the Organization of Trade (a metropolitan Chartist trades' initiative, promoting producer co-operatives) began with this first principle: 'That the land, being the gift of the Almighty to the people universally, ought to be held in sacred trust by the State for their benefit, and not be exclusively possessed by a fractional part of the community.'[40] Harney, influenced as we have seen by the Spenceans, had espoused analogous arguments in 1845. Feargus O'Connor's sentiments, in the quotation that heads this chapter, offered a similar radical interpretation of the rights and responsibilities of private property and the state. O'Connor did not promote the Land Plan with the intention of creating a socially conservative alternative to, or deviation from, Chartism. Rather, he conceived its estates as a practical demonstration of how society would be reconstituted under the Charter, and he dared to hope that in time these estates might be so successful that even an unreformed government might be persuaded of the desirability of a small farm system. In this respect he found support from the unlikely quarter of John Stuart Mill, the first edition of whose *Principles of Political Economy* praised O'Connor's 'well-conceived arrangements' as offering a model for land reform in Ireland.[41]

Bronterre O'Brien's interest in land nationalization pre-dated Chartism and had first been aired in the pages of the great unstamped paper *Poor Man's Guardian* which he edited from November 1832 until it closed in 1835. O'Brien first hinted polemically at the case for land nationalization in December 1833: 'to attack property is … to attack a robbery'. By 1835 his argument was well refined:

> What the Irish want … are what nature requires, and justice entitles them to … they want their rents lowered to one-half or one-third their present amount or if they are to pay competition prices for the use of the land, they want that ALL shall profit by these prices. They require that the fee-simple of the land shall revert to the rightful owner, viz. THE NATION, from which it could never be alienated without the general consent expressed by the majority – that the nation shall therefore resume its proper position as grand landlord of the whole country, and receive the rent henceforward in behalf of the people, to be divided share and share alike among every inhabitant, rich and poor, after defraying the expenses of government, this is the only just way of holding land.[42]

Even O'Brien, however, was cautious about applying comprehensive land nationalization in the English context. This is particularly apparent in his support for Thomas Bowkett, an active Chartist and secularist, in the promotion of building societies.[43] Plebeian land and building clubs had existed since the 1790s. From the 1820s practical interest in the agrarian ideal led to the formation of a small but growing number of land societies. In Bowkett Building Societies members' subscriptions were pooled to make an interest free loan to each member in turn to enable them to buy a property, 'turns' being decided by ballot. In legal and actuarial terms there was absolutely nothing to distinguish Bowkett's initiative from that of O'Connor in the Chartist Land Plan, except for one key difference: Bowkett Building Societies were restricted to fifty or a hundred members. Bowkett's scheme grew in effect by cloning societies rather than engorging the sole original. They were far from immune from failure and, like O'Connor's land scheme, they were denied the protection of the Friendly Societies Act because they operated as a lottery. Yet the Bowkett principle endured into the 1930s.[44] The emergence of this associational form out of the Chartist movement (and from O'Brien's circle at that) further alerts us to how closely associated Chartism was, in all its varied facets, with the idealization of small property ownership. Some Chartist localities were contemplating the launch of societies through which their members could acquire smallholdings as early as 1840, the same year that there was a revival of interest in London in the land reform plans of the veteran Spencean Thomas Preston.[45] And from the late 1840s, significant numbers of Chartists became involved in building societies.[46]

The projected organization of land holding within a Chartist polity also turned on Chartists' view of the state. Hostility to the centralization of state power was a strong underlying current in Chartist ideology.[47] Like the promotion of the smallholding ideal, this was one of the elements that bound together O'Connor and his critics in the movement. Reformed government should facilitate and guarantee access to the land, but no more. Prioritizing land redistribution therefore curtailed enthusiasm for land nationalization. The mechanism needed at a national level to administer what, following Spenceanism, was often conceptualized as 'the people's farm', was arguably incompatible with the Chartist concept of light national government and significant local autarchy. The London Working Men's Association's journal, *The Charter*, argued control should be vested in democratically elected local commissioners.[48] O'Brien's response to this, at least in his Chartist phase, was to argue, much as Thomas Spence had done at the turn of the eighteenth century, in favour of parochial control. *Lloyds' Weekly London Newspaper* even alleged that O'Brien 'was the most distinguished … plagiarist' of Spence.[49] But the concept of the parish as the primary mechanism for both government and regulation of property carried diminished conviction in a rapidly industrializing and urbanizing society. Spence remained an authority to whom Chartists favouring outright public ownership continued to appeal.[50] However, it is arguable that the Spencean ideal survived in its purest form in the colonies of the Chartist Land Plan. 'By its accomplishment alone can you now set-up the principle of individualism against that of centralisation.' Chartism's estates were structured round individual land holdings, the only centralized facility being a schoolhouse, and they were promoted as being free of 'NATIONAL EXCISE PARSONS', and having none of the features of 'the present Labour system of England [which] is one huge system of communism; the wealthy idle director living upon the ignorance and dependence of aggregate struggle'.[51]

All Chartists agreed that land reform would be a political, economic and social imperative for a reformed parliament. They were unanimous that the basis on which land should be held for cultivation must be that of smallholdings and small farms. The emergence of arguments in favour of land nationalization was attenuated by a continued disposition in favour of small-scale ownership and suspicion of the state and its centralizing tendencies. This strongly inclined Chartists towards friendly societies and other mutualist organizations in their later careers. It also eased the passage for those ex-Chartists (and they were legion) who wished to secure a place in the Liberal sun.

Was there a single defining feature of the various Chartist positions on land reform? It is a commonplace of Chartist historiography that it appealed particularly to small producers, typically domestic outworkers such as handloom weavers. A disposition towards small-scale production is evident too in Chartist agrarian ideology. It is a disposition that the Land Plan did not create but rather shared with an overarching political outlook that privileged issues of equity and access over ones of equality and ownership. Access to – and control of – the land, rather than the democratization of ownership itself, was the essential basis from which all Chartist land reform emerged. Once this is understood then we can see that Harney was not being disingenuous in espousing Spencean ideals while editing a paper which was vociferous in its support of the Land Plan; nor was there any inherent inconsistency between the Land Plan and land nationalization, or between the latter and building societies. The ostensibly Janus-headed stance of the Chartists, at once critical of private ownership of the soil and yet jealous for rights of property in land, ceases to be problematic once we register that the key issue for all Chartist land reformers was access to, rather than ownership of, the land.[52]

Notes

1   The literature on Chartism is extensive. The most substantial histories are D. Thompson, *The Chartists: Popular Politics in the Industrial Revolution* (London, 1984), and M. Chase, *Chartism: A New History* (Manchester, 2007).

2   J. MacAskill, 'The Chartist Land Plan', in A. Briggs (ed.), *Chartist Studies* (London, 1959), pp. 304-341; A. M. Hadfield, *The Chartist Land Company* (Newton Abbott, 1970); chapter 4 above (first published 1996).

3   For the historiography of the Plan see chapters 4 and 5 above.

4   J. Saville, introduction to reprint edition of Gammage, *History of the Chartist Movement* (New York, 1969); D. J. V. Jones, *Chartism and the Chartists*, (London, 1975), pp. 130-7; J. Bronstein, *Land Reform and Working-class Experience in Britain and the United States, 1800-1862* (Stanford, Ca., 1999);

A. Messner, 'Land, leadership, culture and emigration: some problems in Chartist historiography', *Historical Journal* 42: 4 (1999), pp. 1093-1109; A. M. Hadfield, *The Chartist Land Company* (new edn, Aylesbury, 2000). See also chapters 4 and 5 above.

5   For the classic exploration of the extent of Chartism's debt to earlier radical tropes and its consequences see G. Stedman Jones, 'Rethinking Chartism', in his *Languages of Class: Studies in English Working Class History, 1832-1982* (Cambridge, 1983), pp. 90-178.

6   *NL* 11 Apr. 1840.

7   Derby Local Studies Library, MS BA/909/16186, items 10 and 11 (Jonathan Bairstow, 14 June 1841).

8   [P. O'Higgins], *Chartism and Repeal: an address to the repealers of Ireland, by a member of the Irish Universal Suffrage Association* (Dublin, 1842), p. 5. See also 'On the law of primogeniture', [Scottish] *Chartist Circular* 21 Dec. 1839.

9   Alfred League advertisement on back cover of 'Effiax', *The Tax-Payer's Catechism, or Dialogues between Mentor and Telemachus on the Causes of Chartism* (Liverpool, 1848).

10   C. Hill, 'The Norman Yoke', in J. Saville (ed.), *Democracy and the Labour Movement* (London, 1954). See also A. Briggs, 'Saxons, Normans and Victorians', in *The Collected Essays of Asa Briggs: Volume II* (Hassocks, 1985), pp. 215-35.

11   E. Jones, *Evenings with the People 2: The Hereditary Landed Aristocracy* (London, 1856), 4. M. Taylor, *Ernest Jones, Chartism and the Romance of Politics, 1819-69* (Oxford, 2003) identifies land reform as a consistent trope in Jones's political career, stretching from Chartism to the cusp of selection as a Liberal parliamentary candidate shortly before he died.

12   Reissues and pirated editions of John Wade's classic *Black Book* (first published 1820) were frequent during the Chartist period. The leading Lancashire Chartist Reginald Richardson published successive editions of *his Popular Black Book and Almanac,* along with *The Black Book, or Annual Tell Tale* (Salford, 1839), *The Red Book; or A Peep into the Peerage* (London, 1841), and *The Blue Book of the Commons* (1848); see also *The Black Book of England; Exhibiting the Existing State, Policy and Administration of the United Kingdom* (London, 1847); *The Black Book of the British Aristocracy* (London, 1848); *Court Jobbery: or, the Black Book of the Palace* (Strange, 1848).

13   'To the landlords of north England', *NL* 15 June 1839.

14   *Bronterre's National Reformer* 15 Jan. 1837. For O'Brien see A. Plummer, *Bronterre* (London, 1971).

15   Editorial, 'Primogeniture', *NS* 25 Apr. 1840

16   *NS* 2 May 1840

17   Chartists reinforced their case against primogeniture by arguing that it drove the younger sons of the aristocracy 'like so many devouring locusts' into military and naval service, the law and the church: *The Speech Delivered by William Dixon, the People's Candidate, at the Moot Hall, Wigan, 1841* (Wigan, 1841), p. 12. See also P. McDouall, 'Land', *English Chartist Circular* 46 (Dec. 1841); ''Primogeniture', *NS* 25 Apr. and 2 May 1840.

18   W. J. Linton, *The People's Land, and an Easy Way to Recover It* (London, 1850), p. 6; cf F. B. Smith, *Radical Artisan: William James Linton, 1812-97* (Manchester, 1973), p. 68.

19   M. Wollstonecraft, *A Vindication of the Rights of Men, in a Letter to the Right Honourable Edmund Burke, occasioned by his Reflections on the revolution in France* (1790), reprinted in J. Todd (ed.), *Mary Wollstonecraft: Political Writings* (London, 1993), pp. 60-1.

20   M. Chase, *'The People's Farm': English Radical Agrarianism, 1775-1840* (Oxford, 1988), pp. 45-120.

21   Ibid; see also *DLB*, vol. 8 and (for Neesom) Chase, *Chartism: A New History*, 184-91.

22   *NS* 30 Aug. 1845.

23   *An Authentic Report of the Trial of Doctor Peter Murray McDouall* (Manchester, 1848). For McDouall, a figure of considerable influence on northern Chartism, see Chase, *Chartism* passim.

24   F. O'Connor, *A Practical Work on the Management of Small Farms* (7th edition, Manchester, 1845), p. 40.

25   [B. O'Brien], *A Brief Inquiry into the Natural Rights of Man* (London, 1852), 45; *The Poor Man's Guardian and Repealer's Friend* 1 [3 June 1843].

26   C. Doyle, reported in *NS*, 1 Jan. 1848. For Doyle see P. Pickering, *Chartism and the Chartists in Manchester and Salford* (London, 1995), *passim* and 194-5.

27   E. Jones, 'Letters on the Chartist programme', *Notes to the People, Volume 1*, no. 3 (May 1851), 55-6. See also *idem*, 'Our Land: Its Lords and Serfs. A Tract for Labourers and Farmers', *Notes to the People, Volume 1*, no. 5 (June 1851), 103-14.

28   *Birmingham Daily Post*, 27 Nov. 1867, cf. *Labour and Capital: A Lecture* (1867), quoted in J. Saville, *Ernest Jones: Chartist* (London, 1952), p. 230.

29   E. Jones, 'Monopoly and its effects', *Notes to the People, Volume 1*, no. 23 (Sept. 1851), 444.

30   *NS* 14 Sept. 1839; *Charter* 15 Sept. 1839. For the Declaration see Chase, *Chartism*, p. 106.

31   For example at Bolton, The National Archives (Kew), Home Office Papers, HO 45/249, fol. 127 [15 Aug. 1842].

32   Report on the 1843 Convention, *NS* 16 Sept. 1843; see also Chase, *Chartism*, p. 248.

33   *The Times* 29 Mar. 1839.

34   J. Mason, *A Letter to Mr Macaulay, MP, in Reply to the Charges Made by that Gentleman against the Chartists* (Birmingham, 1842), p. 11.

35   Quotation from the programme adopted by the 1851 Chartist Convention, quoted by Jones, 'Letters on the Chartist programme', p. 55.

36   Editorial, 'Equalisation of property', *NS* 2 May 1840

37   See below, chapter 12.

38   G. J. Harney, 'The Charter, and something more!', *Democratic Review* Feb. 1850, pp. 351, 352.

39   'Plan of agitation adopted by the Chartist Convention', *Friend of the People* 18 (12 Apr. 1851). The 1851 programme is also analysed in Chase, *Chartism*, p.

339.

40 *Power of the Pence*, 2 (18 Nov. 1848). For the NAOT see J. Belchem, 'Chartism and the trades, 1848-50', *English Historical Review* 98 (July 1983), pp. 558-87.

41 See chapter 5 above.

42 'O'Connell and the Irish', *Poor Man's Guardian* 13 June 1835.

43 *National Reformer* 14 Nov. 1846, 6 Feb., 1 and 15 May 1847.

44 S. Newens, 'Thomas Edward Bowkett', *History Workshop Journal* 9 (1980), 143-8; E. J. Cleary, 'Starr, Richard Benjamin (1813–1892)', *Oxford Dictionary of National Biography*, Oxford University Press, 2004 [http://0-www.oxforddnb.com.wam.leeds.ac.uk:80/view/article/47865, accessed 8 March 2008].

45 *NS* 16 May, 29 Aug., 12 Sept. and 31 Oct. 1840. See also Pickering, *Chartism and the Chartists*, pp. 117-19.

46 J. West, *History of the Chartist Movement* (London, 1920), pp. 282-3; Chase, *Chartism*, pp. 26, 245, 349 and 353-7. See also 'James Maw', in *DLB*, vol. 10, and on convergences between late Chartism, building societies and other forms of mutualism J. Saville, *1848: The British State and the Chartist Movement* (Cambridge, 1987), pp. 208-11.

47 F. C. Mather, *Chartism and Society* (London, 1980), pp. 26, 58-9, 83-5; E. Yeo, 'Some problems and practices of Chartist democracy', in J. Epstein and D. Thompson (eds), *The Chartist Experience* (London, 1982), pp 345-80.

48 'The land of England belongs to the people of England', *The Charter* 1 Dec. 1839.

49 *Lloyds' Weekly London Newspaper* 5 Oct. 1845. On O'Brien as a land reformer see especially Plummer, *Bronterre*, pp. 179-84.

50 For examples of appeals to Spence's authority see *London Dispatch* 18 June 1837 and *NL* 30 Dec. 1837 (Place); *NS* 16 June 1838 (calls for increased 'Spencean knowledge'); *Operative* 25 Nov. 1838 and *NS* 8 Dec. 1849 (O'Brien); *NS* 3 Feb. 1849 (Nottingham Chartists); 30 Aug. 1845 and 31 Aug. 1850 (Harney).

51 *NS* 9 Nov. 1844, 16 Oct. 1847, 18 Nov. 1848.

52 On this point within English agrarian radicalism generally see Chase, 'The People's Farm', pp. 183-4; Iorwerth Prothero makes the same point with reference to English and French artisan radicalism in his *Radical Artisans in England and France, 1830-70* (Cambridge, 1997), pp. 140-41.

12

OUT OF RADICALISM:
THE MID-VICTORIAN FREEHOLD LAND MOVEMENT

'It was usual', F. M. L. Thompson has suggested, 'for mid-Victorians to think of house-ownership as the preserve of a section of the upper working class … a quirk of a small minority of skilled artisans who set especial store on thrift and respectability, saw them as ideally embodied in house-ownership, and successfully pursued their ambitions through the machinery of local, terminating, building societies.'[1] The roots of such popular aspirations to homeownership deserve attention. Whilst the mechanism of small terminating building societies was important, it was significant chiefly during the early nineteenth century, and cannot fully account for working-class owner-occupation in the Victorian period. A key part of the explanation is to be found in the freehold land movement, a loose confederation which emerged in the late 1840s, causing a short-lived but illuminating flurry in political circles. A study of this movement is useful both because of its intrinsic importance as a provider of cheap owner-occupied housing, and for the trends in popular politics and attitudes which it reveals.

Freehold land societies provided their members with freehold properties, together with the associated advantage of a parliamentary vote. In the years following the embarrassment of Chartism in 1848, the freehold land movement came close to dominating popular politics. Its roots were those common to Chartism: the imperative need to extend the franchise, working-class self-respect and mutual improvement, and agrarian idealism. The last peaked towards the end of the 1840s, notably but by no means exclusively in the Chartist Land Plan. 'The wish to improve their condition by the possession of land is taking root in the universal heart of the working classes', observed Thomas Cooper.[2] At the 'Labour Parliament' of 1854, the number of land societies formed during the previous three years was put at over 300, a growth not implausibly described by an early historian of Chartism as 'the most productive of ideas and the least studied in the history of the English working-classes'.[3] Of these societies, the freehold land movement formed the largest single constituent, certainly more than half.

Such societies were a powerful means of converting thrift into consumption, and historians have primarily emphasized their contribution to urban, and especially suburban, housing development.[4] However, their political and social aspects no less deserve scrutiny, but have been largely ignored because the movement fits uncomfortably into the brisk progressivism that still characterizes much of the historiography of working-class politics.[5] Two phases of growth can be identified. The first, commencing with the Birmingham Freehold Land Society [FLS] in 1847, saw the formation of at least seventy societies by the end of 1851. Almost all were provincial and rooted in the working-class ethic of self-help. A second and more overtly commercial phase, largely complete by 1854, comprised mainly metropolitan societies. The London-based National Society, however, belonged to the first phase, though its branch structure (unusual in the movement, and among building societies generally at this time) meant that it too had strong provincial roots. Significant both for its size and its political complexion, the emergence of the National in 1849 accelerated the process whereby the movement became an important vehicle for the spread of advanced liberalism, assuming a pressure-group function through the formation in the same year of the Freehold Land Union. In this respect it can be seen as a significant departure in popular politics, though middle-class liberalism's attempt to incorporate what remained an essentially working-class movement was never complete.

In 1850 one of the five newspapers founded exclusively to serve the movement asserted: 'A new era has commenced with the FREEHOLD LAND SOCIETIES.'[6] The alleged 'discovery ... in practical politics', which formed the basis of their operations, was the facility to create forty-shilling freehold votes in the counties:

> Why should an Englishman henceforward supplicate parliament, in vain, to grant him a vote, when he may owe to his virtuous prudence and economy his own enfranchisement? The cost of a single pint of beer a day, from the time of the promulgation of the 'People's Charter' to the present time, amounts to more money than would buy a county qualification.[7]

The purchase of a county qualification was a relatively simple exercise, made possible by the retention in the 1832 Reform Act of the ancient forty-shilling freehold franchise, by which all owners of freehold property in the counties worth £2 or more (at a notional annual rental of 5 per cent) were eligible to vote. The reaffirmation in 1832 of what even reformers acknowledged as an anachronism was a conscious attempt to counter the £50 tenant-at-will franchise (the Chandos Clause), and the threat it embodied of undue influence by landed interests over tenant farmers.[8] Although the forty-shilling franchise did not extend to the parliamentary boroughs, residents of the latter possessing land of appropriate value were permitted to participate in the elections of the county in which the borough was situated. This had obvious implications for the growth of an urban electorate. Furthermore, no residential qualification was entailed, and an Act of 1696 (7 & 8 Wm. 3 C. 25) remained on the statute book to uphold the franchise of those who mortgaged forty-shilling freeholds.

During the 1840s a number of court cases established the legality of subdividing a property for sale in parcels of sufficient value to qualify their new owners for the forty-shilling freehold franchise, provided that the transaction was made at full market price, that is to say not implicitly subsidized by the vendor, which could constitute fraudulent intent to manipulate voting. Like all franchises, the forty-shilling freehold had to be proved to the district revising barrister, to whom the electoral roll was submitted in the autumn of each year.[9]

The cautious architects of the 1832 Reform Act thus bequeathed to Victorian England a charter of uncharacteristic generosity, especially in those urban centres where buoyant demand enhanced land prices. It has been observed of County Durham that 'it did not take much more than a paddock and a pigsty to qualify'.[10] Henceforward much effort in county politics was devoted to securing the registration of those who were ignorant of, or indifferent to, their right to vote. The courts of the revising barristers became a focus of action by the agents of Whigs and Tories, protectionists and free-traders, liberals and conservatives, and other interest groups – for example the Society for the Liberation of Religion from State Patronage and Control, which had a specially-appointed committee, 'to work electoral machinery as far as possible for anti-state-church purposes'.[11]

Such agents operated openly under the aegis of an organization or interest group, with a view to enfranchising existing property owners. By contrast, early attempts actually to create new voters are somewhat obscure. From at least the 1780s building clubs, typically composed of a few tradesmen and small masters, had operated in certain towns. Some at least must have been mindful of a political dimension to their activities. The first documented land society in the capital to have had an explicit enfranchising intent emerged in 1829. By the mid-1830s, even before case law had affirmed the legality of mortgagor voting, clubs 'wishing to make purchases for votes' existed in Birmingham, whilst the Owenite movement discussed a similar strategy as part of its communitarian plans.[12] Chartists likewise combined to exploit opportunities in this way. Partly because the legal position had yet to be clarified, but also because of the dilution of broader principles that it implied, this aspect of early Chartist organization was little publicized. A report of 1840 from the London Charter Association's committee on electoral tactics, chaired by the veteran Henry Hetherington, gives the first firm indication of the manipulation of the forty-shilling freehold franchise:

> Another effective mode of creating Chartist voters might be, by establishing among the members of the [Metropolitan Political] Union societies of working men; each contributing a certain sum per week to form a fund, the sole object of which fund should be to take houses, and place therein a number of members to be joint proprietors; by such means the members would not only have a direct and permanent interest in the movement, but would, both by their votes and interest, render powerful aid to the cause.[13]

In the changing climate of opinion after 1842, from which the Land Plan ultimately emerged, Chartists were more explicit about the potential for vote-creation. During the mid-1840s, the Central Registration Committee, with the land-owning radical MP for Finsbury, Thomas Slingsby Duncombe, as its president, worked quietly but efficiently to create both county and borough voters.[14] Before it emerged that allotments on the Chartist colonies were effectively tenancies rather than freeholds, the Plan had an explicitly stated aim of enfranchising its members: 'the Land Plan at one and the same time will confer both political and social freedom', the Registration Committee confirmed in 1845. The same objective was adopted by the East London Boot and Shoemakers' Mutual Protection Society, an organization which eventually dissolved itself in order to re-form as a branch of the Chartist Land Plan.[15] Beyond Chartism, but firmly within the radical tradition, the National Land and Building Society similarly emphasized the political advantages of freehold property,[16] as did the less overtly political Oddfellows' Land and Building Society.[17] By the late 1840s, therefore, the radical credentials of forty-shilling freehold vote creation were well established. Besides the possibility of enfranchisement, these societies explicitly endorsed the idea of property ownership. Building society principles attracted an active popular political constituency, the most obvious indication of this being the Starr-Bowkett Building Societies, another product of the late 1840s with a distinct radical pedigree.[18] The primary function of even the Chartist Land Plan itself may for many have been that of a building society: a survey of its Teesside membership, for example, reveals both large numbers of lodgers, and a higher propensity (compared with local Chartist activists as a whole) for married members to reside with a partner's parents. This suggests that many perceived the Plan as a building society as much as an agrarian scheme per se.[19]

Liberal patrons of freehold land societies tended to credit free trade rather than popular radicalism with the discovery that 'the price of political emancipation is down in the market',[20] the first concerted campaign fully to exploit the vagaries of the county freehold franchise having been organized by the Anti-Corn Law League. In 1841 both free-trade candidates for the West Riding of Yorkshire were defeated soundly by protectionists. Defeat in this important constituency, the largest in the country, was a blow to Whig-Liberal morale, and was ascribed as much to the superior organization of the Tories as to the intrinsic appeal of protection to the electorate. Cobden, at the suggestion of a Rochdale Chartist and League supporter Charles Walker, initiated a scheme whereby 2,000 names were added to the electoral roll in a little over two years. Land was purchased and subdivided for sale to supporters in parcels of sufficient value to confer the vote. No attempt was made to establish a cadre of either smallholders or homeowners: in many cases the purchased property was immediately leased back to the vendor. The success of the strategy was so apparent in the revising barrister's court that the Tories failed to contest a by-election in 1846 and Lord Morpeth, the sitting member defeated in 1841, was returned unopposed. At the general election the following year Morpeth was returned with a substantial majority in the company of Cobden himself.[21] The same strategy was successfully applied by the League in East Surrey and Lancashire, and used to sustain the free-trade vote in a number of other counties through the 'Quarter of a Million Fund', raised by subscription for the purchase of properties in targeted constituencies. Cobden, in his own words, was converted to 'the opinion, that if they wanted to make another change constitutionally and legally, it would be by the 40s. freehold plan, and by no other means'.[22]

The success of the initiative arguably engendered over-optimism in Liberal ranks. The Anti-Corn Law League had pursued an ad hoc strategy to secure specified electoral goals. The vast majority of votes had been manufactured for conspicuously absentee patrons without recourse to mortgages. Free-traders from Scotland (where electoral law differed), for example, were invited to purchase freeholds in Northumberland and Durham.[23] However, support for the freehold land societies was drawn from more localized and humbler backgrounds. The delivery of monolithic slabs of Liberal support was never part of their agenda. Whilst many members were sympathetic to Liberal parliamentary candidates, others were not; and the motives of nearly all of them reflected not only political, but also economic, and more directly personal, considerations.

The freehold land movement was an archetype of the ethic of self-help. 'This Society was established to improve the social, promote the moral, and exalt the political condition of the industrial population', stated the Birmingham FLS in a typical formula.[24] The vote was only one of several attractions, others being the ownership of real property, secure investment of savings until such time as a freehold became available, and the acquisition of the social status which accompanied both land ownership and the exercise of 'political manhood'. Furthermore, membership of such societies itself carried status:

> The Freehold Land Society as a depository for future requirements, as a stepping stone to an honourable independence, as offering the means for a noble resistance to the invitations of the poorhouse, as a machine to effect man's political redemption, is without parallel in the history of this great Empire.[25]

All the constituents of Victorian self-help are present in this extract from the *Prospectus* of the Bradford FLS: thrift, honour, and independence, underlined by a mistily-perceived nationalism and a rather more sharply-focused fear of the workhouse. The central concern is status, social and political. The origins of the forty-shilling freehold electoral strategy in the labour movement suggest that the consensus achieved from the mid-1840s onwards, between middle-class liberalism and working-class radicalism, was not the fruit of a hegemonic imposition of 'bourgeois' values on a compliant workforce. Nor was it contingent upon the incorporation of an 'aristocracy of labour'.[26] The freehold land movement did largely cater for small tradesmen and skilled artisans, but its history helps clarify how a labour aristocracy evolved, not from the consciously manipulative work of the middle class, but rather from the drawing out of strands from within working-class experience. Just as it cannot be divorced from working-class political radicalism, so it was linked to the complex spectrum of popular mutual improvement. At its simplest level this spectrum manifested itself in the universal popularity of burial clubs, an insurance against the ultimate loss of status in a pauper's grave. The quest for homeownership was itself closely linked to the workman's concern to provide against death: 'The sting of calamity is in a great measure extracted by the provision which he has by a rigid economy and prudent foresight been enabled to secure against the day of trouble'.[27] One need not look hard for the roots of working-class materialism: every new possession stifled fear, and after the indignity of a pauper's grave, the greatest fear was eviction.

The freehold land movement also demonstrates two further elements central to an understanding of post-Chartist popular politics. The first was the continuing search for political advancement after both physical and moral force had been baffled; the second was the increasing sympathy this met from politicians of an advanced Liberal persuasion. 'Sympathy' is used advisedly here, for this was a reaction to indigenous popular values rather than an attempt to impose alien ones. The emergence of the freehold land movement was both an indication and a result of these trends.

It is significant, then, that the first and most influential freehold land society, founded in 1847, arose in Birmingham, a city with a tradition of class co-operation on radical political issues and a high concentration of skilled workers. Both its MPs, G. F. Muntz and William Scholefield, were advanced Liberals sympathetic to the People's Charter, and both took an active interest in the freehold land movement, appearing on public platforms in its promotion and serving the Birmingham society in the offices of trustee and president. There they were joined by a vice-president whose participation reveals the freehold land societies' close connections with Nonconformity, municipal pride, and social improvement: the Reverend George Dawson, father of Birmingham's civic gospel.[28] The Society's prime mover, however, was an associate of Dawson, its secretary James Taylor. A reformed drunkard of working-class background and secretary of the Birmingham Temperance Society, from 1848 Taylor devoted himself full-time to the freehold land movement nationally.[29]

These brief biographical details of supporters of the Birmingham FLS illustrate the movement's roots in Dissent, temperance, and liberalism; but the self-help ethic was no less important, and in pronounced contrast both to the philanthropic character of many contemporary allotment societies, and the non-commercial provision of working-class housing. In an interesting comparison, one writer claimed in 1860 that the retail co-operative movement did 'for the articles of the workman's daily consumption what Freehold Land and Building Societies have done for land and houses'.[30] From its commencement, the emphasis of the movement was on self-improvement:

Working men of Bradford – of England! To you the Committee appeal. Your own enfranchisement is within your reach. Be independent and noble minded. The British legislature, by a great majority, told Joseph Hume, Esq., M.P., that you are unworthy of the 'Vote', and denied you the right to possess it! Cease to ask for that which by your own frugality you can obtain! To the cause of your own freedom you are invited, to the brilliant deed of your own political redemption you are now challenged.[31]

Freehold land societies were frequently connected with existing agencies for working-class self-improvement. Along with temperance societies these form a familiar pattern. The London Mechanics' Institute spawned its own society, the Birkbeck, as did institutes at Coventry, Peterborough, and Sheffield. 'Literary Institutes' played host to societies in Lambeth and Southwark, the Christian Brethren to a Batley society, and the Wesleyan school to Clayton West's. At Oldham aspiring freeholders met 'in the school-room of the Working Men's Hall', whilst Northampton's society formed round the nucleus of local Owenite secularists.[32] Other societies were closely connected with another familiar focal point for self-improvement, the public house. Licensed premises had long accommodated burial and friendly societies, building clubs and trade unions. Freehold land societies conformed to this well-established pattern. The freehold land movement was genuinely popular, with antecedents considerably broader than temperance and Dissent alone. Whilst the members of the Attercliffe Fruits of the Soil FLS were meeting in a Methodist New Connexion schoolroom, their neighbours of the Attercliffe Freedom Hill Society were in the Coach and Horses.[33] Like Owenite and Chartist groups before them, societies also assumed ancillary social functions. Weekly meetings were held on topics which were often tangential to the movement's central aims. Elaborate celebrations on a society acquiring an estate, or upon the first allottees taking possession, were customary, and closely resembled those of the Chartist Land Plan. For example, the first street of houses developed by the Uxbridge branch of the National FLS was named Walmesley Terrace after the Bolton MP and president of both the Society and the National Reform Association. On taking possession in September 1850, the property was decorated with banners and flags, and a sports day held, 'enlivened by an excellent brass band'.[34] As developers, freehold land societies were well geared to the scale of the mid-Victorian construction industry. Whilst the number of large firms grew during the century, the typical house-builder was a small master. In London, for example, during the period 1840-70 some 80 per cent of building firms were responsible for six or fewer houses per annum; fully one-third of all firms built only one or two houses in any one year.[35]

The fact that freehold land societies offered plots of land grouped on estates and, in the case of the larger municipal societies, developed houses on them had particular attractions. Not only building but also legal costs were kept to a minimum, an important consideration, since the cost of conveyancing was generally considered a major disincentive to working-class purchases of real property.[36] Second, as Crossick suggests in his survey of artisan housing in Kentish London, such developments were status-defining residences, and 'added a spatial dimension to social separation'. The titles of many streets sponsored by these societies themselves proclaimed residents' sense of community and unity of purpose. There were countless Bright, Cobden, and later Gladstone streets. Leicester, Northampton and Ludlow were just three of the towns which boasted a Freehold Street or Terrace, whilst Sheffield societies developed both a Liberty and a Freedom Hill.[37] In his evidence to the Royal Commission on Friendly Societies in 1871, Taylor emphasized the concentration of freeholders' homes in refuting a suggestion that the origins of these houses, and their being purchased through a mortgage, rendered them unattractive to the working class. These factors, he insisted, together with the superior sanitary arrangements in such developments, rendered them particularly attractive.[38]

However, to treat the freehold land movement solely as a housing developer is to pass over several other important facets of its character. In their initial phase these societies were, first and foremost, *land* societies: many remained so. They should therefore be seen in the context of the long and vital history of English radical agrarianism, and of the particular acceleration in popular interest in land schemes of all kinds in the mid-1840s.[39] Ostensibly this may seem implausible, given the urban roots of the movement and its function as a developer, especially of suburban housing. Yet few things so closely underline the psychological unity which still obtained between rural and urban England in the mid-nineteenth century than the emergence of the freehold land movement. Many publications and speeches generated in its cause reflected the extent to which questions about the land and its ownership were still felt to be pressingly relevant to society in general:

THE FREEHOLDERS UNION are engaged in the two-fold labour of extending the Franchise and multiplying the number of landed proprietors. We hardly know which of these two is the more important and needful. The monopoly of political power and the monopoly of the land are the two parent evils in this country, from which a multitude of lesser ones grow; and it is not possible to attack the one but through the other, or to effect any great or beneficial change in the condition of the mass of the people, until both these monopolies are abolished.[40]

The significance of such a statement lies in its resonance with the sentiments of both Chartism and advanced liberalism on 'the land question'. Freehold land societies were born at the same historical moment as the Chartist Land Plan and a plethora of other schemes such as the National Land and Building Society. For many urban workers, the land was historically distant enough to be alluring, yet sufficiently close – spatially and psychologically – still to seem attainable. Furthermore, the Reform Act of 1832 was increasingly seen less in terms of the downward extension of political rights to 'the middle class' than as the successful arrest of the drift of political control away from landed property. Neither petitions for the Charter, nor the truncated concept of 'Complete Suffrage', had met with any success. Though an important element within the NCA sought to consolidate the radical agrarian tradition through the adoption of land nationalization, most looked to policies of greater access to the land through widening ownership.[41]

The freehold land movement sought to achieve this both by societies' practical operations, and by acting as a focal point for agitation for free trade in land. It linked its activities to a widening gulf in society: 'Our towns are unnaturally filled – our villages are as unnaturally drained. As a consequence fearful evils are perpetrated. These can only be removed by a restoration of a proper balance, and this can only be effected by free-trade in land.' Prospectuses for the Birmingham FLS were headed with the biblical quotation (Joshua I: 2), 'POSSESS THE LAND', and prominent among the slogans therein, as elsewhere in the literature of the movement, were 'freeholds for the people' and 'land for the people'. The Birmingham society also conspicuously deployed one of the most emotive terms in the radical agrarian vocabulary, jubilee, in connection with its anniversary in 1854. James Taylor headed his propaganda with the alluring cry: 'County votes for working men and freeholds for the million'.[42]

That the freehold land movement set out to restore 'a proper balance' between towns and villages may seem ironic, in view of its substantial contribution to suburban development. However, the suburban retrospect should be set against the contemporary view that the societies offered an escape from urban chaos, congestion, and rented property. Membership was a means to counter the rural/urban imbalance in personal life, through the acquisition of an allotment or a home with an adjoining garden. Many societies left it to individual decision whether or not to build on a plot. The disparate building styles of those freeholder streets still untouched by redevelopment in Sheffield, for example, bear witness to a piecemeal approach to building somewhat akin to twentieth-century 'plotland' development (where agrarian impulses were likewise a key motivating factor). The process by which the Sheffield suburb of Walkley, 'the working man's West End', developed was described by one contemporary thus:

> Scarcely had plots been staked out and allocated before owners were busy digging, fencing, or building, in the early morning and late at night, Saturday afternoon and often all day on Sundays, until rough plots took the shape of gardens with vegetables and flowers ... and every conceivable adjunct to agriculture and horticulture on a small scale. ... Soon crude huts gave place to detached houses – hundreds of which studded the hillside.[43]

Even the National FLS, in time one of the greatest metropolitan housing developers, initially shared in the objective of simple land provision, a fact which Cobden, in launching the Society in 1849, was at pains to emphasize. Contemporaries commented on the function of allotment provision: 'The erection of houses is seldom or never to be attained in these societies.'[44] Even when the movement became consistently focused upon housing development, space was still found in its journals for horticultural articles. In the smaller societies the function simply of providing land was never eclipsed. This was the case in Sheffield as late as the 1870s, whilst in 1881 the influential advocate of land reform, G. C. Brodrick, noted that 'the acquisition of minute plots by the working classes has been facilitated of late by the agency of freehold land societies ... and may hereafter be developed into a modified form of peasant proprietorship'.[45]

Even as the larger societies concentrated on building development there was sometimes a tendency to provide large gardens at the expense of domestic amenities (inside lavatories, for instance). Whether houses were erected by a society, the individual, or not at all, in almost every case it is possible to discern vestigial agrarian sentiments in the largely urban membership. Psychologically, the mid-Victorian working class was never far from the countryside. The early growth of homeownership can be interpreted as an attempt to diminish the gulf between town and country, and to vouchsafe an element of real control over a key aspect of personal life in the face of diminishing independence at the workplace. Just as suburbia compensated for urban working conditions, so owner-occupiership can be seen as a compensation for the deference integral to both industrial and commercial labour, and the increasing popularity of gardening as balancing the loss of control over the process of production. Because working-class experience remains largely defined by historians through workplace, trade union, and political activities, the importance of home life and domesticity to Victorian workers has been significantly underestimated.[46] Until these are put back into the historical equation, the growth of building societies will be imperfectly understood. The comforts of home, and the contribution such societies might make to securing them, were a recurring theme.[47] In the words of the *Freehold Land Times and Building News*:

A detached or semi-detached house gives one more fresh air and breathing space, such privacy as is consistent with independence, room for children to run about in and for the wife to discharge her household duties.[48]

This passage might epitomize Victorian middle-class aspirations, were it not for its emphasis on the wife as a worker rather than ornament in the home. The independence of which it speaks is that aspired to in the Chartist Land Plan rather than of bourgeois respectability. In an attenuated form the ideals of the English radical agrarian tradition thus lived on in the freehold land movement – attenuated, because the function of this vestigial agrarianism was to compensate for the direction of economic and social change rather than, as previously, to subvert it.

Chartist critics similarly regarded the freehold movement's position on the franchise as severely compromising the radical political tradition.[49] The failure of successive radical agitations to secure even partial satisfaction had however created a climate in which any extension of the electorate, however modest and however achieved, was attractive to many who still supported the principle of universal suffrage:

The majority of 'Freehold Land' supporters do not concede one iota of their claim for Universal Suffrage ... but they think, nevertheless, that until this moral right be made a legal one (hopes, the realisation of which twinkles dimly in the distance), something has to be done to increase and consolidate the strength of the people, in order to provide a counterpoise to the power of the aristocracy, and gain another point in the mountain of progressive reform.[50]

Official pronouncements often emphasized that the freehold land movement was an alternative strategy to Chartism:

it is now clear that the people can obtain a Reform Bill for themselves through the medium of these Societies. The law is with them. Judges have decided in favour of the principle this Society adopts. The individual interests of the people will be promoted by supporting it. Shall it be said, therefore, that they claimed from the Government that which they had not the perseverance nor the consistency to obtain for themselves when clearly placed within their reach?[51]

It was precisely on this basis that the freehold land movement was supported by radicals as varied as G. J. Holyoake,[52] Henry Hetherington,[53] Thomas Beggs,[54] the former Chartist Robert Lowery (like Beggs active in Lovett's 'People's League'),[55] and, later, Charles Bradlaugh.[56] Even the *Northern Star* felt obliged to balance its highly critical editorial position with lengthy objective reports of Freehold Land Union conferences.[57] Where a distinct rift did emerge between the freehold land movement and Chartism was over the former's wish to disassociate itself from Feargus O'Connor and the Land Plan, the protracted and inelegant demise of which coincided with the formative years of the movement:

With Mr O'Connor's political principles we have no controversy, but every friend of Land or Building societies has a right to complain of the odium which his blundering mismanagement is calculated to bring on all such Associations.[58]

The potential for confusion between Chartism and the freehold land movement increased after 1849 with the appearance of the National Freehold Benefit Building Society, set up by the Land Plan to seek to circumvent legal problems, and of a further two societies with Chartist promoters, the British Empire Freehold Land and Building Society (in which Duncombe was involved), and the United Patriots' National Benefit and FLS (whose promoters included O'Connor, George Julian Harney, and W. J. Linton).[59] A less equivocal source of support for the freehold land movement came from the radical caucus in Parliament. The involvement of Muntz and Scholefield in Birmingham has already been noted. Charles Gilpin, MP for Northampton (1857-74) and one of the foremost campaigners for the ballot, was an enthusiastic early patron.[60] Thomas Slingsby Duncombe was president of a society in his Finsbury constituency. The former Anti-Corn

Law League activist and noted anti-slavery campaigner, George Thompson (MP for Tower Hamlets, 1847-52), was a trustee of both the British and Westminster Societies; in the latter he was joined by the remarkable member for Peterborough, G. H. Whalley, whose outspoken support of the Tichborne Claimant was to take him to prison in the 1870s. The Lambeth FLS enjoyed as its patron one of the most persistent campaigners for electoral reform, Locke King.[61]

The brightest constellation of Liberal patrons was to be found on the board of the National FLS. It was originally conceived in 1849 as an offshoot of the Metropolitan (later National) Parliamentary and Financial Reform Association, a body which had involved both Francis Place and Feargus O'Connor in its early months. In practice, the council of the Association became dominated by former Anti-Corn Law League activists. It was this body which delegated twelve of its members to form the initial steering committee of what, following the style of the parent organization, was at first titled the Metropolitan and Home Counties FLS. Among the twelve were Sir Joshua Walmsley (president of both the Association and the Society); Cobden; Joseph Hume, the promoter of 'the Little Charter'; Samuel Morley; and Gilpin.[62] John Bright joined as director a year later, having initially devoted his energies to an abortive 'Commons' League' (whose objectives likewise included the exploitation of the forty-shilling freehold franchise).[63]

The freehold land movement thus gave the impression, as George Thompson remarked, of being 'a confederacy mainly of Liberal politicians'.[64] By any standards the contingent of Liberal parliamentarians involved was both sizeable and important, and it provides perhaps the fullest index of the movement's initial political seriousness. For Cobden especially, freehold land societies were more than merely a vehicle for stiffening the Liberal spine of county electorates: 'In proportion as this 40s. freehold movement made progress, in the same proportion would they find the votes of the House of Commons on all liberal questions would make progress.'[65] Their presence, and especially that of Cobden, should be seen in the context of that sense of isolation and frustration experienced by Anti-Corn Law Leaguers in the decade following repeal. As McCord some time ago observed, 'the disappearance of Corn as an immediate political issue put the initiative in British politics back firmly in the hands of the established parties'.[66] It was this cadre which pushed for the formation of an umbrella body, the Freehold Land Union, and for a newspaper, *The Freeholder*, which like *The League* before it was distributed gratis to the influential as well as sold to the faithful.[67]

Yet these moves to place the freehold land movement on a professional footing similar to the Anti-Corn Law League were also an indication of a failure of political imagination. Cobden especially was incapable of thinking in terms of a wider reforming movement: his lukewarm response to the Commons' League, with its broad parcel of reforming policies, suggests a loss of political nerve, whilst his fixation that the freehold land movement could reinstate him and his followers at the pivotal point of political action reveals a misreading of both the mood of the working class and its capacity for action on the issue. 'The forty-shilling scheme alone will not do the work, and alone it will not work extensively,' wrote Bright to Cobden, 'I think you exaggerate the extent to which people will adopt the system, especially as no definite object or battle is before them.'[68] In a private letter, the Sheffield MP John Arthur Roebuck was more forthright: 'Cobden is a poor creature, with one idea – the making of county voters. He is daunted by the country squires, and hopes to conquer them by means of these votes.'[69]

If Cobden intended the freehold land movement to absorb political energies largely baffled since Repeal, he also meant it to serve the same function as the League in clothing an attack on the landed interest:

I want it as a means to all that we require, and upon my conscience it is, I believe, the only stepping-stone to any material change. The citadel of privilege in this country is so terribly strong, owing to the concentrated masses of property in the hands of the comparatively few, that we cannot hope to assail it with success unless with the help of the propertied classes in the middle ranks of society, and by raising up a portion of the working class to become members of the propertied order; and I know of no other mode of enlisting such co-operation but that which I have suggested.

The requisite 'portion of the working class' Cobden defined as 'teetotallers, non-conformists and rational Radicals'.[70] Whatever its shortcomings as a grand political strategy, the participation of prominent advanced Liberals in the movement visibly set a seal of approval on the working-class ethic of self-help, whilst avoiding any offensive suggestion of charity or patronage. Much of the movement's significance lay in its extending that code of self-improvement, which had hitherto been largely confined to the labour movement, into the new context of liberalism.

'The citadel of privilege' was assailed both at the polls and through the routine functioning of the societies. Their very modus operandi advertised the virtues of free trade in land. Supporters argued for the social necessity of the sale and dispersal of landed property unhindered by the laws of settlement, primogeniture, mortmain or entail. In the counties, though few electoral victories could positively be ascribed to the movement, societies formed the nucleus for constituency organization and broadened awareness of Liberal policies and personalities.

There are also grounds for suggesting that the movement to some extent did undermine the confidence of landed interests. At its simplest, evidence of this can be found in proceedings before the revising barristers' courts, where the franchises created through these societies were vigorously contested by protectionist interests. The quality of land, building construction, and services such as mains drainage, were all disputable when a franchise was initially registered, and most societies took care to retain the services of both builders and surveyors to attest on such issues.[71] Still more indicative of Tory disquiet was the formation in 1852 of a 'defence Society (for it really was a defence movement on our part, and we were driven to it)'. The Conservative Land Society copied the very procedures of the societies it opposed, and like the National and other municipal societies developed large suburban estates, similarly evolving into a permanent building society:

FREEHOLD LAND SOCIETIES have done good service to the Radical cause at the late election. Lancashire has long since been secured through their means, and the West Riding all but converted into the pocket borough of the Cobden family. In East Surrey and Middlesex the Conservative candidates were defeated solely by their means, and in many other counties there would not have been a contest, much less a hard battle, had it not been for the exertions of radical Freehold Land Societies ... Why should not the 'CONSTITUTIONAL PARTY' have their LAND SOCIETIES, and raise up a counteracting body of intelligent freeholders to poll against those of their destructive rivals? This course ought to have been pursued years back.[72]

The most realistic attempt to counteract the impact of the freehold land movement was made in the form of proposals for legislative intervention to curtail the scope of its political activity. Disraeli discussed such a project, 'which will probably be the key to future power', as early as 1850. It was the end of the decade, however, before he presented a package of reforms to Parliament which would, if passed, have nullified the movement's additions to the electorate. The 1859 Reform Bill was the most eloquent testimony to the impact of the freehold land movement. It is now largely remembered as the occasion of the collapse of Derby's second ministry, and for what Bright contemptuously described as 'fancy franchises' – electoral qualifications based upon educational criteria, and on savings bank investments.

However, the Bill also proposed the abolition of the forty-shilling freehold county vote, transferring existing voters to the boroughs in which their property was situated, but disenfranchising those whose qualification lay in a county constituency alone.[73] The ministry's defeat came with the division on Russell's amendment that it was 'neither just nor politic to interfere' in the forty-shilling freehold franchise.[74] The contemporary Tory response to the freehold land movement suggests that Cobden's enthusiasm for it may not have been as tactically inept as his recent biographers, and before them Roebuck and Bright, implied.[75]

None the less, it failed 'to effect a breach in that fortress of landlordism, the county representation', as the 1852 *Reformers' Almanac* had predicted. The political appeal of the movement depended heavily on its being seen as a cognate organization within a concerted campaign for reform. The steady decline of 'Liberal' interests in the counties (from a peak of 71 in 1835 to 36 in 1847) was hardly arrested by the movement at the general election of 1852, which saw a total of only thirty Radical Liberals returned for the English counties.[76] Parliamentary patrons reassessed their support in the light of both the election and the difficulties experienced by the Parliamentary and Financial Reform Association that year. Bright was the first to decline re-election to the board of the National FLS (by 1858 only Gilpin remained). A careful estimate of the allotments created by freehold land societies, made by Thomas Beggs the following year, put the total at 19,500 – an impressive figure but, diluted over 44 counties, unlikely to force a rout at the polls. Seven years later, in a speech opposing Disraeli's Reform Bill, Bright estimated the total votes created at 36,000. The only specific victories ascribed to the movement by its supporters were East Surrey (where the National Society consolidated Locke King's thin majority), Middlesex ('though by the hair of his [the Radical member's] head'), and North Warwickshire.[77]

If election results disappointed parliamentary Liberals, they only reflected the experience of the Freehold Land Union and the *Freeholder* in trying to marshal the constituent parts of the movement. The Union had no coercive powers, and it was a frequent complaint that societies' officials failed to take it seriously, or provide statistical data to enable the movement's progress to be monitored. Cassell, editor of the *Freeholder*, another casualty of 1852, voiced similar complaints.[78] Middle-class liberalism had failed to hijack what was essentially a working-class movement. As such its aims and aspirations differed from those of its patrons, as the authors of *Progress of the Working Classes* observed:

Freehold Land Societies started with the intention of manufacturing forty-shilling freeholders ... That objective is now quite a matter of secondary consideration. The shareholders may not care less for the freehold, or the political power it confers; but their leading desire is to add a house to the land, and thus secure free homes.[79]

From the mid-1850s the direction of freehold land societies' literature increasingly emphasized the building function. This was not an abrogation of their pedigree, since mutual improvement had always shared with radical politics the shaping of the movement. Even the most commercial societies continued to advertise an intention to help 'prevent ... the evil operation of those laws that fostered the possession of large estates, and gave to the few an undue influence over the many'. If this was bravado, it was none the less bravado that seems to have sold shares.[80] Likewise, the *Freehold Land Times*, which commenced in 1854 and was, in contrast to the earlier *Freeholder*, a strictly commercial venture, maintained a policy of editorial and news coverage of a Liberal bent, in support for example of land reform and free trade, and attacking the conduct of the Crimean War. What militated most against the ambitious agenda parliamentary Liberals tried to impose on the movement, was the range and character of the societies it awkwardly embraced. Not only were certain societies uninterested in Liberal parliamentary aspirations; some were actively hostile. There was little in common between the National and even the larger provincial societies, and still less between the latter and the small groups, based on local and workplace communities, which were the typical form the movement took, for example, in Sheffield. These contrasts themselves reflected the often sharply-differentiated experience of labour in the major industrial cities. To a significant extent Chartism had exposed such differences rather than reconciled them: it was hardly likely that a modest venture like the Freehold Land Union would succeed.[81]

With the leviathan National very much an exception to the pattern, the overwhelming majority of societies were modest in size and scope and directly controlled by their memberships, a major reason why they proved so resistant to the centralizing aspirations of the Freehold Land Union. Many were so small and/or vigorously independent that they failed to register under the Friendly Societies Act and as a result were (and remain) practically invisible. However, at least 184 societies can be established as operating between 1847 and 1854, a total which is significantly larger than the 'approximately 130' identified by Beggs, the most scholarly contemporary commentator. Even the higher figure, however, is almost certainly incomplete: 'I have found it no easy matter to get particulars of the various societies, or even to ascertain the existence of some of them. Many of them are doing a very small business, and seem to be loosely conducted.'[82]

The distribution of the 184 societies is informative. First and foremost, there were none in Scotland and Ireland, where different electoral law applied, though a Scottish Forty-Shilling Freehold movement was set up to agitate for the extension of the franchise to counties north of the border.[83] In Wales, where English law applied, freehold land societies were founded in Abergavenny, Cardiff, Pontypool, Pontypridd and Swansea. No other Welsh building societies were registered at this point, and it would seem that at a time when such organizations were proliferating in England, the freehold land movement may have been a prime mover in their extension into Wales.[84] A similar situation existed in some English centres. In 1854 freehold land societies accounted for all registered building-society activity in Barnstaple, Bolton, Burton-on-Trent, Hanley, Ipswich, Newcastle, Norwich and Sunderland. Small building clubs on the terminating principle probably existed in all these towns; but to such provincial centres the freehold land movement extended the concept of the permanent principle, as well as the social base of building-society operations. Lincoln furnishes a good example of this: its first building club was founded in 1847, but building-society activity there only became significant with the formation two years later of the Lincoln and Lincolnshire FLS. A branch of the Conservative Land Society followed in 1853. Between them the two societies extended owner-occupation across a far broader social spectrum than a building club could ever have done. For example in 1855 the Conservative society bought five and a half acres which were made available to members at a cost of 1s. 6d. per yard, inclusive of road costs. Hitherto, purchasers could expect to pay upwards of 5s. a yard, and still have to make their own roads.[85]

The most striking feature of the regional distribution of these societies, however, concerns London. Before 1852 only four had emerged in the capital, against some seventy in the provinces, (with particular clusters in the West Riding and West Midlands). The London-based National, admittedly, was of exceptional size, yet at least thirty other societies predated its formation. By 1854, however, the geographical balance had shifted drastically. Fifty-eight societies now operated from addresses in the capital: on the other hand, few provincial societies were registered in the 1850s. The new London societies exhibited a very different character. They tended not to be focused on a geographical area, and combined a calculated appeal to the readiest market for cheap suburban housing with the character of speculative commercial ventures. This is evident in the titles of several: City of London Provident Clerks'; Freemasons'; Government Officers'; United Tradesmen's; Suburban Villa and Village. The Ancient Order of Foresters' Friendly Society found its title assumed without permission by a purely commercial undertaking. In the competitive atmosphere that surrounded the development of estates on the metropolitan fringe even those societies with ulterior political motives encountered frustration. The Temperance FLS dissipated its energies trying to create voters for South Essex, only to be confronted by apathy on polling day. Its first estate, at Stratford, was its last, and henceforward it operated purely as a building society.[86]

Jobbing was by now rife in the shares of metropolitan societies, as estates were acquired for development ahead of the extension of railway lines from the capital.[87] The *Freehold Land Times* printed the share prices of nearly every London society, along with market intelligence. As a consequence, there emerged a contrasting pattern of shareholding between capital and provinces.[88] In the latter most shares were held singly by largely working-class memberships. The ratio of members to shares was rarely less than 70 per cent in the provincial societies. In some, such as Northampton (79 per cent), Dudley (82 per cent), Bradford (84 per cent), and North Staffordshire (88 per cent), it was even higher. By contrast, as early as 1850 the membership/ share ratio of the National was only 53 per cent, the lowest of any society from which statistics were collected by the Freehold Land Union that year.[89] Dissenting voices were raised at trends within the Society,[90] but already it was set on the path that would take it to become 'the largest land company to operate in London generally during the nineteenth century'.[91]

The commercial basis of such societies, so soon after the movement's inception, calls into question the social constituency it served. The freehold land movement was never exclusively working class, but nor was it exclusively middle class. Chapman and Bartlett's analysis of a Birmingham FLS development of the early 1850s, Victoria Road, Aston Park, suggested that around a quarter of households employed at least one living-in servant. Skilled artisans and independent masters made up the rest of the household heads who did not. Victoria Road, an infill development of relatively low-density housing, was not typical of the Birmingham Society's activities, and the proportion of working-class residents was probably greater elsewhere. Most societies which attempted large-scale developments built a variety of housing types, like any large commercial developer, with cheaper working-class homes forming the bulk of the units constructed.[92] In evidence to the Royal Commission on Friendly Societies, James Taylor stressed the working-class base of the movement in Birmingham, though since he explicitly included Victoria Road allowance must be made for his having exaggerated:

They mostly belong to the working population of the town. We have some 10,000 or 12,000 members in our offices, all of whom are working men, certainly 95 out of every 100 … We have 13,000 houses in Birmingham belonging to working men. We have streets more than a mile long, in which absolutely every house belongs to the working-classes of Birmingham – Albert Road, Victoria Road, Gladstone Road, Cobden Street, Bright Terrace, and so on.[93]

Four years before, Ludlow and Jones, in *The Progress of the Working Classes*, estimated the total of 'working men's homes' erected in the city at between 8,000 and 9,000; 'fully 90 per cent of the persons enrolled were working men, whose wages varied from 12s. to 40s. per week'. A contemporary Birmingham historian described the freehold land movement quite simply as 'for the benefit and elevation of the working-classes'.[94]

Even the National Society enjoyed a sizeable popular enrolment. Its working-class membership was estimated at one-third of the total, a proportion smaller societies almost certainly exceeded.[95] Whalley described the membership of the British FLS as 'chiefly of the working classes'. In Northampton, Bradlaugh's electoral base was widely ascribed to the success of the local FLS in creating household qualifications for the borough.[96] A Chartist described the membership of the Stafford FLS as 'small tradesmen, warehouse clerks, lawyers' clerks, shoe clickers, and the higher paid class of mechanics – the aristocracy of labour'. Another Chartist concurred, describing the supporters of the movement generally as 'a small portion of the best paid operatives and a few enterprising tradesmen'. A further general assessment, compiled by an actuary in 1851, found that freehold land societies were 'extensively taken up by the class of small retail dealers, employés [sic], and the superior class of workmen'.[97]

The freehold land movement retained a working-class base, therefore, whilst its middle-class membership was overwhelmingly drawn from the newly socially mobile stratum of small retailers and tradesmen. For the remainder of the middle class home ownership was the exception, rather than the norm. If, as Thompson suggests, such 'institutions ... retained from their origins more than a whiff of radicalism and vulgarity', the freehold land movement might well have reinforced social distinction.[98] This was not incompatible with the enhancement of social consensus. The ties that bound the mid-Victorian consensus were generated as much from within working-class experience, as they were imposed from without. Freehold land societies served to infuse into the middle classes the popular aspiration for home ownership. They, and the building societies into which they evolved or which replaced them, became part of the fabric of a viable class society, assuaging middle-class nervousness of the highly mobile urban working-class householder, ostensibly rootless and bereft of civic pride. 'Building societies are much more than societies for building,' explained a speaker to the 1859 conference of the Social Science Association. Their

> tendency must be to raise the character and condition of the operative; to increase his repugnance of strikes … They foster a spirit of self-denial, of prudence, and forethought. By increasing each man's interest in the State, they directly promote the stability and permanence of its institutions. Still more, I believe them to exercise a powerful educational influence, to teach, in the long run, self-control and mutual forbearance, thus contributing above and beyond their financial uses to the intellectual and moral elevation of the people.[99]

The close links between the freehold land movement (and building societies generally) with temperance reinforced this tendency: as the movement shed overtly political aspirations, so the moral aspects of self-improvement through home ownership were increasingly emphasized:

> In a late report of the Committee of the Coventry Society we read that 'one of the most pleasing results of the society's operations is the improved moral habits of many of its members'. The North and East Riding society also reported: 'The society's operations produce the best effects on the habits of the poorer members by encouraging them to save money from the public house.' Similar testimony was also borne by the Newcastle Committee; and at Darlington we learn that the society has been the means of converting many of its members into steady members of society, and instead of finding them at the ale-house … you may now see them at our Mechanics' Institution, gaining all the information they can. Thus, then, the Freehold Land Movement is creating everywhere a great moral revolution.[100]

In any explanation of Victorian social stability working-class home ownership, slight though it was, provides an important element.[101] It was concentrated in a manner which inflicted maximum damage on labour's capacity to mobilize on the housing issue. 'Along with unemployment, housing was the most intractable of problems with which the labour movement had to deal.'[102] Yet this centrality is not reflected in the popular politics of the period. The likely leadership of any working-class campaign on the issue – skilled, educated, and enjoying regular employment at a wage above subsistence level – was continually being siphoned off into homes of its own. The emergence of the freehold land and building society movements effectively eliminated urban rents and housing as a grievance for the most politically articulate of the working class; and, in addition, this cadre extended beyond actual homeowners to those saving to become so. Moreover, the increasingly common pattern of building society mortgagors taking on two houses, one for themselves and the other for letting to cover the cost of building, converted lower-middle-class and labour-aristocrat owner-occupiers into urban landlords as well.[103]

Goldman has pointed to the importance of the Social Science Association, and similar organizations, in laying the foundations of that 'public opinion ... both broad and deep' to which Gladstonian liberalism owed its existence. The freehold land movement was similarly one of the 'symbolic institutional engines of the liberal consolidation'.[104] It was a milestone in the emergence of that spirit of class co-operation, cemented by specific personal contacts, upon which the electoral effectiveness of radical liberalism so much depended. Into liberalism it injected a tradition of politically-orientated mutual improvement which had hitherto been almost exclusively working class in character. It was also a significant vehicle for promoting free trade, most obviously in land, and for sustaining the radical-liberal critique of the landed interest. However, Cobden's optimism that the movement was 'a means to all that we require ... the only stepping-stone to any material change', was misplaced.[105] Bright's hesitant support for the National FLS, and his early desertion, were a more accurate evaluation. His presidency of the society in his Rochdale constituency, though, was a long-term commitment and precisely that kind of involvement on the part of advanced Liberal figures which was of the greatest value. It set a visible seal of approval on working-class mutuality; it widened the dissemination of ideas and publicity; helped to consolidate constituency organization; and narrowed the divide between those urban areas where liberalism was traditionally strongest with the rural counties where it was weakest. Disraeli's 1859 Reform Bill suggests that the freehold land movement had disturbed the status quo. It may not, except in two or three instances, have actually won seats, but in a period of massive and enduring structural change in English popular politics it widened the electoral rolls, through a scheme also capable of satisfying both material and social aspirations.

Those material and social aspirations focused upon the ownership of real property, an ambition which in turn derived from the agrarian impulse that was deep-seated still in the urban workforce. The freehold land movement can be seen as a watershed: between, on the one hand, the plethora of popular land schemes which had arisen within the early working-class movement (and of which the Chartist Land Company was simply the largest); and, on the other, the building societies. The latter, the single most effective force in dispersing real property in Britain, thus derived more than a little of their impetus from the demand for a reform in the ownership of land which had been an enduring feature of English popular politics.

Notes

1   F. M. L. Thompson, *The Rise of Respectable Society: A Social History of Victorian Britain, 1830-1900* (London, 1988), p. 168.

2   *Cooper's Journal,* 17 Jan. 1850.

3   J. West, *A History of the Chartist Movement* (London, 1920), p. 223.

4   S. D. Chapman and M. Bartlett, 'The Contribution of Building Clubs and Freehold Land Societies to Working-Class Housing in Birmingham', in S. D. Chapman (ed.), *The History of Working Class Housing: A Symposium* (Newton Abbot, 1971), pp. 240-4; M. Doughty, introduction to id. (ed.), *Building the Industrial City* (Leicester, 1986), p. 11; H. J. Dyos, *Victorian Suburb: A Study of the Growth of Camberwell* (1961), pp. 114-17; P. Gallimore, 'Building Societies and Housing Provision in North Staffordshire (1850-1880)' (University of Keele M.A. thesis, 1985), pp. 176-222; S. M. Gaskell, 'Yorkshire Estate Development and the Freehold Land Societies in the Nineteenth Century', *Yorkshire Archaeological Journal,* xliii (1971), 158-66; J. M. Rawcliffe, 'Bromley: Kentish Market Town to London Suburb, 1841-1881', in F. M. L. Thompson (ed.), *The Rise of Suburbia* (Leicester, 1982), pp. 58-9; D. A. Reeder, 'Capital investment in the western suburbs of Victorian London' (University of Leicester Ph.D. thesis, 1965), pp. 176-82; F. Sheppard, *London, 1808-1870: The Infernal Wen* (London, 1971), p. 156; H. F. Tebbs, *Peterborough: A History* (Cambridge, 1979), pp. 161-3.

5   The principal political studies of the period which consider the movement are: F. E. Gillespie, *Labor and Politics in England, 1850-1867* (Durham, N.C., 1927), pp. 83-8, 94-5; J. Prest, *Politics in the Age of Cobden* (London, 1977), pp. 106-21; N. C. Edsall, 'A Failed National Movement: the Parliamentary and Financial Reform Association, 1848-54', *Bulletin of the Institute of Historical Research,* 44 (1976), 109, 112, 116-17, 120, 127-8; Edsall, *Richard Cobden: Independent Radical* (Cambridge, Mass., 1986), pp. 198, 204-9, 217, 236, 259; D. A. Hamer, *The Politics of Electoral Pressure: A Study in the History of Victorian Reform Agitations* (Hassocks, 1977), pp. 89-90, 95, 347; W. Hinde, *Richard Cobden: A Victorian Outsider* (New Haven, Conn., 1987), pp. 196-7.

6   *Freeholder* 1 Jan. 1850.

7   'The Freehold Franchise', *Reformer's Almanac* (1849), p. 64.

8   Norman Gash, *Politics in the Age of Peel* (London, 1953), pp. 91-4; D. C. Moore, *The Politics of Deference* (Brighton, 1976), ch. iv, passim; Morley, *Life of Cobden*, pp. 304-5

9 The fullest study of radical Liberal practice regarding electoral registration remains Prest's *Politics in the Age of Cobden*. The relevant legal cases are also detailed in E. J. Cleary, *The Building Society Movement* (London, 1965), p. 50.

10 T. J. Nossiter, *Influence, Opinion and Political Idioms in Reformed England* (Brighton, 1975), p. 58.

11 The Society's journal, *The Liberator*, endorsed the freehold land movement, and encouraged dissenters to avail themselves of the opportunity it presented to obtain the vote: see 3 (Sept. 1855). See also 'The Revising Barrister', *The Liberator*, 16 (Sept. 1856); William H. Mackintosh, *Disestablishment and Liberation: The Movement for the Separation of the Anglican Church from State Control* (London, 1972), p. 57. For a detailed account of registration activities in the West Riding see F. M. L. Thompson, 'Whigs and Liberals in the West Riding', *English Historical Review*, 74 (1959), 214-39.

12 M. W. Beresford, 'The back-to-back house in Leeds, 1787-1937', in Chapman (ed.), *The History of Working Class Housing*, pp. 102, 123; Lambeth General Union – *Weekly Free Press of Trades, Manufactures and Commerce*, 197 and 206 (25 Apr. and 20 June 1829); and see also M. Chase, *'The People's Farm': English Radical Agrarianism, 1775-1840* (Oxford, 1988), p. 153. *Birmingham: Aris's Birmingham Gazette*, 23 Jan. 1837, and G. J. Johnson, 'On the Benefit Building and Freehold Land Societies of Birmingham', *Journal of the Statistical Society of London*, xxviii (1865), 507; see also Chapman and Bartlett, 'The Contribution of Building Clubs and Freehold Land Societies to Working-Class Housing in Birmingham', pp. 236-40. For Owenite discussions in 1838 about the forty-shilling franchise and its applicability to their communities see *Weekly Tribune* 11 (15 Dec. 1849).

13 *NS* 25 Apr. 1840; see also 17 July 1841.

14 *NS* 25 May, 22 June 1844, 26 Apr. 1845, 3 Oct. 1846, 20 Jan. 1847; A. R. Schoyen, *The Chartist Challenge: A Portrait of George Julian Harney* (London, 1958), p. 152; cf. *The Movement and Anti-Persecution Gazette*, 30 (6 July 1844). For the work of Chartism's metropolitan registration committee, *NS*, 22 June, 10 and 17 Aug., 12 Oct. 1844. The major radical publisher James Watson issued a *Handbook of Registration*: 'Chartist committees should see to its circulation' (*NS*, 4 May 1850). Also see above, chapter 8.

15 East London Boot and Shoemakers: *NS* 25 Jan. 1845, 24 May 1845, 24 Jan. 1846; Chartist Land Plan: *NS* 24 May 1845.

16 Promoted by James Hill, a Wisbech landowner and socialist, the National Land and Building Society enjoyed the support of a number of prominent radicals, including William Carpenter, Bronterre O'Brien, Goodwyn Barmby, and the Spencean, Charles Neesom: see *Lloyds Weekly London Newspaper*, 8 and 15 June 1845, B[ritish] L[ibrary] (Department of Printed Books), Place Collection Set 56, fo. 405; see also Chase, *'The People's Farm'*, p. 171.

17 *Utilitarian Record* 1846, p. 3.

18 For the Starr-Bowkett movement see Cleary, *Building Society Movement*, pp. 101-15, and B. T. Robson, *Urban Growth: An Approach* (London, 1973), pp. 154-65. There were close links between Bowkett's movement and certain radicals: see *Reasoner*, vol. I (1846), 263, 270; *Utilitarian Record*, vol. ii, 20

Jan. 1847, p. 24; 17 Feb. 1847, p. 24; *NS* 19 and 26 Aug., 2 Sept. 1848; *New Moral World* 2 Nov. 1844; *English Chartist Circular* 138 (31 Oct. 1843), p. 341; *National Reformer* 7 (14 Nov. 1846) and 31 (1 May 1847); also S. Newens, 'Thomas Edward Bowkett: Nineteenth Century Pioneer of the Working-Class Movement in East London', *History Workshop Journal* 9 (Spring 1980), 143-8.

19   M. S. Chase, 'Chartism, 1838-1858: Responses in Two Teesside Towns', *Northern History* 24 (1988), 163-4.

20   W. J. Fox, *Lectures Addressed Chiefly to the Working Classes*, vol. iv (London, 1849), pp. xiv-xv.

21   Anti-Corn Law League activities in the West Riding are fully discussed in Thompson, 'Whigs and Liberals'. For Walker's role see *The Times*, 27 Nov. 1849, and for his Chartist connections *NS*, 27 Nov. 1841.

22   *The Times* 27 Nov. 1849; *Gateshead Observer* 31 Jan. 1846.

23   *Gateshead Observer* 10 Jan. 1846.

24   Rouse's Building and Freehold Land Societies' Directory and Almanac (London, 1853), p. 54.

25   Bradford Equitable Building and FLS, *Prospectus* (Bradford, 1849).

26   The debate on the labour aristocracy has been wide-ranging. For a survey of the literature before 1980, see R. Q. Gray, *The Aristocracy of Labour in Nineteenth-Century Britain, c. 1850-1914* (London, 1981). Significant subsequent treatments of the concept include: E. Hobsbawm, 'Artisan or Labour Aristocrat?', *Economic History Review* 37 (1984), 355-72; id., *Worlds of Labour* (London, 1984), pp. 214-72; M. R. Holbrook-Jones, *Supremacy and Subordination of Labour: The Hierarchy of Work in the Early Labour Movement* (London, 1982); P. Joyce, *Work, Society, and Politics: The Culture of the Factory in Later Victorian England* (Brighton, 1980); G. McLennan, *Marxism and the Methodology of History* (London, 1981), pp. 206-32; T. Matsumura, *The Labour Aristocracy Revisited: The Victorian Flint Glass Makers, 1850-1880* (Manchester, 1983); C. More, *Skill and the English Working Class, 1870-1914* (London, 1980); R. Price, *Unions and Men: Work Control in Building and the Rise of Labour, 1830-1914* (Cambridge, 1980); A. Reid, 'Intelligent Artisans and Aristocrats of Labour: the Essays of Thomas Wright', in J. Winter (ed.), *The Working Class in Modern British History* (Cambridge, 1983); R. Dennis, 'Class behaviour and residence in nineteenth century society: the lower middle class in Huddersfield in 1871', in N. Thrift and P. Williams (ed.), *Class and Space: The Making of Urban Society* (London, 1987), pp. 73-107; T. Spencer, 'Trade Unionism and Socio-Economic Development in the Yorkshire Glass Industry circa 1840-1940' (Open University D.Phil. thesis, 1988).

27   C. Havercroft, *How Can a Man Become His Own Landlord?* (Manchester, 1876), p. 3 (a paper first read to the Lincoln Land and Building Society); cf. J. H. Salkeld, 'Building societies, their use and abuse', *Co-operator*, 29 5 (25 Mar. 1871).

28   Entries for Muntz and Scholefield in M. Stenton (ed.), *Who's Who of British Members of Parliament* (Hassocks, 1976), vol. 1; J. Langford, *Modern Birmingham* (Birmingham, 1873), ii. 8-9, 162; E. P. Hennock, *Fit and Proper Persons* (London, 1973), ch. iv: 'George Dawson and the Civic Gospel'.

29   J. E. Ritchie, *Freehold Land Societies* (London, 1853), p. 10; Langford, *Modern Birmingham*, pp. 8-9.

30   'Co-operative Societies', *Meliora* 4 (1860), cited in P. Hollis, *Class and Conflict in Nineteenth-Century England, 1815-1850* (London, 1973), p. 315.

31   Bradford Equitable Building and FLS, *Prospectus* (1849).

32   This list is necessarily selective: *The Birkbeck Freehold Land Societies Simplified and Explained* (London, 1855); Coventry FLS: TNA, FS6/210/52; Peterborough FLS: TNA, FS6/189/4; Sheffield Reform FLS: TNA, FS6/215/66; Lambeth FLS: *Provident Times*, 15 Mar. 1854; Southwark FLS: ibid. 1 Feb. 1854; Second Batley FLS: TNA, FS6/105/83; Northampton FLS: *Northampton Mercury*, 15 Feb. 1890 (I am indebted to Edward Royle for this reference); and see the entry for Joseph Gurney in *DLB*, vol. 5.

33   Attercliffe Fruits of the Soil FLS: TNA, FS6/217/140; Freedom Hill FLS: TNA, FS6/217/113.

34   *Freeholder* 1 Jan. and 1 Oct. 1850; *Freehold Land Times* 1 Sept. 1854.

35   H. J. Dyos, 'The Speculative Builders and Developers of Victorian London', *Victorian Studies* 9 (1967), supplement, p. 659; E. W. Cooney, 'The Building Industry', in R. Church (ed.), *The Dynamics of Victorian Business* (London, 1980), p. 157; P. Kemp, 'The transformation of the urban housing market in Britain, c. 1885-1939' (University of Sussex D.Phil. thesis, 1984), pp. 20-21, 71-2.

36   E.g. comments on the Birmingham FLS in *Co-operator* 298 (15 Apr. 1871).

37   G. Crossick, *An Artisan Elite in Victorian Society* (London, 1978), p. 145; RC Friendly Societies, 'First Report', *Parliamentary Papers* 1871, c. 452, col. 3666; *Freeholder and Commercial Advertiser* 19 Apr. 1852; Attercliffe Freedom Hill FLS: TNA, FS6/217/113; Freedom Hill FLS: TNA, FS6/216/94; *Reasoner* 15 Dec. 1852; Ritchie, *Freehold Land Societies*, p. 10; M. Elliott, *Victorian Leicester* (Chichester, 1979), p. 109.

38   RC Friendly Societies, cols. 3666-71; cf. operations of the Coventry Freehold Land Society, described by C. H. Bracebridge, 'Paper read to F Section, British Association, Newcastle-upon-Tyne, on the Coventry Freehold Land Society', *Journal of the Statistical Society of London* 26 (1863), 455-7.

39   J. MacAskill, 'The Chartist Land Plan', in A. Briggs (ed.), *Chartist Studies* (London, 1959), pp. 304-41; D. Hardy, *Alternative Communities in Nineteenth Century England* (London, 1979), pp. 65-105; I. J. Prothero, *Artisans and Politics in Nineteenth Century England* (Folkestone, 1979), passim; J. Epstein, *The Lion of Freedom: Feargus O'Connor and the Chartist Movement, 1832-1842* (London, 1982), pp. 249ff.; D. Thompson, *The Chartists* (London, 1984), pp. 299-306; Chase, *'The People's Farm'* passim.

40   *Freeholder* 1 June 1850.

41   For the popular-radical view of 'the land question' see Chase, *'The People's Farm'*. For general discussions of the politics of the issue see F. M. L. Thompson, 'Land and Politics in England in the Nineteenth Century', *Transactions of the Royal Historical Society*, 5th ser. xv (1965), 23-44; and B. English and J. Saville, *Strict Settlement: A Guide for Historians* (Hull, 1983), pp. 105-15.

42   *Freeholder* 2 Feb. 1852; Birmingham FLS, *Prospectus* (1855); *Freehold Land*

Times 15 Jan. 1854; *Sheffield and Rotherham Independent,* 23 Dec. 1848, cited in Gaskell, 'Yorkshire Estate Development', p. 159; M. Chase, 'From Millennium to Anniversary: The Concept of Jubilee in Late Eighteenth- and Nineteenth-Century England', *Past & Present* 109 (1990), 132-47.

43   C. Hobson, 'Walkley', *Town Planning Review,* vol. iii (1912), 41. See also S. Pollard, *A History of Labour in Sheffield* (Liverpool, 1959), pp. 22-3. For the plotlands of the twentieth century see D. Hardy and C. Ward, *Arcadia for All: The Legacy of a Makeshift Landscape* (London, 1984).

44   *The Times* 27 Nov. 1848; J. H. James, *Guide to Benefit Building Societies* (London, 1849), p. 27; cf. V. Scully, *Mutual Land Societies: Their Present Position and Future Prospects* (Dublin, 1851), p. 13. Charles Kingsley believed that such societies aimed to encourage the creation of working-class absentee rentiers, rather than home-owners: see his *Application of Associative Principles and Methods to Agriculture* (London, 1851), p. 57.

45   RC Friendly Societies (1871), cols. 6886-965, 7776-8; G. C. Brodrick, *English Land and English Landlords: An Enquiry into the Origin and Character of the English Land System, with Proposals for Its Reform* (London, 1881), pp. 154-5.

46   But see M. J. Daunton, *House and Home in the Victorian City: Working Class Housing, 1850-1914* (London, 1983), pp. 263-85; N. Kirk, *The Growth of Working Class Reformism in Mid-Victorian England* (London, 1985), pp. 216-17; P. Williams, 'Constituting class and gender: a social history of the home, 1700-1901', in Thrift and Williams (ed.), *Class and Space,* pp. 154-204; B. Harrison, 'Class and Gender in Modern British Labour History', *Past & Present,* 124 (1989), 121-58.

47   *The Co-operator* 65 (July, 1865); 'A Journeyman Engineer' [Thomas Wright], *Some Habits and Customs of the Working Classes* (London, 1867), esp. pp. 188ff.; W. A. Abram, 'Social Conditions and Political Prospects of the Lancashire Workmen', *Fortnightly Review,* new ser., xxii (1 Oct. 1868), 429; W. Marcroft, *The Inner Circle of Family Life* (Manchester, 1886); *Co-operative News* 2 Sept. 1899.

48   *Freehold Land Times and Building News* 15 Aug. 1854.

49   See for example the opinions of W. J. Linton, *English Republic,* vol. 1 (1851), 65; G. J. Harney, *Democratic Review of British and Foreign Politics* Feb. 1850, p. 350; Thomas Cooper, *Cooper's Journal* 17 Jan. 1850; and James Orange of Nottingham, *Labour League* 9 (30 Sept. 1848). The main anti-Freehold Movement editorials in the *NS* are as follows: 11 Nov. 1848, 7 Apr., 16 June, 1 Dec. 1849, 29 Nov. 1851; see also articles and letters in 16 Mar., 6 and 20 Apr., and 18 May 1850.

50   Westminster FLS, Rules (1849), pp. viii-ix.

51   *Cooper's Journal* 16 Feb. 1850.

52   G. J. Holyoake, 'Who originated the Freehold Land Plan?', *Reasoner* vol. vi, 6 (8 Aug. 1849), also *Freethinker's Magazine* Feb. 1851.

53   Hetherington was an officer of two of the three societies which operated from the Owenite Institute in John Street, London: John Street Provident Society for Obtaining Freehold and Leasehold or Real and Personal Property, *Rules* (1847); John Street Economic Loan Association, *Rules* (1850); advertisement

for the Economic Freehold Land Association, *Reasoner*, vol. xv, 10 (7 Sept. 1853).

54   T. Beggs, 'Freehold Land Societies', *Journal of the Statistical Society of London*, vol. xvi. Besides his active membership of the People's League, Beggs was a full-time agent of the Complete Suffrage Union. See F. Boase, *Modern English Biography* (London, 1892), and B. Harrison, *Dictionary of Temperance Biography* (London, 1973), entry 36.

55   B. Harrison and P. Hollis, 'Chartism, Liberalism, and the Career of Robert Lowery', *English Historical Review* 82 (1967), 510.

56   J. M. Robertson, 'Bradlaugh's Parliamentary Struggle', in H. B. Bonner (ed.), *Charles Bradlaugh* (London, 1894), ii. 208. For Bradlaugh's close association with the promoters of the Northamptonshire FLS, see E. Royle, *Victorian Infidels: The Origins of the British Secularist Movement, 1791-1866* (Manchester, 1974), pp. 181, 311; id., *Radicals, Secularists and Republicans: Popular Freethought in Britain, 1866-1915* (Manchester, 1980); and D. Tribe, *President Charles Bradlaugh* (London, 1971), *passim*.

57   *NS* 17 Nov., 1 Dec. 1849.

58   John Cassell], 'Mr. O'Connor's Land Scheme', *Freeholder* 1 Mar. 1850. For other attacks on Chartism from within the freehold land movement see: *Freeholder* 1 Nov. 1850 and 12 June 1852; *Provident Times* 8 Mar. 1854; Ritchie, *Freehold Land Societies* pp. 8, 16, 22; *Birkbeck Freehold Land Societies*, p.3; *Freehold Land Times* 15 Dec. 1854; William Peplow, letter to the editor, *Cooper's Journal* 9 Mar. 1850.

59   *NS* 4 Apr., 21 July and 18 Aug. 1849; *Star of Freedom* 4 Sept. 1852; cf. the entry for Thomas Clarke, a director of the National Freehold Benefit Building Society, in J. Bellamy and J. Saville (ed.), *DLB*, vol. 6. The Reform FLS also had close Chartist connections: see G. R. Sims, *My Life: Sixty Years' Recollections of Bohemian London* (London, 1917), p. 12.

60   B. L. Kinzer, *The Ballot Question in Nineteenth-Century English Politics* (New York, 1982), p. 62.

61   Duncombe, *Freehold Land Times* 1 May 1854; Thompson, ibid., and *Household Narrative* Apr. 1853; Whalley, *Household Narrative* Feb. 1853; Locke King, *The Times* 27 Nov. 1850, and *Weekly News and Chronicle* 9 Apr. 1853.

62   F. E. Gillespie, *Labor and Politics in England*, ch. iii, passim; H. Bellman, *Bricks and Mortals* (London, 1949), pp. 33, 205; *NS* 18 Aug. 1849.

63   Gillespie, *Labor and Politics in England*, p. 30; Bellman, *Bricks and Mortals*, p. 38; N. C. Edsall, 'A Failed National Movement: The Parliamentary Financial Reform Association', pp. 108-31.

64   *Freehold Land Times* 1 May 1854.

65   *The Times* 27 Nov. 1849; cf. ibid., 28 Nov. 1850, 25 Nov. 1851 (reports of annual conferences of the Freehold Land Union).

66   N. McCord, 'Cobden and Bright in Politics, 1846-1857', in R. Robson (ed.), Ideas and Institutions in Victorian Britain (London, 1967), p. 95.

67   *The Times* 14 Nov. 1849, 27 Nov. 1850; Cobden to Bright, 1 Oct. 1849, BL. Add. MSS, 43649, also cited in Morley, *Life of Richard Cobden*, pp. 514-17.

68   Edsall, *Independent Radical*, pp. 205-6.

69   Ibid., p. 205.

70   Cobden to Bright, 1 Oct. 1849, loc. cit.

71   See, for example, *Freeholder's Circular* 1 Oct. 1853; cf. Prest, *Politics in the Age of Cobden*, pp. 111-14.

72   *Freehold Land Times* 1 Aug. 1854; *Britannia and Conservative Journal* 28 Aug. 1852.

73   Disraeli to Stanley, 11 Jan. 1850, cited in W. L. Monypenny and G. E. Buckle, *The Life of Benjamin Disraeli* (6 vols., London, 1914), iii. 238; *Hansard's Parliamentary Debates*, Third Series, vol. 152, cols. 966-1043; vol. 153, cols. 389-481, 532-623, 692-792, 825-903, 916-1004, 1044-1120, 1157-1264.

74   Ibid., vol. 153, col. 405; division on Russell's amendment, cols. 1157-1264.

75   Edsall, *Independent Radical*, pp. 205-6, 208-9; Hinde, *Cobden*, pp. 195-8.

76   *Reformer's Almanac for 1852* (London, 1851), p. 71; J. Vincent, *The Formation of the British Liberal Party, 1857-1868* (new edn., Harmondsworth, 1972), p. 26.

77   T. Beggs, 'Freehold Land Societies', *Journal of the Statistical Society of London* xvi (1853), 338-46; *Hansard*, vol. 152, col. 1026; *Reformer's Almanac* p. 97; N. C. Edsall, 'A Failed National Movement', pp. 119-20.

78   *Household Narrative*, Nov. 1851, p. 256; *Freeholder*, 8 Mar. and 28 Aug. 1852.

79   J. M. Ludlow and L. Jones, *Progress of the Working Classes* (London, 1867), p. 126.

80   Prospectus, the Liberal Permanent FLS, *Freehold Land Times* 1 Aug. 1854.

81   Cf. D. Smith, *Conflict and Compromise: Class Formation in English Society, 1830-1914, a Comparative Case Study of Birmingham and Sheffield* (London, 1982), p. 60.

82   Beggs, 'Freehold Land Societies', pp. 340-1. The main problem in assessing the total of freehold land societies arises from the indifference of many of them to registering under the Friendly Societies Act of 1834. Registration was not compulsory, although there were clear legal benefits in doing so. However, many smaller societies eschewed registration. As with the co-operative movement, it is unlikely that the full extent of the freehold land movement will ever be ascertained. A further problem posed by the files of the Registrar of Friendly Societies is the compulsory use of the titular formula 'Benefit Building Society'. Usually the registered title was discarded by freehold land societies for business purposes; but it does mean that, except where the Registrar's files reveal a society's initial ignorance of this provision of the Act, they are not an infallible guide even to the number of freehold land societies to register. For a discussion of the same issue with reference to the co-operative movement see R. C. N. Thornes, 'The early development of the Co-operative Movement in West Yorkshire, 1827-1863' (University of Sussex D.Phil. thesis, 1984), pp. 126-7.

83   P. Hume Brown, *History of Scotland* (Cambridge, 1911), iii. 361-2; H. J. Hanham, 'Mid-Century Scottish Nationalism', in Robson (ed.), *Ideas and Institutions*, p. 175.

84   This discussion of the regional distribution of societies is based on data collected from the *Freehold Land Times*, the *Building Societies Almanac* (1847),

Rouse's Building and Freehold Land Societies' Directory and Almanac (1853), and on the files of the Registrar of Friendly Societies in the Public Record Office, London.

85   J. W. F. Hill, *Victorian Lincoln* (Cambridge, 1974), p. 130.

86   RC Friendly Societies (1871), evidence of James Phillips, col. 6139; *Freehold Land Times* 15 June 1854.

87   The co-ordinated expansion of the National FLS in parallel to railway development is well documented in the Society's periodical, the *Freeholder's Circular*. See esp. 4 (1 June 1852), 16 (1 June 1853), and 20 (1 Oct. 1853).

88   *Freehold Land Times*, 1 Aug. 1854; cf. *Chambers' Edinburgh Journal*, vol. xx, Dec. 1853, pp. 377-9, for an attack on speculation in freehold land societies' shares.

89   Data calculated from figures in the *Reformer's Almanac* and the *Democratic and Social Almanac* for 1850.

90   *The National Freehold Land Society, as it is, and as it must be* (London, 1853); *Freehold Land Times* 1 Aug. 1854.

91   H. J. Dyos, *Victorian Suburb: A Study of the Growth of Camberwell* (London, 1961), p. 117.

92   Chapman and Bartlett, 'The Contribution of Building Clubs and Freehold Land Societies to Working-Class Housing in Birmingham', pp. 242-4. The Peterborough society developed an estate purchased from the Church Commissioners: Westwood Street, a terrace of small houses for labourers, was adjacent to the railway line; larger houses for engine drivers in Gladstone Street included a number that were acquired in pairs; superior houses in Cromwell Road were taken by foremen, clerks, and some small business men – see Tebbs, *Peterborough*, p. 162.

93   RC Friendly Societies (1871), cols. 3652, 3666, 3670.

94   Ludlow and Jones, *Progress of the Working Classes*, p. 126; J. Langford, *A Century of Birmingham Life* (Birmingham, 1871), ii. 569. The Leicester FLS made 2,550 allotments in the period 1849-81, approximately one-fifth of the city's new housing stock erected in these years: see Elliott, *Victorian Leicester*, pp. 115-16.

95   Beggs, 'Freehold Land Societies', p. 340. Because of escalating land prices on the fringe of the capital, developments by the National FLS for its working-class membership tended to be in inferior situations. *Tait's Edinburgh Magazine*, for example, observed that 'you have only to go to Stoke Newington, and at the back of Coach and Horses Lane you will see the newly-fledged freeholders all working like negroes to raise up a modern Utopia ... in a large pit, about fifteen, and in some parts even twenty feet below their neighbours'. The reply to the allegation in the *Freeholder's Circular* was evasive, see 2 (1 Apr. 1852).

96   *Weekly News and Chronicle* 26 Feb. 1853; J.M. Robertson, 'Bradlaugh's Parliamentary Struggle', in H. B. Bonner (ed.), *Charles Bradlaugh* (London, 1894), ii. 208; A. L. Thorold, *Life of Henry Labouchere* (London, 1913), pp. 128-9.

97   *Cooper's Journal* 9 Mar. 1850; *Reynolds's Political Instructor* 5 Jan. 1850; A. Scratchley, *Industrial Investment and Emigration* (London, 1850), p. 92;

cf. J. Hole, 'Dwellings for the Lower Classes', *Transactions of the National Association for the Promotion of Social Science for 1871* (London, 1872), 523 – 'they [building societies] have enabled thousands of the superior portion of the artizan class to become house owners'.

98 F. M. L. Thompson, *Hampstead: Building a Borough, 1650-1964* (London, 1974), p. 373.

99 J. A. Binns, 'Benefit Building Societies', *Transactions of the National Association for the Promotion of Social Science for 1859* (London, 1860), 684-5.

100 Ritchie, *Freehold Land Societies*, p. 19.

101 It is unlikely that an accurate figure for the total of working-class homeowners could ever be calculated. The freehold land movement was not the only agency in the field. In 1900 the Co-operative Union estimated that 30,000 workers had been housed in homes they owned by co-operative building societies. Provision was heavily concentrated in the north-west. See S. M. Gaskell, 'Housing and Estate Development, 1840-1918, with particular reference to the Pennine Towns' (University of Sheffield Ph.D. thesis, 1974), p. 169. For other useful discussions of the issue see Daunton, *House and Home*, p. 198; id., *Coal Metropolis: Cardiff, 1870-1914* (Leicester, 1977), pp. 107-8; A. Offer, *Property and Politics, 1870-1914' Landownership, Law, Ideology, and Urban Development in England* (Cambridge, 1981), pp. 119-20; P. Kemp, 'The transformation of the urban housing market in Britain'; D. Rose, 'Home ownership, subsistence and historical change: the mining district of West Cornwall in the late nineteenth century', in Thrift and Williams, *Class and Space*, pp. 108-53; P. Williams, 'Constituting class and gender', pp. 196-201.

102 D. Englander, *Landlord and Tenant in Urban Britain, 1838-1918* (Oxford, 1983): quotation from p. v.

103 Against his better judgement George Howell was converted into just such a landlord when he acquired his own home through the Temperance Permanent Benefit Building Society (formerly the Temperance FLS) in 1867. There is an illuminating discussion of his 'reckless' tenantry in his unpublished autobiography: Bishopsgate Institute, Howell Autobiography, volume D (i).

104 L. Goldman, 'The Social Science Association, 1857-1886: A Context for Mid-Victorian Liberalism', *English Historical Review*, 101 (1986), 95-134. Working-class homeownership was an occasional subject of discussion by the Association – see for example Binns, 'Benefit Building Societies'; Hole, 'Dwellings for the Lower Classes'; and A. Arnold, 'Free Trade in Land', *Transactions of the National Association for the Promotion of Social Science for 1872* (London, 1873), 460-75.

105 Cobden to Bright, 1 Oct. 1849, cited by Morley, *Life of Cobden*, p. 514.

INDEX

Malcolm Chase is Professor of Social History at the University of Leeds and the author of *Chartism: A New History* (2007), a major narrative account. His other books include *Early Trade Unionism: Fraternity Skill & the Politics of Labour* (new edition 2012) and *1820: Disorder & Stability in the United Kingdom* (2013).